SUNSET ON THE LOCH

Rubha Ré
Lighthouse

Gruinard
Bay

Laide
Aultbea

Ullapool

Melvaig

Loch Ewe

Dundonnell
An Teallach

Loch
Broom

Poolewe

Strath

Inverewe

The Gairloch
Gairloch

Loch Maree

Badachro

Letterewe
Slioch

Red Point

Loch Torridon

Ben Alligan
Diabaig

Beinn Eighe
Kinlochewe

Isle of
Rona

Torridon

Achnasheen

Applecross

Loch Monar

Loch Carron

Stromeferry

Loch Mullardoch

Kyle of
Lochalsh

Dornie

Kyleakin

Loch Duich

Loch Affric

Isle of Skye

Glenelg

Sound of Sleat

WESTER ROSS

N

Loch Clunie

Scale approx. 12 miles to inch

SUNSET ON THE LOCH

BEE JAY

Author of
And it Came to Pass, 1963
The End of the Rainbow, 1964

STRATH · GAIRLOCH · ROSS-SHIRE
1965

PRINTED IN GREAT BRITAIN
BY R. & R. CLARK, LTD., EDINBURGH

CONTENTS

*Dedicated
to the
Gairloch people
and all
lovers of Gairloch*

CHAPTER I

INTRODUCTION

SUNSET on the loch; on the Gair Loch, the Gairloch in Western Ross. The country of the *Real* Highlands of Scotland in which I live and in which I suppose I shall pass the remainder of my days—and then, 'Sunset'. Sunset in Shangri-La.

This story borders mainly on the Gairloch area, little known to those in the south, but a district that needs to be written about, for its peaceful nature, its unlimited—and at times, wild—majestic scenery, and its friendly people ... the Highlanders.

The author's earlier book, *And It Came to Pass*, dealing with Western Ross and Skye, having met with such resounding success all over the world, has prompted the writing of *Sunset on the Loch*; so those who did not have opportunity of reading that former saga of the north-west—or even those who did—may be able to learn yet something more of this enchanting and romantic land at the end of the rainbow, which offers so much of everything to everybody at all times of the year.

Those who *do* know of this land (west of Garve, *where nobody hurries*) return here year after year. In that they *do* come, there *must* be something that draws them. Maybe it is the grandeur to be seen round every corner; maybe the way of life of its folk; maybe of the innumerable uncrowded *safe* beaches and coves with their limitless stretches of clean golden sand, and where—if you come across a footprint—you suddenly pull yourself up like a Robinson Crusoe, wondering who on earth this stranger could be, in such oceans of sand; maybe because these coastal waters are swept by the Gulf Stream; maybe because we are the same latitude as Labrador; maybe because of the *indifference to Time* here ... maybe 'tis something else? Who knows? Maybe 'tis the glens, bright in the sunlight, or fresh and green after soft, warm rain.

In this book, Highland life has been given even greater prominence than in *The End of the Rainbow*; so this volume may be said to rank as the 'Triple Alliance'; maybe a concerto to end all concertos?

Those whom we have known to come here as strangers, certainly never leave as strangers; we won't let them! They return home with a joy they have never experienced before, not only in the Fàiltes (welcomes) met with throughout the land—found not just in the hotels, but on the croft and guest-house gates—but in the captivating scenery nature has seen fit to reveal. Their only regret is they have never seen the like of it before.

This book is written honestly and with no attempt at exaggeration. Should one be able to pay a visit early spring or late autumn (in fact even from December to April) out of the seasonal rush of July and August, when all Britain seems to go holiday mad, one's appreciation of this quiet, vast and spectacular area of our beloved island (totally unrelated to any other part of Britain ... a district possessing 'Europe's finest coast-line' as one eminent and travelled Scottish B.B.C. personality told me) will be talked of for years to come, whilst sitting at one's fireside at home. Yes, have no doubts at all, this is perfectly true.

After reading this book, I make bold to say, you *will* want to visit us; and as I record later on "we're friendly people in Western Ross; we laugh and we chat, and none of us posh. We share our joys and sorrows too, and life is richer because we do."

I term this as God's own country. I am not a special reporter but I do feel licensed to write and print my honest convictions; my strong beliefs.

I maintain you *will* see, and you *will* be conquered by it all. *Veni, Vidi, Vici.*

Onwards then to the land of the Fàiltes and Slàinte Mhaths, where almost anywhere is a viewpoint where you behold some of the most incredible scenery in all Europe; shapely peaks at every turn soaring up from loch-fretted moorland; straths galore, heather galore, bracken galore, and where no concrete hands have been allowed to come along to spoil everything with so-called 'motorways'—and therefore speed is the last consideration (for have I not said, once you pass Garve, *nobody hurries!*) None of the dozens of postcard-cum-gaudy trinket ('made in Birmingham') shops that one meets with in seaside resorts up and down the country. No; for this is a land of beauty, a land of peace, a land of quiet movement; and whilst there are acres upon acres, and stretches upon stretches of moorland and glen, there is—parodoxically—no room for anything but Nature.

And Nature can be very grand.

NUNQUAM NON PARATUS

CHAPTER 2

HAIL CALEDONIA!

O NE hazard of the Highlands in Scotland is, that in looking
at a mountain, you may miss something else wonderful,
or pass a turning which leads back into history or legend,
or even miss a highland wedding which might be happening
in some outlying village.

It is in such a thought that I would slow down your car and
take you along these turnings, bringing you face to face with history, superstition, folk lore, the grandeur of the lochs and rugged
coast-line, which eventually gives one a feeling of timelessness.
This we must have if we are to know anything of the wonderland
of Wester Ross; of its heart-warming people and their ways,
and to capture the elusive poetry of this unique countryside,
which in a previous book I have termed 'the end of the rainbow'.

For those who pick up this book and scan its opening pages,
I would remark it deals for the most part with Gairloch—the
fifth largest parish in Scotland—albeit it brings in some of the
surrounding country (as well as the isle of Skye), all of which is
tantalisingly beautiful in its own way, even when it's raining;
though as one goes further afield, there is not the foliage, the
trees or the glens that are met with in and around the Gair Loch;
the Gairloch of Wester Ross itself, the sunsets of which out-colour
and out-strip *any* of the coloured postcards one sees in the local
stores. If they *did* appear as such on a p.p.c., one would say they
were photo-faked. But no! they are real; the sunsets are not
—indeed they *can* not—be faked by Nature. They have to be
seen to be believed. And I should know, because I live here. . . .

*   *   *

In these days, constantly do we read in the national papers
slogans like 'Let's get away from it all', accompanied by half-

4

or full-page splash adverts of 'Holidays Abroad'. Gaiety, comfort, sunshine and exhilarating sea breezes. One gets tired of reading all the glowing accounts of these heavenly places; these glorious prospects: 'See Europe by Luxury Coach'; 'How Poland answers your holiday questions'; Costa Brava, Majorca, Yugoslavia, the Adriatic. 'Fly to the Sun'; Italy; 'carefree holidays', blue skies. 'Come and share the sun.' ... It's unbelievable. Then again one of the smarter things of journeying into space (going abroad, for foreign holidays no longer fill one with awe) is a luxury liner cruise. 'Young at heart' cruises for those under 35 years of age seem to be the latest urge (birth certificates *not* required!); also 'slim cruises' for those with middle-age spreads. Fancy that; for one can laze and sit down to a menu as long as your arm on such liners and put on weight, and more weight. What will they think up next, in advertising these sea-going ideas to attract newcomers to go sunshine cruising mad; for if not, these liners would of course be laid-up in dry dock during the winter, and one would not wish the shipping companies to go into liquidation. Oh! no. Entertainments of all kinds also 'go to sea' in such soul-reading advertisements. Top cabaret stars are being engaged to entertain you under these constantly sunny skies. Good for them, otherwise *they'd* be on the dole! Even golf professionals are being enlisted to give talks on golfing, whilst sailing in the Adriatic, taking one away from the boat deck, the moon, the blue sea and a lovely girl. More bright dance bands than have ever sailed the seas before, or set out from hot, smoky, small night-clubs in Town, will be there. It will do *them* a world of good to breathe in pure air. All this to allure you from home and to get your money; money out of pleasure, and competition seems to be keener than ever, to obtain passengers to fill a score of big liners cruising *away* from good old Britain. It is estimated at least 100,000 now go a-cruising each year. (They'll be going on a slow boat to China soon!) Sun, fun, good food, pleasure and sight-seeing at breakneck speed, are the spotlights. You arrange to meet your friends in Nice, Copenhagen, Leningrad, and the Mediterranean Islands—indeed any place under the sun (except Britain) in these days of big-thinking, and in keeping up with the Jones's. Personally, I've never kept up with them and feel happier in that respect, for many of the Jones's have 'gone under' (and I don't mean down to Australia!) And as you sit on deck with your luncheon tray don't give it when you've finished to the first man in uniform who chances by to take it away, for who knows he may be the Chief Officer!

Continuing this exciting narrative, one is being intrigued by visiting the islands of the Great, with a capital G. Minorca, reminiscent of Nelson; Corfu, the jewel of the Ionian of Ulysses fame; Malta, the Knights of St John; Sardinia, where patriot Garibaldi lived, and fought for it against the Austrians and helped Italy annex it. Parga, unspoiled it is said, with orange and lemon groves bordering its sandy beaches, which the Roman Emperor, Augustus, founded to celebrate his victory over Mark Antony at Actium. And Elba, where Napoleon was in exile. Verily, emperors, admirals, generals, knights, heroes, patriots— now all dead—for one adventurous reason or another, have identified their names with such places; and you, the average person in Britain, must go there just to say you've been where Napoleon slept and so on and so forth. Amazing! As though we, up in Scotland, hadn't got islands—islands galore, such as Mull, Skye, Tiree, Islay and the Outer Hebrides; to say nothing of Staffa which inspired Mendelssohn to compose an overture.

Then, perhaps, you are invited in these ads. to go where the Germans follow the sun, to Sylt, the millionaire's island play- ground on the North Sea coast off Western Germany and Denmark. And there they jostle nakedly on the beaches, and later on (not nakedly we hope!) in the stylish bars and casinos.

Getting away from it all? It's a great life. 'It's never winter' on the lavish island of Ibiza, one of the Balearic islands, where the spring flowers push their way through the soil long before they do in Britain. I wonder? for I've bulbs shooting up in November, and primroses blooming all through the winter in Gairloch; and forget-me-nots grow almost wild and appear any old time in the winter. 'Forget-me-not'; what a nice name. It apparently came from the tale of a German knight who plunged into a river for a tuft of flowers for his lady-love. He wasn't able to come back to the bank for I'd have you know he was heavily clad in armour (and in *amor*, too) and before he drowned he threw the flowers to his love's feet crying 'forget- me-not'! And tulips, like Persian turbans, shoot up early here, and one's rockery is always in flower one way or another and

certainly never resembles the Clearance's period of 1745 onwards. Everything pert as the breeze, which saucily billows a
petticoat hem, light as the grasses swinging in the estate field . . .
but who would believe me?

Abroad, in these fishing villages, we find cobbled streets
threading under balconies of fishermen's cottages, and you'd
better watch that a few cod's heads are not thrown down on
you; and the usual domed cathedral above the town or village.
Harbour restaurants where, with expensive wine, you can wash
down rich sea foods. And at the night-clubs, foreign bands—
again in a smoke-ladened, fuggy atmosphere—play out foreign
songs and music which you can't understand, but the wine
makes you dance and you tap your feet to this exotic bizarre
brouhaha, clap your hands and nod approvingly to the coloured
conductor, telling the 'lovely' who is dancing in your arms with
care-free abandonment, that this is all so different from dull old
England; and as you go back unsteadily to your reserved table,
hold hands, telling each other 'this is it'. Ah! me. I am not a
cynic, but hold the view that instead of getting *away* from it all,
you're going *in to it all*, good and proper, with both feet; and
in the end with both pockets—empty!

Turning over these fairy leaves still more, one reads that
Belgium is *The* country—Europe's top place; a fascinating land
with the easiest of easy car-ferries from Dover. How gullible
can the British be? There are easy car-ferries in the Highlands.

And the people you meet on such tours, which end all tours!
Nobody knows who you are once you're aboard the lugger—
these floating palaces. You embark with a new character, a new
personality surging through your watery veins. The young
'35' merely puts a Cleopatra kit in her suitcase (borrowed from
a friend) and before the ship reaches warmer climes, emerges
from her cabin in a striking bikini-style outfit and attitude.
Although she may be an ordinary respectable 10 a.m.-5 p.m. typist
in a London office, the 'call of the sea' soon blows all that drab-
ness of her city life away, although goose-pimples may be evident
in the cold draughts outside the over-heated cocktail lounge.
She walks around slowly on deck, with a nonchalant careless air,
eyes discreetly half-closed or lowered in her endeavour to strike
a note of captivation; and with the roll of the supposedly
stabilised vessel, knocks her painted toe-nails (showing through

her open, flimsy sandals) against an odd capstan or davit, which brings forth more than a few naughty, nautical oaths! At boat drill, she will see to it that all the ship's officers demonstrate in minute detail how, or how not, to make the reef knots to her life-jacket, hoping against hope she *will* be in a lifeboat, long before the ship docks again at Tilbury, with the smart junior officer. But Barnacle Bill knows a thing or two, believe me; he knows her type, although in a weak moment forgetting his staid wife at Gravesend, he may invite her up to the boat-deck just to show her the incomparable moon under semi-tropical conditions. As though she has not seen the same old moonlight in her own Surrey or Sussex town before! And should she fall —well, she falls like Lucifer! Fancy-dress costume and all.

Then there is the fellow who is out to impress, and to enjoy every moment in the smoke-room bar, standing drinks all round. A jovial, amusing, generous chap, spending all he can —regardless; until the cruise is almost over and he is down to his last £1 note, whereupon he looks plaintively around at his friends—his friends who are suddenly no more. A bore indeed; and his so-called friends at the golf club at home say the same of him also, if he did but know. There is the young man of mystery, with dark, longish hair, gazing at the stars, smoking an Abdulla cigarette from an ultra-long cigarette holder, waiting for some young 'under 35' to saunter along, who has no partner for a dance, and this is her maiden voyage. She won't be a maiden for long; for he pledges to marry her, once they are back in England. Again, I wonder? I know full well all this happens on board a liner under a semi-tropical—let alone a tropical—sun, for I have travelled abroad more times than I can remember. I know the technique of these young bloods, and I smile ... the camel's inscrutable smile, and I feel sorry for the innocents abroad. Yes, life is different on board ship. Then there is the athletic type, who thinks it is the 'done thing' to tramp around the deck half a dozen times, two or three times a day, just to keep his liver in order, whistling away merrily; then break off for a quick game of deck tennis; whilst everyone else is lolling about in deck chairs and sleeping the sleep of the just, although it may only be midday. Truly it takes all sorts to make a Mediterranean cruise.

'Follow the sun'; and I suppose if you keep advertising,

thousands *will* follow; like sheep in the Highlands of Scotland.
Advertising agents seem to be adept at slick phraseology. And
of course you are constantly reminded that the English (*not* the
Scottish) pound note goes so much further in such and such a
country. Seville, and bull fights! who relishes seeing a gory
bull-fight? Portugal and the great spy city of Lisbon. Property
speculators are today preparing the ground for a D-day that
gets earlier and more populated each year. Girls sunning themselves in scanty bikinis; so much so that coastguards are kept on
the alert giving them a printed card reading 'only one-piece
costumes permitted'. One French girl got over this by removing
the top half of her suit! My! oh, my! Czech roads twist
through fir and pine, with banks knee-deep in blue lupins.
Everywhere, they say, you'll see wild cherries and fairy castles!
Bermuda, with its translucent sea, even more brilliant than the
sun, that washes long beaches of pearly-pink sand or fretted limestone rocks; coral reefs, exotic fish. 'Escape—without having
to count the cost!' Bulgaria, where I'm told you waken to the
whisper of a million roses opening up their petals to the sun;
valleys where grow the musk rose and they produce attar of
roses. Seductive thoughts, all. But then this is a country where
Mata Hari was born, so what can you expect? Canaries, the warm
Atlantic islands, which can be reached in under 6 hours by plane.
'Fortunate Isles', with bananas, palm trees, cacti and sugar cane.
    Well, as I have said, what of it? . . .
    And not content with all this, there is something more offered
to crown everything, namely, a system of 'Pay Later'—or
holidays on the H.P. system. Can you beat it? Most of the
'financing for credit' holidays is carried out by a specialised
travel company. You can obtain such easy-payment holidays
on repayment schemes covering 6 or 9 months. Of course it
will cost you more in the long run, with interest charges and so
forth; but even so, 'holidays on tick' enable you to avoid
paying a hefty slice out of the family's annual budget in one fell
swoop. 'Come to Gairloch; don't bother paying; pay when
you can afford to, in two, three, five or ten years' time! Just
drop us a card to keep in touch after you've been here a fortnight
on tick!' Maybe aye!—or maybe 'och aye!
    Really I am getting so carried away myself with myself
writing of all these luscious places myself, that I'm thinking myself

I must try them out myself, says myself! (Of course 'myself' repeated often, is a saying you always hear up in the Highlands; and it's myself as is telling you, I'd have you know; in case you thought I was unfamiliar with grammar and syntax, myself!)

And we must not forget America; oh! no! 'The fare's right down'; places are great, spaces are wide, and fun's all there. There seems to be sun, fun and games, everywhere *except in Britain*?

Without being a dismal Jimmy, I would remind you of one snag though when coming back from one's glorious Continental holiday; of your meeting with the genial (?) Customs men at Dover—the blue-uniformed officers of the waterguard—and you are shown a thumb-marked battered-looking printed card headed 'Have you anything to declare?' in bold black lettering. Ah! yes, there's films we got abroad, and a camera we got cheap in Naples; some foreign jewellery; cosmetics (for they're so much better than you get at home; these foreigners know more about 'make-up' than we do, y'know; and the highly coloured, decorated jars of cream and wrinkle remover, gives your face a better morale); and yes, a bottle or so of Cognac and one or two liqueurs—quite apart from the light red vino and other alcoholic concoctions you've consumed during those halycon days in Vienna. However, an alcoholic breath is un-Customable! You've got to smile and pay up all the duty levied—and it's not a trifling amount—knowing you've seen, drunk and eaten everything that's worth seeing, drinking and eating abroad; the Mona Lisa; dancing on the Pont d'Avignon at midnight; the ravioli and the zambaglione sauce; you thought you saw and snapped Brigette Bardot, but after the film is developed in a chemist shop in Trieste, you wonder? for the vital statistics don't seem to be in the right place, or in the right perspective, somehow! In the words of the old song whilst 'accentuating the positive, you've eeleemeenated the negative!' Vesuvius erupting and a spark flying on the lens; an earthquake in Sicily —and it looks like it from the angle of the photograph. We have crossed the Rubicon, without being told we have; but still we know Caesar once crossed it, so all's well ('och!' said one wee Scottie in the party, 'that wee burn's nothing; I could spit across it, so what odds Caesar crossing it?') And Rome, teeming with sightseers, Well, if Rome was always as full of foreigners, small wonder the Romans were always marching away from it all! and its ruins. Next, we shall be reading these foreign tourist agents will be arranging chariot races in Rome, or wrestling matches in Athens!

All just to be in a place abroad; and if you're sitting in a multi-coloured flower garden in the Alps, with a sheer cliff thousands of feet high (and thousands of years old, too) looking through the afternoon's mist into the background of Time, what thoughts have you any better than if you were at the top of Glen Docherty gazing westwards to Loch Maree—looking like molten silver—and the sea? Confess it all; you'd have no better thoughts . . . unless of course you were looking at Loch Maree through straight up-and-down Highland rain! Even so, it would still have a picture all on its own.

And there are the lovely scented cigarettes you've smoked and brought back in your baggage. Not Virginian tobacco; oh! no, something far superior to that, these foreigners smoke. To me, the tobacco always seemed to have a good percentage of camel dung mixed up in the golden scented leaf! And a camel has a very characteristic smell. But you don't mind that, for you're in El Dorado!

So, eventually, you come back to England, to the white cliffs of Dover, having parted with your last ten or twenty pounds over the Custom's desk, with—'nothing to declare!' So what?

My answer? My answer to all the foregoing, although I have lived a quarter of a century in the tropics, 'midst waving palms, tropical fish, curry and rice, mangoes, pineapples and coral seas—not forgetting the many beautiful, alluring, flashingly attractive Sinhalese girls—is that, bluntly speaking there is nothing to it'. There is more to it in our own country, up in the Highlands of Scotland: and I write from experience, and experience counts if nothing else does. Or it should do.

Of course to those down in England, this land in which I live, and write, is—compared with abroad—on one's own door-step; and that, I think accounts for it being bypassed and be-littled to some extent. It's too near to think of, is Scotland; let's go further afield, and get more of a change one says. Though is it? When you think of it, we are 500 miles from the Midlands, and over 1,000 miles from the south coast of Britain. Let's buy clothes for the occasion, evening gowns and all the matching

accessories, and look our smartest on board, or on tour. What
fun! Hubby's lounge suit is frayed and he simply *must* get a
new one in the 25-guinea range; and his evening dress is mil-
dewed, so he needs another, and the latest style, as well as new
patent leather shoes; for on the dance floor the lights fairly show
up everything. We simply can't afford *not* to spend our money
on this feast of adventure. . . . So you do, and when you total
all this up, apart from the apparent cheapness in fares, it becomes
a very costly matter; and you return home to Suburbia and begin
to economise trying to save up on the far-more-than-you-thought
expenses. Maybe you'll be saving up for many a month to come
to break even, and perhaps have to deny yourselves of ordinary
essential food. One should read all these brochures carefully,
making yourself *au fait* with all the extras involved which may
not be so self-evident in casually reading the fares, generally in
bold capital letters.

And, of course, it should be remembered you can't take your
pet dog abroad as you can up in the Highlands. So *Chummy*,
that beloved German dachsund—whose back is so long that all
the family can pat it at one and the same time—must be left in
the care of Aunt Eliza (although she abhors dogs!) who lives a
few streets away, and who will tend to its needs and feed it—you
hope—whilst you are away enjoying yourselves basking and
dancing on the shores of the Blue Danube. Darling *Chummy*,
we hope you won't be too lonely without us!

*   *   *

And so, as a prelude to the Highlands and Gairloch, I would
pointedly put the question, why not skip all the bother, fuss,
excitement, much advance arrangements and certainly expense,
adventuring abroad? But simply cross the national boundary;
the Cheviots by Carter Bar, or by so-called romantic Gretna
Green, into Scotland, so near at hand, and head for the 'Wild
West'? It pays to do so in a variety of ways, not the least in
money and health value. Scotland is more tweedier than elsewhere, especially when almost half the British Cabinet potter
about in this land in plus fours carrying guns and dressed as
gillies! The glens and lochs of the West Highlands are incomparable with any others in Britain or abroad.

This is no imagination; no attempt at literary license; IT IS

A FACT. There are innumerable charming and ideal spots for 'getting away from it all'. As I have said, it is all here, on one's doorstep for the taking. Just casually pack a few odd cases, jump in the car and head for the north; north-west of Inverness to Garve and the west. Once you're there, once you're in Wester Ross, you'll want to come and shower your thanks on me for letting you in to a secret—the secret of the finest coast-line in Europe, 'midst towering mountains and silent lochs, 'midst a people friendlier than you've ever met in your life (*and Britishers at that!*); a Gaelic-loving people, a people whose hospitality knows no end; a God-fearing people; a worthy, if not a wealthy, folk. A crofting people; and crofting and farming goes on for ever. Government's come and go, dynasties wax and wane, dictators rise and fall; men, women, children and animals are born and die, machines wear out . . . yet crofting goes on for ever. Nothing can stop it; so why don't town's folk come and watch it all, and cheer it on its wholesome way ? Forget the big, ugly cities, the reek and the grime, and revel in the goodness and purity of the air in your *own* country. You will return full of happy memories, and realise what happiness in living means. I know only too well, the meaning of the atmosphere that evokes what the Gaels call 'the wave in the heart' and the 'dream in the eye'. There is all the difference in the world to that, and the stuffy, smoke-reeking atmosphere of a small dance floor on a luxury liner.

Looking around at Gairloch's rugged, savage coast-line from where these lines are written, on a star-lit clear summer night with a rich flood of silver moonbeams filling the quiet loch, and breaking in shivered gleams upon the little burns (brooks) that murmur away in a Gaelic tongue, I often think to myself in peering up at such a sky and the mountain scenery, "well, if the wrong side of Heaven is so glorious as it seems from here, what —I am tempted to ask—must the right side be like ?" Surely this should make you think. These lofty mountains, the beaches, coves, glens, hillsides and straths (valleys) seem to conspire, one with the other, in unsurpassable beauty.

It is good to know though, that not everyone is leaving these island shores; there are still those in Scotland who head for the usual popular English resorts, whilst in the reverse, English folk still come north to the Scottish Highlands, to find peace of

mind 'midst peace and plenty. In 1963 tourist traffic north and
to the islands increased by over twenty per cent. But again,
how small in comparison to those going abroad. Five-and-a-half
million people took a holiday in Scotland in 1964; and nearly
670,000 tourists came from overseas to sample fresh salmon and
Scotch beef! I once saw a cryptic notice in a Glasgow tourist
agency window, where there was a comprehensive list of
Scottish resorts and Highland tours it was urging one to take.
It read 'GO AWAY FROM HERE'! And another slogan, 'Don't
be a ditherer; be ready to go!' And yet again, travel overland
to Naples and join a luxury liner there and 'sail *from* the sun,
to the sun, *with* the sun to tideless *plages* of the Mediterranean'.

Through these pages, I bring you to Gairloch and Wester
Ross, if possible in May, June, mid-September, even October.
The main holiday season is July to mid-September, and more
often than not it is apt to be wet then; although of course there
may be exceptions. As a rule, spring comes later than in England
and carries on to June. Scotland and the REAL Highlands of
Wester Ross, also the many Hebridean islands, and MULL and
SKYE, offer more beauty and romance, than do the Grecian Isles
and all the foreign advertising put together. One gets a taste of
Scotch mist at times, but what a lovely tangy taste it is; and
Highland straight up-and-down rain, as I have mentioned, just
glances off you!

If you ask the average Sasunnach what he knows of Scotland,
you are most likely to be told it is a land inhabited by the rem-
nants of the Vikings of old, or of bagpipes, whisky, kilts, hairy-
kneed muscular Highlanders, twirling stunted corkscrew sticks,
anti-British patriots; 'neeps'—which they imagine means a
small tot of whisky!—and kippers; thick oatmeal porridge and
haggis (thought to be a wingless bird, or a finless fish; a legless
rodent or a boy's name); or maybe of Bannockburn where King
Alfred burnt some bannocks! 'Och aye; and perhaps a lot
more elevating matter, including the fact that the men have
webbed feet due to so much wet weather; and they sum it all
up by saying there's not a finer country in which to relax with
an umbrella! Seldom are you told of the great scenery, the
uplifting mountains of Torridon—the oldest in the world, old
before the Himalayas even started—the misty green glens, the
many beautiful isles, the mirror-surface of its islet-studded lochs,

the limitlessness of the *safest* golden sandy beaches you can
possibly imagine, set 'midst seclusion and quietude. Even
in the seasonal rush you feel you are still alone on such stretches
of expansive smooth, clean sand; the home of the intriguing
Fair Isle jumpers, sweaters and matching skirts, and a host of
other knitted wear, woven by the wives of crofters, farmers
and fishermen, on looms handed down for generations. Nothing mass-produced on machines can be as beautiful, they tell
you, as home-spun by these craftswomen. Each creation is
a hand-creation; hand-spun, hand-knitted, hand-dyed. Can
you get these things abroad, or on a cruise? If you do and you
look closely at the garment, you'll probably see 'made in Scotland' on a wee tab. So why go away to get what you can
buy here? Why? Fashion magic, woven for the world. Last
year over 10 million yards of Scottish tweed of two hundred
varieties were exported, and much of it used by royal couturiers.
Even ordinary Scottish knitwear sales now exceed £20,000,000
a year. Why suffer delusions in going to a foreign country,
foreign money, foreign food (which may well upset your
tummy), foreign talk, and a feeling that not knowing the English
equivalent of such coinage—or if you do, you need paper and
pencil to work it all out—you may be 'done down'. And should
you find an error in the sum, you get all the excuses under that well-
advertised sun, for same, politely and smilingly given, of course!

And what of the tipping? If you don't give sufficient or
more than sufficient, you'll feel as though you can't make for
the frontier barriers fast enough; in fact the taxi-man may leave
you half-way unless you grease his palm well *en route*.

However, you may not believe me; I don't expect you will!
But at least I have warned you, so the only answer is to go ...
and come back. And when you do come back, you will eagerly
want to read the chapters that follow.

> ... Never the light falls on the bay
> Never a wave breaks in to foam
> But my heart goes with it, on its way
> Looking out from my Highland home ...

*   *   *

So onwards to the land of FÀILTE and SLÀINTE MHATH; GU
ROBH SÌTH AN SO (peace be here) and BEANNAICH-SO (bless here)

—two salutary greetings in the Gaelic; the land where *nobody
hurries*, and to the secret of deep living which lies in the unseen
place where Time and Sense is forgotten. Beyond mere words,
signs, forms or symbols; where you live each day at a time.
And each day can be quite a full day up in the Highlands. Up
in these parts you can tour awhile and stay awhile! Am thinking
this is a good slogan, too! (surely I have not caught the continental germ after writing so much about these advertising
tycoons!) And Aunty, if she hasn't a car can take a seat in a well-
known holiday-coach-touring company's fleet and travel in ease
and comfort along the Road to the Isles, (made famous throughout the world by that song-writer Kenneth MacLeod "By
Tummel and Loch Rannoch and Lochaber I will go; by Ailort
and by Morar to the sea") or the royal route to Gairloch, and
return loaded with Scottish presents, Edinburgh rock, tartan
scarves and knickers, Gairloch jumpers, and so forth, and tell her
neighbours when she gets back with a twinkle in her eye, how
much she enjoyed everything, even the Edinburgh Festival
where she saw a young girl wheeled naked on a TV / lamp
trolley across the McEwan Hall organ gallery; but especially of
a wee drop o' the 'craitur' (that's whisky to you!—'Noontide
Dram' she called it!—) that warmed the cockles of her Lan-
castrian heart from time to time, and which greatly fostered
friendship *en route*. In this respect it made, she said, one feel
at home, abroad! (Surely not *another* advertising slogan ?)
Further, she will tell her friends there are no traffic jams in the
Highlands; no fume-ridden stretches of road. Just plain, good air,
sandwiched between scenery and good-living people. And here
she found peace and quiet, and an air of 'the world forgetting'.

The Scottish Highlands cover one-third of Scotland, equivalent to a fifth of the total area of England and Wales; and in
that area is contained the highest mountains in Britain, and
some of the deepest lochs in Europe. As to scenery—well,
you will read of all this wonderland in these forthcoming pages.
CEUD MILE FÀILTE, a hundred thousand welcomes, is the traditional greeting of the Highlander to any stranger who may stay
with him, even though it be just for one night . . . and another
Gaelic saying 'would that you were coming, instead of going'.

*   *   *

Thus do I urge you to read on; to learn of these parts, and what there is to offer in life in visiting these corners of pure charm and expanse. (Some people have really no idea how big Scotland is; they think it is a little place at the top of England, and that we still employ the pigeon post!) You will be glad you took the chance to do so. You will be sorry to have given it all a miss, and gone elsewhere. Well, not exactly *sorry*, for you will not have known what you *have* missed; but shall I say, you will be the *poorer* by having missed it all.

The purple heather blooming on every ben,
The burns ababbling o'er stones and down the glen;
The misty mountains, towering high
The trees, the bracken, the very sky
Create a picture in the mind
That nowhere else you'll ever find.

Hail Caledonia!

CHAPTER 3

NORTHWARDS—TO THE NORTH-WEST

IN previous writings, I have taken readers carefully on their way from Edinburgh up the Caledonian Canal to Inverness; via Stirling, Callander, Lochearnhead, Glencoe, Ballachulish ferry, Fort William, Fort Augustus, Drumnadrochit. Quite an array of Highland names, through quite a range of varying Highland scenery. There is no need to elaborate on this journey here; so we will now assume we *have* arrived at Inverness; by rail, road or air.

Inverness—via the Caledonian Canal. This canal was a tremendous engineering feat, constructed by Thomas Telford, who started making it in 1803; and nineteen years later, the sloop *Caledonia* was the first ship to traverse the sixty miles from Corpach, Fort William, to Clachnaharry at Inverness. Of the sixty miles, about twenty miles are artificial; the remainder being composed of the three lochs, Loch Lochy, Loch Oich and Loch Ness. The canal has twenty-nine small locks, controlled by the Ministry of Transport. The cost of the project was $1\frac{1}{2}$ million pounds. The main object was to save fishing craft the slow and sometimes perilous journey right up the west coast of Scotland to the top of Caithness through the Pentland Firth ('twixt the Orkneys and Caithness), and down to the east coast ports.

Inverness, Queen of the North; the capital of the Highlands, and really the only town of any size in the north of Scotland. It has a broad river flowing through it, and thus has an advantage over Edinburgh; and there are pretty walks round the River Ness. The city prides itself on the purity of its speech and intonation. Most fascinating. Just as you enter the town, from the S.-W., you pass Tomnahurich, a renowned cemetery, beautifully situated on a hill; known generally as the HILL OF THE YEW TREES, but more correctly the HILL OF THE WHERRY. When, in the Stone Age, torrents burst their way seawards, this hill opposing them stood firm, the waters passing by on either side.

There is a very interesting small book, though now out of print, viz.: *The Prophecies of the Brahan Seer.* This seer was undoubtedly imbued with second sight. He was one Kenneth Mackenzie, better known as Coinneach Odhar Fiosaiche, the Brahan Seer, who was born in the Island of Lewis, in the parish of Uig, about the beginning of 1600, and became possessed of a stone in a remarkable way by which he could reveal the future of man and mankind. He no doubt predicted a great many things; among these may be placed his prophecy, 150 years beforehand, of the making of the Caledonian Canal and that ships would sail round the back of Tomnahurich Hill. In point of fact a paragraph appeared in the *Inverness Advertiser* in 1859 (*i.e.* before Tomnahurich had been made a cemetery) and reads thus:

> Tomnahurich, the far-famed Fairies' Hill, has been sown with oats. According to tradition, the Brahan prophet who lived 200 years ago predicted that ships with unfurled sails would pass and repass Tomnahurich, and further that it would yet be placed under lock and key. The first part of the prediction was verified by the opening of the Caledonian Canal, and we seem to be on the eve of seeing the realisation of the rest by the final closing up of the Fairies' Hill.

This, mark you, was in print before the prediction was fulfilled. The Seer's prophecy was that the day would come when Tomnahurich, or as he called it, The Fairy Hill, would be under lock and key and the fairies secured within. A unique cemetery on the top of a hill and the spirits (of the dead) chained within. The Brahan Seer was the keenest-eyed of all Highland prophets. The Fairy Hill is not quite correctly named; as I have said it is the 'Hill of the Wherry'—a light boat, which upturned, Tomnahurich very much resembles. The Hill of the Fairies may have been very well ascribed to the near-by village of Ballnaferry—'ferry' being sounded like 'fairy'. But this is a small discrepancy surely in the light of the prophecy?

I have made mention of the fact that this Seer became

possessed of his revealing stone in a remarkable manner. Whilst working as a common labourer on a farm in the neighbourhood of Loch Ussie, on the Brahan Estate, his mistress—the farmer's wife—was unusually exacting with him, and he, in return, teased her, and on many occasions spent a great deal of his wit upon her, much to her annoyance and grief. His conduct became so unbearable that she decided upon disposing of him to save her from future annoyance. Love growing cold sort of style! And an opportunity soon arose. The Seer's boss had sent him away to 'cut the peats'—a common source of fuel—and it was necessary to send him his dinner for he was a good distance away from the farm to come home; and his 'girl-friend', the farmer's wife, decided to kill him by poisoning his meal. When it arrived, our friend and prophet, being exhausted from his honest exertions in his master's interest and from want of food, lay down on the heather and fell asleep. He wakened suddenly by feeling something cold on his breast, which he found was a small white stone with a hole through the middle. He looked through it, when a vision appeared to him revealing the treachery of his mistress. To test this 'divination', he gave his dinner to his collie dog; the poor beast writhed in agony and died.

It was indeed a prophetic stone, and as he looked at and through it, he found himself deprived of the sight of his right eye —the eye he looked through—and thereafter he continued *cam* or blind of an eye. If the Brahan Seer *did* possess the power of prophecy (and I am of opinion he did), he more than likely used the stone as a 'gimmick', simply to impress the people who might never believe he was possessed of such a gift of foresight unless they saw and had evidence with their own eyes, the means by which he exercised it.

Going northwards out of the town, there is a fine wide vehicular traffic bridge completed in September 1961, and formally opened on the 28th of that month. There is, too, a notable castle, situate on a high mound overlooking the flowing Ness, which in olden days served as a goodly watch-tower. On the mound standing boldly in front of the Castle entrance, is the statue of Flora Macdonald, whose name—as all must know— was so linked with Bonnie Prince Charlie of the 1745 Jacobite Rebellion. The inscription on the monument is in Gaelic and English and reads . . .

As long as a flower grows on a field
So long will the fame of the maiden endure.

So we say farewell, *slàn leat*, to Inverness, its castle, station and airport (Dalcross), and wend our way to Garve, through Beauly, Muir of Ord and Contin—unless one wishes (after Muir of Ord) to see Dingwall and Strathpeffer. Dingwall is the county town of Ross-shire. It was called in Norse, THING-VILLR, 'Field of the Thing'; the Norse General Court of Justice. Dingwall was therefore in those days the centre of the Norse administration in Ross-shire. Strathpeffer, five miles out of Dingwall, is a very popular resort and centre for tours up north, and is beautifully situated in a fertile strath. It has an equable temperature the year round as it is so near to the Cromarty Firth. It used to be famous for its Spa waters, but now this is almost a thing of the past. The waters were of two kinds, chalybeate and sulphurous, bearing a strong resemblance to those of Harrogate in Yorkshire (now defunct) and Aix-la-Chapelle in France.

The road and journey via Contin, however, is more pleasant and far less congested than the main Dingwall road. At Muir of Ord, a road runs eastwards to the Black Isle; Fortrose, Rosemarkie and Cromarty. Like many isles in Scotland, it is really a peninsula—a very fertile one—the shores of which are bounded on one side by the Cromarty Firth and on the other by the Beauly Firth, both merging into the large Moray Firth. This peninsula is termed the 'Black Isle' because snow seldom if ever lies there. It is famous for its crops and cattle. In the old days it was also said to be 'black' because the greater part of it was black moor, uncultivated.

Shortly after leaving Contin village, we come to the Falls of Rogie, approached through the woods by a few minutes' walk off the main road where a quarry is being worked. These Falls are a famous beauty spot where the Black Water and the Rogie Burn meet in a wild gorge with the waters crashing over the black rocks in a spectacular, natural fall; and when in full flow you may watch, fascinated in the extreme, the salmon hurtling out of the lower pools up into the high torrent in its urge to reach the spawning grounds beyond. Some of the jumps the fish have to make from one pool to the other above them may be as much as 10-foot sheer; yet they make it (maybe after more than one try) in one mighty leap. It is incredible how they manage it; but manage it they do. These Falls are a veritable rockery of nature's own making; the waters tumbling down in a musical cascade. Visitors, *en route*, must NOT miss this great sight.

The salmon, and the trout! Both wily fellows having instincts such as we humans have. Such animal wisdom speaks volumes for some invisible Creator, who infused instinct into otherwise helpless little creatures; and it all makes one think deep down at times that our Universe has been—and surely must have been—designed and executed by some profound Intelligence; but how and when is so frighteningly unexplainable.

Examine this instinct. The young salmon spends years at sea, then comes back to its own river, travelling up the very side of that river into which flows the tributary where he was born. What brings him back so precisely? If you transfer him to another tributary he will know at once that he is 'off target' and will fight his way down and back to the main stream and then turn up against the current to finish his 'destination home' more accurately. There must be some hidden power; truly the firmament sheweth His handiwork.

It is a fascinating story, full of intrigue, starting from the egg, a tiny red globe which lies buried in the gravel bed. From the egg he lives in the dark off the yolk-sac attached to him. The sac finished, he pushes his way out of the gravel, barely an inch long, and as he grows very slowly he may only be an ounce or so or a few inches long after two years there. One day the impulse seizes him, and all his compatriots, and they start downstream to the sea, and when they taste the salt water they head out to sea and vanish, no one knows where. Yet he comes back, maybe in one or maybe in five years' time, but he comes back and to the mouth of the river in which he was hatched. He will now be some 18 inches long and weigh 8 or 10 pounds; should he have been away at sea longer he may be 40 to 50 pounds and strong, very strong. He carries on to his birthplace and never stops to feed, surmounting waterfall after waterfall. Before a salmon leaps over a weir and up a waterfall it judges its height by eye. The Freshwater Fisheries Laboratory at Pitlochry are studying the behaviour of the salmon very extensively. They pair off eventually, and when they reach the right bed the female swims close to the bottom, turns on her side and fans violently with her tail, digging a trench a foot or so deep, and expels her eggs, whereupon the male covers them with milt as they sink to the bottom of the trench. They are covered over, and then new trenches made and so the fertilising goes on, the female laying up to as many as 20,000 eggs. In due course the eggs come to life and the whole cycle commences again.

Recently government research into the spawning habits of salmon has provided a new and fairly accurate method of calcu-lating the number of eggs the fish will lay, and it should now be possible for anyone who knows the lengths of female salmon going up-river to spawn to estimate, with a very good degree of accuracy, the number of eggs these fish will lay. The number of eggs in the ovaries of female salmon has been obtained and worked out on an average according to the size of the fish, and so the fertility of the salmon has been studied almost to a fine art.

To the east of these Falls of Rogie, and south-west of Ding-wall and south of Strathpeffer with Ben Wyvis towering 3430 feet high is Loch Ussie, into which loch it is said the Brahan Seer eventually cast his divining stone.

Earlier, I have mentioned how Kenneth, who was gifted with Celtic second sight (TAIBH-SEARACHD) obtained his powers. There is yet another version as to his receiving the stone, and I quote roughly from *The Prophecies* thuswise: Whilst his mother was looking after the cattle one summer evening on a ridge overlooking the burying-ground in Uig, she saw all the graves of the churchyard opening, and all the people, from newly-born infants to old grey-haired folk, coming up out of the graves and departing in many directions. After a while they returned to their resting places. But she noticed one grave still open, and she went to look at it, placing her distaff over its mouth (for she had heard from old stories that if she placed that upon it, the spirit of the dead one would not be able to enter). Shortly she noticed a fair woman coming rushing inwards. The spirit said 'lift your distaff off my resting-place so I may enter'. 'That I will do', said Kenneth's mother, 'if you will tell me why you did not come along with the others; what delayed you ?' The spirit replied that her journey to Norway was much longer than theirs, for she said 'I am the daughter of the King of Norway and was drowned whilst bathing in that far-off country, and my body was found on the beach nearby here; and so my grave is here. As a small reward and token of your courage' she said, 'I will possess you of a valuable secret. You should go and find in the loch nearby, a small round blue stone, which you should give to your son, who by its powers can reveal the future.' The mother did as commanded, found the stone and gave it to her son Kenneth. No sooner had he obtained this stone of divination, than his fame spread far and wide; being sought after by the gentry. And no special meeting of theirs was considered complete unless Coinneach Odhar was present. So to those who had some belief in premonitions and the supernatural, he was looked upon as a living authority.

* * *

So leaving the Falls of Rogie (and reminiscences of the Brahan Seer) we wend our way onwards to the tiny village of Garve, set in the colourful wonderland of the north-west. At Garve, with a lovely cosily-tucked-in hotel, of fishing and food renown and wonderfully managed and owned by my great Highland champion—Miss Helen Mackenzie of the third generation from the time the hotel was built close on 310 years ago; the days of stage-coaches and carriers, when it took many days to get through to Ullapool, only thirty-odd miles away. And if through snow, then perhaps weeks. At Garve, you breathe in a completely different atmosphere—indeed a different world comes upon you, suddenly and with no warning whatsoever. The Garve Hotel, an inn in the old days, was a posting house, used by the drovers of those days whilst journeying to and from the west coast to the stock sales at Dingwall.

From Garve then, we really embark on our true journey to Wester Ross, where—I would repeat—*nobody hurries*. A mile out, at the hamlet Gorstan, one road turns right—to Ullapool by Strath Garve and the course of the Black Water river and the vast forests which cover this strath (Strathvaich in particular), the haunts of the red deer; the other straight on is *our* road to Gairloch. From Garve to Loch Maree by way of Strath Bran is our way, and you are now embarking on seeing landscapes of the wildest, high mountains, rock-streams, moors, lochs and glens; colours galore made either by the setting sun or rain, or both with the attendant rainbows caressing you and the roadway you follow. No towns; only villages or hamlets, consisting mostly of scattered crofts and homesteads with a church and a post office—clachans, in fact. A 'clachan' may be said to consist of a school, a church and an hotel, surrounded by unproductive moorland. Hotels few, roads narrow, winding and hilly; no garages to speak of, certainly none boasting first-class repairs. That is the picture, the glorious panorama in technicolor as the film people would say; and I feel sure when you do reach journey's end you will say I have not exaggerated; that it is even more spectacular than words can describe.

Leaving Garve we make for Achnasheen (Field of Storm) 16 miles, the one and only road, twisting and turning, passing the long 6-mile Loch Luichart, utilised in the hydro-electric scheme, the magnificent power station being at Grudie Bridge. Should you be interested to view the power house, and visitors are welcome (you are asked to sign the book on leaving), you should take a look to see if your shoes are clean; or even take them off as though you were entering a mosque, for as soon as you open its portals you would think you were in some beautiful stately home, with red polished floors and not a speck of dust to be seen anywhere. There were two men using a Hoover polisher on the floors when I made an unexpected entrance; and this in a building, an industrial building, at the back of beyond; polishing the station floor and wearing soft slippers so as not to mark their handiwork! It is a beautifully built house blending well with the hills and valley, the dense foliage and fast running burns. Very spick and span and elaborate indeed; and its erection and upkeep has no doubt put 'nought point something' on to the cost of current production *ex* Grudie.

Thence by Loch Achanalt, Strath Bran (already named), to Achnasheen, a road and country packed full of breathtaking interest.

From Achanalt by the banks of the river Bran the mountains tower on either hand, hemming in the verdure-fringed river which winds its way through this rugged stretch of country. On the left is Sgurr Vuillin, 2845 feet high; and ahead Fionn Bheinn, 3060 feet, its lower slopes rising abruptly from the shores of Loch Rosque.

As for Achnasheen, it is only noted for its railway station, a very busy one; for there, goods and mail to Gairloch and the north-west are unloaded; the main line carries on to Kyle.

From Achnasheen our journey is even more exciting than before. The road to the left just out of Achnasheen takes you via Loch Carron to Strome Ferry and Kyle; to the right we go. The road for three miles travels alongside the north bank of the desolate Loch Rosque. It then mounts 800 feet and descends Glen Docharty 1-in-12. Just past the summit, shortly passing the A.A. box and suddenly coming round a bend and without warning, there comes into view the majestic panorama of Loch Maree and the country for miles beyond.

Should you be privileged to have a nice bright day, you will look down on this famous watershed open-mouthed, with miles of apparently molten-silver reflecting the morning's sun, with —it seems—scores of fir-clad islands floating on its waters, the haunts of much bird-life, gulls and grey geese whose homes are sheltered by the feathery trees rising from the loch itself; you will look down on all this and look up to Slioch on the right (3217 feet) and Beinn Eighe (Ben Eay) to the west (3309 feet)— a white quartzite mass. It is a dazzling view, this silvery setting, the more so I think because you are looking 800 feet down on everything. You may search the dictionary tumbling over all the superlatives you can find; search your mind for all the appropriate epithets, but none I feel sure can adequately or justly describe the sudden and terrific impact of the occasion. Nothing short of seeing it for yourself will suffice. It is not as though you are on the edge of a precipice looking sheer down; nothing so frightening as that, but you are looking down and across to the great expanse of the west, and what it has to offer. A breath-taking panorama of that initial moment when everything appears before you fresh and new and shining; a herald of things to come; grandeur of stark simplicity. It beggars all description. The sight is compelling. At that instant you feel you have a sense of being a member of that company of original explorers and pioneers who opened up this country of the north-west. Of all the countless lochs in Scotland—or in Britain —none possess this commanding, arresting approach. None. A loch whose still and polished surface reflects as a mirror every detail of the enchanting scene, flawlessly. . . . The County Council should erect an attractive wooden chalet at this vantage point, for visitors to rest awhile, and to take note at leisure of what is in store for them.

The Gaelic name of Glen Docharty is GLEAM DOCHARTAICH, and from the negative prefix DO and CARTACH—scoury or place of scouring—we get the term 'glen of excessive scouring', which describes it well.

Cruising down Glen Docharty (sometimes spelt Docherty) in third gear—there's no hurry, you know!—you soon reach Kinlochewe, a typical Highland village, with its neat little kirk erected by public subscription in 1878. Kinlochewe means 'the head of Loch Ewe'. There is a nice, cosy well-managed hotel there, with food at its best. A few yards beyond this hotel (the original part of which was built over 300 years ago as a posting house) the road divides; the left, or south-western branch entering Glen Torridon and the renowned Torridon range, whereas straight on, the main road continues to the head of Loch Maree —thence to Gairloch.

*   *   *

Before leaving Kinlochewe, I would tell you of a cairn; a rough mound of stones on a hillside. Many such cairns are to be seen dotted here and there in the Highlands, built by children or a family as they romp the moorland. It is just something to do, something unusual to that of making sand-castles on a beach. But this *is no ordinary cairn*; perhaps not in design, but certainly in origin and in family memories.

On coming down to the bottom of Glen Docharty, and just before crossing a small bridge at a bend, a quarter of a mile from Kinlochewe village itself (and the bridge there, built 1843), should you look to the right, this cairn is seen a little way up the rocky hillside. . . . It is to the memory of one, Major Angus James Donald Macdonald, M.C., of the 1/6th Gurkha Rifles, who was killed in Malaya in June 1952.

Angus was born in Newtonmore shortly after his father's death, and his mother then brought him and the three other young children in the family to live in Kinlochewe, where he attended the village school and later went on to Dingwall Academy. He made the army his career, but always spent as much time as he could in Kinlochewe, roaming around Loch Maree and Slioch. He received the M.C. whilst serving in Burma in the Second World War; then he married. Going east again, he won his second M.C. in Malaya in action against

B

the terrorists, and many times was he mentioned in despatches; all of which the Kinlochewe folk greatly admired. His wife and two young sons were with him during the Malaya campaign, but in May 1952 she had to bring the younger one, Roddy (a babe in arms, who was stricken down with severe poliomyelitis) to England for special medical treatment and operations. The following month, June, her husband Angus was killed near Taiping, Perak. He was shot whilst leading and shouting to his men to attack a terrorist camp. His personal gallantry, to quote his commanding officer, far and away exceeded the call of duty; he had no thought for his own safety, only that for his men under him. He was a fine tall fellow (cut down in life at only thirty-five years of age), with Highland looks, dark hair and the bluest of blue eyes. In uniform he resembled the familiar Canadian Mountie.

His wish had always been, if anything were to happen to him in Malaya, for his remains to be placed in that cairn at Glen Docharty, so that he could for ever be near 'his' Loch Maree and Slioch. His wish was carried out in July 1953, the service being conducted by the Rev. Macdonald of the Church of Scotland, Gairloch. The cairn was built up more firmly by the village folk of Kinlochewe, who all loved and esteemed him; and then they hauled the heavy granite plaque up the hillside. The inscription thereon (headed with the crest of the 6th Gurkha Rifles) reads:—

In memory of

MAJOR ANGUS J. D. MACDONALD, M.C.

1/6 Gurkha Rifles

Killed in action Malaya 3rd June 1952
Dearly beloved husband of Jean
and daddy of Andrew and Roddy.

"If it be life that waits
I shall live for ever unconquered;
If death—I shall die strong
In my Faith and Free." ...

Am not sure from where this quotation comes (it was suggested by a Mr. Macdonald, ex-Chief Constable of Arbroath, now curator of the Clan Museum, Newtonmore) but almost the same words appear on the Scottish/American War Memorial in Princes Street Gardens, Edinburgh.

For myself, I could add these lines . . .

> Softly the leaves of memory fall
> Gently we gather and treasure them all.
> Unseen, unheard, you are always near
> Still loved, still missed and very dear.

The then babe-in-arms, Roddy, is now 13 years old; still having to be carried, still undergoing operations, yet still brave and courageous as his daddy, and nothing daunts him. His elder brother Andrew is 15 years of age, and they all live in Edinburgh. A long, long time since tragedy struck this Kinlochewe family in the jungle of Malaya in June 1952. Whenever I pass that cairn, I turn and salute, not only the bravery of the man whose ashes lie there, but the bravery of his widow and of his two sons, whom I know. As the French would say: ÇA DONNE BEAUCOUP À RÉFLÉCHIR ('it makes one furiously to think').

With feelings of British pride, we leave Kinlochewe.

Ten miles brings us to Loch Maree Hotel; and here, and at Loch Maree itself, there is much to claim our attention. The road along Loch Maree follows the western shore. Loch Maree is a gem if ever there was one; a real Highland loch over 12 miles in length, 30 feet above sea level. Embracing beauty, romance, superstition, and of course—salmon and sea trout; mostly the latter. The Scottish Council of Physical Recreation now runs a course of learning the art of angling at Loch Maree Hotel.

We stop at the hotel, which was built in 1872. From it one may see the loch is adorned by a number of wooded islands.

This hotel claims distinction on account of the visit of Her Majesty Queen Victoria who occupied the house from 12th to 18th September 1877. This visit called forth the reverential loyalty of all in Gairloch parish.

As we enter the doorway and look up we see a plaque bearing the translation of the Gaelic words on a boulder, 'Torridon Red' sandstone, Sir Kenneth Mackenzie, Laird of Gairloch, caused to be carved to mark the occasion, and which is to be seen just across the roadway from the hotel door.

The Gaelic inscription is as follows:

AIR AN DARA LATHA-DEUG DETH MHÌOS
MEADHONACH AN FHÒGHAIR, 1877, THÀINIG

BAN-RIGH BHICTORIA A DH'FAICINN LOCH-MARUIBHE,
AGUS NAN CRÌOCHAN MU'N CUAIRT. DB'FHAN I
SÉA OIDHCHE S'AN TIGH-ÒSDA SO THALL; AGUS
'NA CAOMHALACHD, DHEÒNAICH I G'UM BIODH
A' CHLACH SO 'NA CÙIMHNEACHAN AIR AN
TLACHD A FHUAIR I 'NA TEACHD DO 'N CHEÀRN
SO DE ROS.

And the literal translation thus:

On the 12th day of the middle month of autumn 1877 Queen
Victoria came to visit Loch Maree and the country around it. She
remained six nights in the opposite hotel and in her kindness agreed
that this stone should be a memorial of the pleasure she experienced
in coming to this quarter of Ross.

The hotel, purely one may say a fishing hotel where good
attention and good food is the order of the day, is beautifully
placed in a sheltered bay backed by a hill called Sron a Choit,
970 feet high whose rocky tops rise above most beautiful natural
birch woods. A small jetty was built in 1884 as a landing-place
for the steamer which in those days plied up and down the loch,
from Loch Maree Hotel to its western end near Loch Ewe,
Tollie pier.

This steamer ceased to operate many years ago, but at the
time, afforded an easy comfortable way of viewing the beauties
of this 'Queen of Highland Lochs'.

The waters of Loch Maree are exceptionally clear, owing to
the rocky and gravel nature of the bed and shores. It never
acquires the dark and peaty tinge which very often characterises
Scotland's many other lochs. Loch Maree's greatest depth is
360 feet; mean depth 125 feet, and the volume of water contained in the loch is some 38,000 millions of cubic feet.

The steamer, Mabel, used to berth at the north-western
corner of the loch, at Tollie ('a place of holes') just near Tollie
farm, and you can see some of the jetty posts to this day, nestling
under trees and rock, beneath the rugged grey cliffs of this wild,
yet 'gentle' beauty spot. This pier was erected in 1883; and on
leaving it, Fox Point is on the left; a low small promontory
terminating in grey-white rocks, deriving its name from some
legend of a fox closely pursued by dogs, taking to the water
here; either that or of some fox of unusual size being killed
there. Behind here, the river Ewe leaves Loch Maree, where

Inveran House and farm are situated. There are stepping-stones across the narrow waters and legend calls them 'sweethearts stepping stones'. Giant Fingal himself is supposed to have planted them. (Oh yes, there are dozens and dozens of legends up Wester Ross way!)

About half-way up the loch, the woods of Letterewe appear ('the Slope to the Ewe'). Near here may be seen the mouth of a canal and on the hillside above, the track of a tram line which brought limestone from a large quarry further up; now defunct. Thence we see Letterewe House, a delightful setting, and used as a summer residence by one of Britain's tycoons. Both in and out of season, Mr. MacPherson, head gamekeeper and general factotum, keeps the estate with its red deer under control. Just beyond Letterewe, the Furnace burn falls into the loch; the hamlet takes its name from the old iron-smelting established there by Sir George Hay about 1605, using ore shipped from Cumberland to Poolewe and brought down the loch to the forest at Loch Maree which was burnt to make charcoal. In all, seven iron furnaces were so situated until all the trees were felled. The furnaces consumed over 100 acres of forest annually. 'Tis good this is all defunct, for who would wish this countryside to be labelled 'The Black Country'?

There is a story—still told to this day—of the first Presbyterian minister who came one summer across to Letterewe to 'convert' the people there. The folk in the wee parish were so incensed, they stripped him naked and tied him to a tree to be literally eaten alive by midges. He suffered agonies and was half demented when he was finally released one night by an old but kindly woman. He fled as best he could, laying a curse upon the hamlet to the effect that no godly people would ever inhabit Letterewe.

We then pass under Slioch's dominating gaze. Slioch, composed mainly of Torridon sandstone, resembles, from some angles of its conical shape, a spear-head and that is its Gaelic meaning; an ancient spear or lance and also that of an ancient flint arrow-head. As you sail close by and look up, it has the appearance of a vast wall, a mighty Gibraltar in Wester Ross. Cold, austere Slioch, whose blue, purple and grey flanks shimmer in the heat haze, or stare vividly at you from the mist before plunging steeply sheer down into the loch. Loch Maree is never frozen over. The red deer mentioned previously are often seen to swim across from their forest to the many islands on the loch, just for a few months; then back again. From Letterewe and near by, the steamer would cross over to Loch Maree Hotel, and as it tied up you would get a good view looking up the glen down which the Talladale flows emptying itself into the loch. From Loch Maree Hotel, the steamer would wend its way along the south shores of the loch, passing Slattadale, thence onwards till it came to Tollie again; its starting-point.

There are twenty-seven islands in Loch Maree, all beautifully wooded; the principal ones are Isle Maree (named after St. Maelrubha, who came from Ireland in 671 to found a monastery at Applecross (A.D. 673), below Torridon, and which has a ruined chapel and burial-ground; and of which I will have more to say shortly); Eilean Suthainn ('isle of fairies' or 'the everlasting island') the largest, nearly 1 mile long and within it there is a small loch with two tiny islands; Garbh Eilean ('the rough isle'); Eilean Dubh na Sroine ('the black isle of the promontory'); and Eilean Ruaridh Mor ('the big island of Rory') and called after a celebrated chief of the MacLeods. On this island, as well as on some of the others, no doubt, the illicit distillation of whisky took place during the good old days of the 1800's.

I have already said there is much superstition up in the north-west country; this generally seems to be the case in most mountainous countries. The supernatural comes to light and takes on form in many ways: mountains and the weird shapes they throw out in the dark and closing mists; old gnarled and twisted trees; lochs with inky-black, deep, still waters; and the long drawn-out still nights—all go to make up legends, yarns and superstitions.

There was the belief that a draught of Loch Maree water was a sure cure for many a disease; in fact it is on record that many invalids had bottles of such water sent them in the certain belief of its curative powers. Nowadays I suppose it would be whisky from Loch Maree, should there ever be such a brand or blend! Recently I heard of an American millionaire who obtained a bottle of Loch Ness water by air mail, as he wished, in opening an old folk's home (whose Scottish ties were of the Caledonian Canal district) to give each resident a glass of real Loch Ness water. Verily there are no ends to ingenuity!

Among older superstitions were the Druidical sacrifices of bulls on Isle Maree which continued as late as 1678. The afore-mentioned St. Maelrubha, who brought Christianity over to these parts in the 7th century, allowed this, giving it a Christian aspect! In those later years the sacrifices seemed to have been connected with the resort to the island for the cure of insanity. This is recorded in the Presbyterian annals.

Yes, there are legends by the score: of a Wester Ross woman who had spent one year with the fairies; that certain peculiar noises and moving lights foreshadowed a death; that plants bedded when the moon was on the wane would never survive; that a stick cut from the bird-cherry tree prevents one being lost in the mist; that whales attack boats newly tarred, and that breaking of the Sabbath brings swift retribution.

On Isle Maree are the remains of a chapel, the successor of an early hermitage of St Maelrubha. Close by is the sacred well long famous for its cure of mental disorders.

Queen Victoria visited Isle Maree on 16th September 1877, whilst she was spending the six days at the hotel. It was the Sabbath day and Her Majesty graciously read a short sermon to her Gairloch gillies. She then fixed her offering in the wishing-tree, it being understood that a wish silently made when making such an offering would be realised; and that should anyone remove or steal any such offering, a misfortune to the person would follow in its wake.

Near the celebrated wishing-well stands this oak tree studded with nails and hundreds of copper coins. To each of these was originally attached a piece of clothing belonging to some patient who had visited, or been brought to the spot. I must confess I have plugged more than one penny into that famous tree myself over the years.

In all probability coming to the island for the cure of insanity dates back to the time of the saint. The procedure was for the party to row several times round the island and those next to the afflicted forcing the lunatic three times into the water covering his or her head. They then stepped on the island, the patient knelt before the altar, then went to the wishing-well, drank some of the water, and finally attached some offering to the tree. They all then rowed back again to the mainland.

This well, so legend has it, lost much of its power later on, because a shepherd who had a mad dog took it to the well and pushed it headlong in. The following day the dog died, and a few days later the shepherd also died!

An American poet once visited this sacred well and was so impressed with what he saw and of the stories he was told as to the healing-powers attributed to the well that he wrote these lines:

> And who so bathes therein his brow
> With care or madness burning
> Feels once again his healthful thought
> And sense of peace returning.
> Of restless heat and fevered brain
> Unquiet and unstable
> That holy well of Loch Maree
> Is more than idle fable.

After St. Maelrubha's death, he became the patron saint of this district. His name is variously known as Malrubius, Murie, Mourie and latterly the corruption Maree. There can be no question but that this island and this loch bears the name of this saint.

In respect of St. Maelrubha's death, four parishes lay claim to the honour of being that in which his remains lie: Applecross, Ferintosh, Gairloch and Farr. There is no doubt he was the greatest of Celtic saints, and by whom throughout Scotland some twenty-two churches were founded around the north-west coast, Skye, Harris, Argyll, Islay, Loch Fyne and up at Lairg in Sutherland.

There is yet another and sweet love-story attached to Isle Maree that I simply must relate. It was told me over thirty years ago by 'Willie the Gillie' of Badachro, a tailor in those days.

After St Maelrubha's death at Applecross, 21st April, A.D. 722, the holy College of Iona appointed a successor to his hermitage on Isle Maree. He was an aged religious man reputed to have great sagacity and piety, one to whom the local folk, as well as the Norse Vikings, could call upon frequently for ministrations of religion, as well as to obtain his wise counsel. The Vikings held this district in subjugation, but to all alike, Celt or Norwegian, he gave his blessings.

There was a young Norwegian prince, Prince Olaf of royal blood, who was the chief of the Vikings in this part of the north-west coast. Not only did this parentage warrant him being their chief, but his personal bravery and daring also enamoured him to his fellow clansmen to be their leader.

They all lived in the prince's war-galley, but during the winter months they would seek shelter and comfort in some of the islands of Loch Ewe. The prince would oftimes come to Isle Maree to see the venerable saint and solicit his advice and blessing.

In due time our noble prince fell in love with a Norwegian princess, but he hesitated to bring his lady-love away with him to live on board a rough war-galley, as a life of that nature and in such surroundings was not befitting such a lady of rank. He accordingly sought the advice of his friend on Isle Maree. This blessed saint suggested the building of a high tower and enclosure near the west side of the isle, so that the prince could bring his bride there, surrounded in peace and quiet by her maid-servants and still be close to his royal highness' galley on Loch Ewe.

This was done and Olaf brought his beautiful fair bride to Isle Maree where they were married by the aged hermit. The princess and her servants were enraptured with such a romantic secluded setting. Everyone was happy and life for the young lovers was one round of passionate delight.

His comrades, however, were planning another expedition and begged their leader to join them on board and sail away to plunder. His young wife was distressed beyond all measure when he told her he had to go and join his comrades and that he must leave forthwith. Shedding copious tears was of no avail to our warrior, who was impetuous and highly strung and so after hours of sorrow she allowed him to go off on this exploit.

But what if something dreadful should happen to him; or for that matter, if something should happen to her during his absence?

In talking over such grievous ideas they both thought of a plan to let each other know in advance how the other had fared.

When the prince was returning up the loch, he should hoist a white flag from his barge on Loch Maree should he still love her and all was well; if not, then a black flag would be flown.

This was arranged; and the princess too, when she saw her master's boat approaching was to leave her retreat in her barge and to fly a white or black ensign accordingly. Both then would know in advance each other's thoughts.

The years went by, as they do in all fairy-tale books, and in due course being victorious, the prince and his party returned safely and anchored at Poolewe. With feverish haste he got into his barge all ready for Isle Maree, raised his white flag of success and love, and urged his oarsmen to row fast to his beloved.

But all through these years, the princess had been filled with anxiety and foreboding. Did her lover, she wondered, prefer his exploits of war and plunder to that of the quiet and stillness of Isle Maree—their home where they could raise a family—or in fact was he really faithful to her when out of her sight? Was this exploit, and others too, a mere pretence for him to court the love of another woman? Under this spell of jealousy and distrust she thought of a plan to test her darling's affection.

When the prince's barge was sighted the princess and her maidens set off in her barge with a black flag amast; not only that but a bier was placed in the middle of the barge on to which the princess stepped, and reclining with the apparent sleep of death on her, a white shroud was spread over her still body. Then her attendants feigned utter grief in all this play-acting.

As Olaf's boat drew nearer he could see a black flag was waving from his beloved's barge—the flag of death; and he was beside himself with anguish and despair, being quite unable to control his agony of mind. When the barges drew alongside the prince leapt aboard, raised the shroud, and seeing that his dear wife was dead, flung up his hands to heaven, drew out his dirk and plunged it straightaway into his heart, dying instantly.

Now this was certainly not what the princess had expected, albeit she had assumed a posture so deathly real; full of grief and stricken beyond all measure, she drew the dirk out of Olfa's heart and plunged it into her own bosom.

She did not die until her barge turned back to Isle Maree, where the holy man was waiting at the slipway, and was able to administer the last prayers of comfort; then she silently passed away to join her beloved Olaf.

The two bodies lie buried in the grounds of the now ruined tower of the island; and a stone and two ancient crosses mark the grave to this day.

Truly a sad, sad story, but one that many old locals seem to have heard of in their bygone youth. We will treat the legend as true, for it will then lend a special air of romance to that lovely saintly island ('the eye of Loch Maree') set amidst the loch bearing its name—a gem within a gem.

As in J. M. Barrie's play, *Mary Rose*, there is one island in particular that 'likes to be visited, and where one never grows old'—and I would say that island should be Isle Maree.

Loch Maree was probably once a sea-loch; the river Ewe which links it with the salt water of Loch Ewe is only 3½ miles long—doubtless the shortest river in Britain.

Anent Loch Maree, a story is handed down from generation to generation that one day after Culloden's disaster to Prince Charlie, a stranger with fair hair and clad in tartan, came to a wee farmstead near the present Loch Maree Hotel, asking for food and shelter. On the morn's morn he left and gave the wifey a gold piece. News that a stranger with gold was in the neighbourhood spread as fast as news *does* spread in the Highlands! The next night, a shot rang out in the stillness, and later on the dead body of the young man was found, robbed of everything. It was subsequently learnt that the young laddie was Prince Charlie's valet, who was carrying French gold pieces. A day or so before this event, two vessels had been sighted in Poolewe bay, and it was assumed they had come to pick up this man and his gold.

So much so for entrancing Loch Maree, most of the northern side of which is privately owned and reserved as a sportsman's paradise.

As I write these lines, there is a scheme on foot to connect up Fionn Loch with Lochan Fada (behind Slioch) for a hydro-electric project involving 6½ million pounds; but the lairds are objecting, on grounds of 'spoilation'. It is said the power-line insulators would glitter like electric-light bulbs in the sunshine and so affect amenities: and the argument continues, much to solicitors' advantage!

We now carry on along the final ten miles of our journey to Gairloch. It has taken quite a while to reach from England, but metaphorically speaking 'it is better to travel than to arrive'. Life is like climbing a mountain; the climb is what matters, and we have climbed our way so far through a wonderful region of the British Isles, soon to arrive at our haven. Everything we have left behind us is not only far away in terms of miles, but far away in terms of spirit.

So we wind our way, passing Slattadale (which we had seen

from our dream-boat a short while ago) thence we leave the
shore of Loch Maree which we have followed for more than
half its length, and cross inland—'westward to the sea', through
narrow Kerrysdale. Rising a little to catch the last glimpse of
Loch Maree through a little forest clearance, kindly thought of
and made for the tourists' benefit by the Forestry Department,
we drop down into Kerrysdale where, at Kerry Falls, there is a
small yet prettily built hydro-electric power station.

From there, skirting the Kerry river (said to be the Norse for
'the copse river'), passing the small stone Kerry bridge on the
left (the turning off for Badachro, Port Henderson and Red
Point) we soon come to the sign GAIRLOCH; then passing the
factor's house, down the brae to the post office and the Old Inn
(completely modernised and excellent accommodation) when we
catch sight of the harbour and pier on the left, and Flowerdale
House—for long, long years, the west coast residence of the
Baronets of Gairloch, the Mackenzies—through a grand avenue
of trees on the right.

We have reached Gairloch.

We have in fact arrived OUT of this world, and IN to Gairloch;
and when that has been said, all else is but repetition ... clear
air; a sense of space and timelessness; scenic treasures all around,
and on a golden summer's night—a general hush.

GAIRLOCH

GAIRLOCH; the Gairloch of Wester Ross, the land of the FÀILTES and SLÀINTE MHATHS; a village and district possessing one of the loveliest settings in the north-west Highlands, a 'resort with a difference'—the REAL Highlands of Scotland—overlooking beautiful horse-shoe GAIR LOCH (with the islands of Eilean Horrisdale, Dry Island, Longa); the Minch, the Cuillins of Skye, the wild Torridon mountains; and on clear days and nights, Stornoway in Lewis, and the south end of Harris. Gairloch with its ever warm climate, even in winter, due to the Gulf Stream lapping its shores; limitless stretches of golden, sandy beaches (the safest imaginable), a small golf course; a district where Time is of really no account, and villagers typically Highland and hospitable to the last degree; a hospitality that is not just a cliché, but a way of life. A coast-line said to be the finest, not only in Britain, but in *Europe*; a friendly people with that old-world Highland courtesy and charm; a God-fearing Gaelic people who keep the Sabbath as few others do in this land of ours; and all this 'midst crashingly beautiful scenery, peace and quietness . . . could one ask for more? For the scenery is not merely viewed—but lived in.

I simply put it to you, to think of all this. True, there are no elaborate cinema or dance halls, no bright neon lights, no rush of traffic, no pavements, no No. 9 buses, no city germs, but just Nature as it was created, and as it is meant to be preserved. An air of purity; an air of Highland respectability; an air of difference and uniqueness; an atmosphere far removed from that of the hurly-burly life of towns. Does not all this make for contentment; for a life worth living, a holiday that is worth one's while? One's ambition is to live. Coming even for a brief sojourn up in the midst of all I have detailed, must surely help and brace one—both materially and spiritually—to live on. Not only that, but to appreciate the *need* to live on; for whilst here one feels thankful one is alive and able to drink in all that peacefulness can offer in this outpost of Empire; this Scottish Wild West. And up in these parts you have to accustom yourself to the fact that no sooner have you seen one surpassingly beautiful place, but another one looms up. Adjectives and adverbs lose their meaning west of Garve ... *where nobody hurries*!

Enough of this though, or else readers will think this is a slice of Tourist Board propaganda!

We are in Gairloch, at the post office which is the hub of the postal service for distribution of mail bags for both the north and the south sides of the bay, *i.e.* for the Strath/Melvaig and the Badachro/Red Point districts. These post and sub-post offices are under the jurisdiction of the Chief Postmaster, Dingwall. The mail bus from Achnasheen railway station (where all mails for this area are unloaded, those remaining go on to Kyle) continues on to Poolewe, Aultbea and Laide. *En route*, of course, this Wells-Fargo mail coach stops at many wayside houses and crofts, handing out letters and packages to folk who are on the wait, not only for this great event of the day, but to hear the latest news and gossip; and that can be plenty! The Gairloch post office at mail times is a very busy place, but everything works out smoothly to time-table and dove-tails in perfectly. Nae bother at a'. A fine old Highland lady, Mrs. Mackenzie, now 85 years of age, was in charge of the post office for some 60 years. In 1953 she received the Coronation Medal in recognition of her services. Even today, she manages to take a hand at odd times, helping and relieving her daughter who is the postmistress. She still knows and keeps in touch with all the latest about forms and regulations; and I salute such a wonderful woman.

From the post office then, we come to Gairloch proper, and after crossing the bridge with the harbour on the left, its fishing boats in from the Minch, and its gaily lighted wharf at nights, we see on the right—through an avenue of trees—the approach to Flowerdale House, for many years, as I have said, the west-coast residence of the Baronets of Gairloch—the Mackenzies. *Flowerdale House*, being a private residence needs its privacy respected, so I will say little personal about it; for nothing is more annoying than to be infested with tourists, complete with cameras, barging in and out wanting to look around; for it is not as though it were Balmoral, Inverary or Dunvegan Castle. The east coast residence of the Gairloch family is at Conan House, Conon Bridge, Ross-shire. The first laird was *Hector Roy Mackenzie*, born 1440, who succeeded to the title in 1494, and died 1528. It was he who received a grant of Gairloch from King James IV. This old wattled house of Gairloch was called An Tigh Dìge (moat house) from it being surrounded by a ditch. The present house is called in Gaelic Tigh Dìge nan Gorm Leac (moat house of the blue flags, *i.e.* slates) and is a few hundred yards above the stone bridge which crosses the Ceann-an-t-Sail river at the head of Gairloch bay.

Flowerdale House is built in two sections; the old part erected by the ninth Laird and second baronet of Gairloch (and so called because of the profusion of wild flowers), was the very first slated house in the district. In the First World War it was used by Prime Minister Lloyd George and his Cabinet, who several times met here. In those days Winston Churchill was only a junior secretary and was given a tiny attic room, whilst David Lloyd George, of course, had the biggest room of all, together with a luxurious adjoining flat! The house has a large vegetable garden and luscious strawberries are grown and sold locally. The whole house and 'policies' are very well sheltered from the south-west winds here in the winter. There is a saw-mill on the estate; for during the years many forest trees are cut down and sawn up for general marketing.

The name, as I have said, was due to flowers being so plentiful in that no sheep ever were allowed to come near the grounds, except on a rope to the slaughter-house.

The Gairloch lairds have Norwegian blood in their veins, for Tormod MacLeod, second of Harris and Dunvegan, was a grandson of Olave the Black, the last of the Norwegian kings who owned the Isle of Man. He died about 1237. In the early part of 1400, Gairloch belonged to the MacLeods. The Mackenzies' Gairloch ancester was Eachainn Ruadh (Red Hector Roy), as I have indicated.

The 'Mackenzies of Gairloch' family was descended from Alexander Mackenzie VI of Kintail, by his second wife Margaret, daughter of Roderick Macdonald III of Moydart and Clanranald, the famous 'RUAIRIDH MACALAIN', by Margaret, daughter of Donald Balloch of Islay, son of John Mor Tanastair, second son of John, first Lord of the Isles by his wife Lady Margaret Stewart, daughter of King Robert II, and brother of Donald, second Lord of the Isles and first Earl of Ross. By this lady, the sixth Baron of Kintail had one son . . . Hector Roy Mackenzie.

When Hector Roy was a young man, his brother-in-law, Allan MacLeod, resided at Gairloch, but the two brothers MacLeods of Lewis, closely connected with Allan, swore that no one with Mackenzie blood should hold Gairloch, and they came over to conquer. Allan, having some inkling of this venture, placed his family on a small island in Loch Tollie (Poleweways). The MacLeod brothers caught Allan asleep whilst he had gone fishing on the near-by river Ewe, and on the banks of the river, at CNOC NA MI-CHOMHAIRLE without any warning, they killed him; they 'made him short by the head'. They then went to the isle and told the wife as to what had happened to her husband. They tore her two stepsons from her knees (the other stepson and her daughter were away at the time, luckily), took them ashore, and carried them along to a small glen through which the Poolewe road now passes, about a mile to the south of the loch, and there at a spot still called CREAG BHADAIN AN AISC (the rock at the place of burial), stabbed them to the heart with their daggers, and carried their blood-stained shirts along with them to the Tigh Dige. Their stepmother managed to secure these shirts through the strategy of one of her husband's retainers, who at once proceeded with them to the boys' grandfather, Alexander Mackenzie the sixth of Kintail at Kinellan, who sent his son (our aforementioned ancestor Hector Roy) with the shirts, as evidence of this atrocity, to report the murder to the King at Edinburgh. His Majesty, upon hearing of the crime, granted Hector a commission of fire and sword to wage war against the murderers (the MacLeods) of his nephews, and then gave him a Crown Charter to the lands of Gairloch in his own favour, dated 1494, as previously recorded. The two assassins were soon afterwards slain at a hollow still pointed out between Port Henderson and South Erradale (vide The South Side chapter), nearly opposite the northern end of the island of Raasay, where their graves are. This was the first step that

Hector Roy got to Gairloch. Allan, however, was loathe to give up the custody of Gairloch, but after several skirmishes in which he was beaten by Hector Roy, he was content to allow him two-thirds of Gairloch, provided Hector would let themselves —the MacLeods—possess the other one-third in peace; which he did, and they kept possession till Hector's great-grandchild put them from it.

The MacLeods made various unsuccessful attempts from time to time to regain Gairloch, and eventually peace was restored.

But for the tragedy of that small island in Loch Tollie, the Mackenzie's may never have been the 'Mackenzies of Gairloch'.

Hector Roy was betrothed to a daughter of the Laird of Grant, but she died before the marriage was solemnised. He, however, had a son by her called Hector Cam, he being of blind eye. After the death of Grant of Grant's daughter, Hector Roy married his cousin Anne, daughter of Ranald MacRanald, generally known as Ranald Ban Macdonald V of Moydart and Clanranald. By this marriage with Anne, Hector had four issues, namely (1) John Glassich, his heir and successor, (2) Kenneth of Meikle Allan, (3) John Tuach of Davochpollo, (4) Dougal Roy, who inherited Scatwell near Dingwall. (It was here, in a pool of the river Conon that one of the Fingalian heroes, Finn MacCoul, caught a salmon in which he found the tooth of knowledge, which gave him powers of clairvoyance; similar to later times of the Brahan Seer attributing *his* prophetic gifts to a stone.) Hector had also another son, John Beg, who was illegitimate according to some authorities, from whom descended several Mackenzies who settled in Berwick and Alloa. Hector Roy, when he died in 1528, was succeeded by his eldest lawful son, *John Glassich Mackenzie*, who was a minor at his father's death. John Glassich married Janet Agnes, daughter of James Fraser of Phoineas, brother of Hugh, sixth Lord Lovat, and had three sons and a daughter. He had also two natural sons before his marriage, Alex Roy and Hector Caol. The latter left a numerous tribe in Gairloch, still known as Clann Eachainn Chaoil, and said to be distinguished by their long and slender legs. John Glassich was assassinated in 1550 at Eilean Donan Castle, and buried in the Priory of Beauly. He was succeeded by his eldest lawful son, *Hector Mackenzie*.

Although Hector Roy obtained a charter of the lands of Gairloch in 1494, the MacLeods continued, as I have said, for a time to hold possession of a considerable part of the district. They had all to the east and south-east of the hill situated on the west side of the churchyard of Gairloch, between the Free and Established churches. At the east end, on the high and easily defended rock, stood the last stronghold occupied by them in Gairloch—to this day known as the 'Dùn', or Fort. Various localities may be pointed out in Gairloch where desperate skirmishes were fought between the MacLeods and the Mackenzies. There is the 'Fraoch Eilean', a small island in the bay between Shieldaig and Badachro, opposite LEAC-NA-SAIGHID—as it was spelt in those days (Leacnaside, see 'South Side'), where a naval engagement was fought. Of this engagement and of many others, thrilling accounts have been handed down through the centuries; especially of the prowess of many Kintail heroes who were mainly instrumental in establishing the Mackenzies of Gairloch permanently and in undisputed possession of their beautiful and romantic inheritance. Many of the MacLeods, after they had been driven from Gairloch, settled in Skye.

After the death of Hector Mackenzie (John Glassich's eldest son) without issue in September 1566 we can record the following successions: *Alexander Mackenzie* (who, however, died a few weeks after succeeding to the estate, and therefore it is seemingly unnecessary to count him as one of the Barons of Gairloch); *John Roy Mackenzie*, John Glassich's third son came next, and lived till he was eighty years of age and was buried in the old churchyard of Gairloch in 1628; *Alexander Mackenzie* who was well advanced in years at his father's death, was most active in the duties pertaining to the head of his house during his father's lifetime, and he led the Mackenzies of Gairloch against the MacLeods in their repeated incursions to repossess themselves of the estate lands. He died in January 1638 in his sixty-first year, and lies buried in Gairloch; *Kenneth Mackenzie*, a strong Loyalist during the wars of Montrose and the Covenanters, died in 1669 and was buried in Beauly Priory; *Alexander Mackenzie*, died aged but forty-two in 1694; *Sir Kenneth Mackenzie* (Alexander's only son by his first marriage) created a Baronet of Nova Scotia by Queen Anne on 2nd February 1703. He died at the early age of thirty-two in December 1703, and buried in Gairloch; *Sir Alexander Mackenzie*, the second Baronet, a child of only three-and-a-half years old when he succeeded Sir Kenneth. In 1730 he married his cousin, Janet Mackenzie of Scatwell, on which occasion a fine Gaelic poem was composed in her praise by John Mackay, the famous blind piper and poet of Gairloch, whose daughter became the mother of William Ross, a Gaelic bard even more celebrated (as recorded later) than the blind piper himself. The marriage did not turn out a success and in 1758 she separated from her husband. Sir Alexander came of age in 1721, and in 1738 he pulled down the old family residence of Staukhouse, or Tigh Dige at Flowerdale, which stood in a low, marshy, damp situation, surrounded by the moat from which it derived its name, and built the present house on an elevated plateau encompassed by woods and hills with a southern frontal aspect. He did not participate in the 1745 Jacobite Rebellion for he had no sympathy with that cause. There were nine children of his marriage. He died in 1766 in his sixty-sixth year and his eldest son, *Sir Alexander Mackenzie*, third Baronet, succeeded him. He was known as 'AN TIGHEARNA RUADH'—the red-haired laird. He built Conan House between 1758 and 1760 during his father's lifetime. He was married twice and died in 1770, being succeeded by his eldest son (by his first marriage) *Sir Hector Mackenzie*, the fourth Baronet, generally spoken of amongst the Highlanders as 'AN TIGHEARNA STORACH', the buck-toothed laird. He was only twelve years of age then. Sir Hector married in 1778, but there was no issue, and by arrangement the marriage was dissolved in 1796. Within a month of the separation he married Christian, daughter of William Henderson, Inverness, a lady who was very popular with the Gairloch people. There were five children of the marriage. He died April 1826 and was buried in the Priory of Beauly; *Sir Francis Alexander Mackenzie*, fifth Baronet, came next and he was twice married. He died in 1843 and was followed by his eldest son of his first marriage, *Sir Kenneth Smith Mackenzie*, sixth Baronet, who was born 25th May 1832, and was considered then to be one of the best and most enlightened landlords in the Highlands. Following the example of his father and grandfather, he dealt directly with his people without any factor or other intermediary, except for an estate manager at Gairloch. In December 1860 he married Eila Frederica, daughter of Walter Frederic Campbell of Islay, by whom he had two sons and one daughter. He died 9th February 1900. His eldest son, *Sir Kenneth John Mackenzie*, born 6th October 1861, seventh Baronet, was the next to succeed to the Gairloch estates. He died 4th December 1929. He married in April 1891 the Hon. Marjorie Louisa Murray, eldest daughter of Viscount Stormonts', eldest son of the Earl of Mansfield, K.T. They had two sons, Hector David (heir) born 1893 and Roderick Ian—who died in the First World War—and one daughter, Marjorie Kythe. The latter married, becoming Lady Stirling. *Sir Hector David Mackenzie* succeeded his father as eighth Baronet. He subsequently became heir to the Conan estate. He died 10th May 1953.

The present lairds of Gairloch are *Brigadier and Mrs. Mackenzie* (the latter being a daughter of Sir John and Lady Stirling of Fairburn, *i.e.* Sir Hector's niece; she married Brigadier Stevenson, D.S.O., O.B.E., changing their name back to Mackenzie). When not in residence in Gairloch they live at Conan House, Conon Bridge. They have a family of three sons, and two daughters. Brigadier Mackenzie was made a Deputy Lieutenant for Ross and Cromarty (along with seven other distinguished personages) in 1964.

It will be noticed the mention of Beauly Priory has been made more than once in connection with the interment of several Baronets. As one will read further on, Sir Kenneth's son, Roderick, whose name appears on the Gairloch War Memorial, was also interred in the Priory. Beauly (from the French 'BEAU-LIEU', meaning a beautiful place), a small historic, but busy market town today, is thirteen miles out of Inverness and just before reaching Muir of Ord. The red-stoned ruined Priory of St. John Baptist, was founded in 1232 by Sir John Bisset of Lovat, for a French religious order. Bisset was a young man when he came north from England to seek his fortune in the service of William the Lion. When Alexander II succeeded to the throne, he established a number of religious brotherhoods throughout Scotland, and Beauly Priory was one of three in his kingdom belonging to the Valliscaulian Order. The first coterie of eight monks and a Prior came from Burgundy. They devoted their time to reading, prayer, contemplation and gardening; and their rules and regulations were austerely strict. They had to wear hair shirts next to the skin, and their habits were of the coarsest wool. In that clothing, and fully shod, they had to sleep in beds without mattresses. Fare was plain. They were allowed neither meat nor gravy, and from Easter to September, they ate only two meals a day with only bread and water and one relish on Fridays. Strict silence was observed, and no women were allowed to enter the bounds except to see the Prior on the business of the Order.

All that remains of the Priory today is the roofless shell of the Church, consisting of nave, chancel and transepts. The former St. Catherine's Chapel is the family vault of the Mackenzies of Gairloch, a link going back to the 15th century, when the Prior was a natural son of Alexander Mackenzie of Kintail. The Mackenzies of Gairloch re-roofed their vault and rebuilt part of the walls and tower during this century.

The late Lord Lovat, who built buttresses around part of the ruins, had plans to re-roof the east end of the building and make it into a chapel, but stories of desecration of the graves, somewhat exaggerated, led to such local agitation that this and other works of renovation were abandoned. The old Mercat Cross standing outside the Priory gate was found lying in a coal yard nearly thirty-five years ago. Consisting of a single column with a square head, which was patched up and raised on the present site, its restoration was made possible by funds subscribed publicly.

At the Reformation, the Priory had possession of lands many miles around Beauly as well as valuable salmon fishings. There was an orchard attached to the Priory. Some old Beauly residents can remember apple trees growing in the now deserted area. The oldest tree within the Priory bounds is a 600-year-old sycamore.

Set amongst stately elms and sycamores, this ruined Priory is a reminder of the simple lives of those French monks who once lived there in contemplative peace.

Apart from the Mackenzies of Kintail and Seaforth there are some forty other *Cadet* families of Mackenzies (of which the Mackenzies of Gairloch form one) all of which make interesting reading.

The *Coat of Arms* of the Mackenzies of Gairloch is thus: Quarterly: 1st and 4th, azure, a buck's head cabossed or (gold); 2nd and 3rd, azure, three frasers argent (silver). *Crest*—a Highlander wielding a sword, proper. *Mottoes*—over crest, 'Virtute

et Valore' (by Virtue and Valour); under, 'Non sine periculo'
(not without danger).

And so we leave the history and the genealogy of 'the Mackenzies of Gairloch'—highly beloved and respected lairds; and
carry on with our narrative of Gairloch and Gairloch district.

At the time of the '45 rebellion, many Government ships
were searching all over the western seaboard of Scotland for
Prince Charlie. One such warship came into Gairloch bay, and
the captain sent a message ashore for the laird to come on board
and dine. Not many in this district followed the colours of the
Bonnie Prince, so the laird of Gairloch made an excuse from
accepting that invitation. The captain was grievously annoyed,
and as his ship weighed anchor, it fired a heavy shot in to TIGH
DÌGE, which hit the gable wall but did little damage.

Paraffin was unknown in those days, so Flowerdale House
was lit by candles. All the table and bed linen for the house was
woven in Conon village, from the spun flax which grew pro-
lifically on the east coast.

I have already referred to the Brahan Seer's prophecies.
This remarkable man makes several references to Gairloch
which form interesting reading. The first is anent Gairloch
House, wherein he records (early in the 1600's be it noted) 'A
dun, hornless cow (supposed to mean a steamer) will appear in
the Minch off Carr Point, in Gairloch and make a "geum" or
bellow, which will knock the six chimneys off Gairloch House'.
Gairloch House, the Tigh Dìge of the seer Coinneach's day, was
the old house which stood in the park on the right as you went
from the bridge in the direction of the present mansion. The
walls were of wattled twigs, wicker work or plaited twig hurdles,
thatched with turf or divots and surrounded with a deep ditch,
which could, in time of approaching danger, be filled with water
from the river, hence the name 'Tigh Dìge', 'house of the ditch'.
It has been suggested the seer's prediction referred to this stronghold, although the ancient citadel had no chimneys to fall off.
The present mansion, however, is called the 'Tigh Dìge' and
strangely enough it *has* the exact number of chimneys—six!

Then again he predicted that 'a bald black girl will be born
at the back of the church of Gairloch', which has been fulfilled.
During one of the usual large gatherings at the sacramental
communion a well-known young woman was taken in labour,

and before she could be removed she gave birth to the dark baby, whose descendants are well known, I believe, and pointed out in the district to this day as the fulfilment of Coinneach's prophecy.

Another prediction that duly came to pass was that 'a white cow will give birth to a calf in the garden behind Gairloch House' also that in 'Flowerdale, a black hornless cow will give birth to a calf with two heads'; it, too, came to pass. And he prophesied that 'the buck-toothed laird will leave the estate of Gairloch without the rightful heir'. Sir Hector Mackenzie, the fourth Baronet of Gairloch, *was* buck-toothed. Now do you believe in Celtic second sight? Sir Hector was the grandfather of that great personality, Osgood Mackenzie of Inverewe Gardens fame, and author of that most interesting book, 'A hundred years in the Highlands', and who died in 1922, eighty years of age.

There were in those old days, many famous pipers of Gairloch named Mackay. The most famous was one Rory, who had one son John, born in 1656 at Talladale (Loch Maree). Both these men lived to the ripe old age of one hundred years. John was struck blind by smallpox in his very early youth, and was later known as Iain Dall (Blind John, or the celebrated Blind Piper) and learnt most of his art from the Macrimmon School of Piping in Skye. He was piper to the first Baronet of Gairloch, Sir Kenneth Mackenzie; and when Sir Kenneth died, to his son, Sir Alexander, 2nd Baronet and ninth laird of Gairloch. He was a bard (poet) as well as a piper. One song he made is said to be still unsurpassed in the Gaelic language. Rory and John are buried in the same grave in the Gairloch old cemetery. The blind piper had one son, Angus, who became piper to the tenth laird of Gairloch. Angus also lived to be nigh on ninety years of age, and he had one son, also called John—grandson of Iain Dall, born in 1755—who on the death of his father, became the family piper to the then laird, Sir Hector Mackenzie of Gairloch. Young John lived at Slattadale (Loch Maree), married, had a large family, and later decided to emigrate to America. On his departure, there never was another piper to the lairds of Gairloch. Piper John made good in America and died there (*circa*) 1840. So ended the illustrious régime of 'the pipers of Gairloch'. The four named, all of whom lived to such advanced ages, were pipers to the lairds of Gairloch for almost two hundred years; during which time there were eight lairds in Flowerdale.

And so we leave Flowerdale ... but whilst on the subject
of pipers and songs, it is very necessary to mention the name of
William Ross, a very celebrated poet, universally known towards
the end of the eighteenth century as 'The Gairloch Bard'. The
Celtic inhabitants of the north-west Highlands have always been
enthusiastic over *poetry* and *music*.

William Ross was born at Broadford in Skye in 1762. His
mother was a native of Gairloch and daughter of the renowned
blind piper and poet Iain Dall, just mentioned. His father built
a small house on Aird the site of which, Leas-a-Rosaich, surrounded by rowan trees, can still be pointed out. It was the
headquarters of the Ross family from which they came and
went; and here it was that Ross died. He was educated in Forres
and later joined his parents who had moved to Gairloch. His
father was a pedlar and young William went along with his
father in his journeyings through Lewis and the Western Isles,
and so became acquainted with the Gaelic language in all its
different dialects. At the age of 24 he was put in charge of the
Gairloch parish school and was most successful in his work there
and his reputation grew. He studied Latin and Greek and
became quite a master of those difficult languages. He acted as
precentor in the Gairloch church. From his youth upwards he
was never a robust lad and he died in 1790 in Badachro near Aird
farm at the early age of 28.

He was buried in the churchyard at Gairloch and it is recorded
the whole population of the district were present to pay their
last respects to a very clever man. He was of their race, their
blood and bone. They knew and loved him well.

Many years later, in 1850, a handsome monument was erected
over his grave through the efforts of Mr. George Ross, a clansman
of his, who for many years was head keeper at Flowerdale House,
Gairloch.

The monument bears inscriptions in both Gaelic and English
and reads:

In memory of *William Ross*, sometime schoolmaster of Gairloch,
better known as the Gairloch bard, who died in 1790, aged 28 years,
this monument is erected over his grave by a few of his countrymen
and others headed by the amiable and accomplished proprietor of
Gairloch, in testimony of their respect and admiration of his extraordinary genius and great native talent 1850.

His name to future ages shall descend,
While Gaelic poetry can claim a friend.

He was truly acknowledged as the foremost Gaelic scholar of his day, and his poetry, it is said, came from the heart.

It should be remembered that a song is composed under two conditions—the air or sound (Gaelic fonn) and the metre or measure. The air is the melody holding the words in a smoothly-flowing order; the metre is the number of syllables in the line. Both these elements occur, and must occur, in the same song.

In a tour Ross made to Stornoway he met one Marion Ross —mayhap a kinswoman of his own—and fell in love with her. His passion or infatuation was only on his part, not on hers. It is believed there was, however, a secret engagement and Marion invoked fire from heaven to consume her if ever she proved unfaithful.

Not long afterwards she married a sailor, a Captain Clough, and went to Liverpool, his port, residing there. But her thoughts constantly turned to her real lover, Ross; and it is thought that when her husband was away on long voyages she wrote to Gairloch suggesting that Ross should meet her. He journeyed as far as Stirling on this secret mission but there his better sense prevailed and he retraced his steps to Gairloch. He spent many nights in the open before reaching his father's cottage and broken in mind and body, took to his bed for the last time. When the unhappy Bard was breathing his last, his thoughts and soul went to far off Liverpool to make claims on Marion, the fulfilment of her promise to wed or the end which she had invoked heaven to send upon her. She was at that moment with the help of her maid dressing in white preparing to attend a ball. A knock was heard at the door and she turned white with fear. The maid answered and told her that a tall young man in Highland dress was waiting without. She heard her mistress whisper 'William Ross'. Marion went to the door but there was no one to be seen. She was holding a lighted candle in her hand, and that very instant the flame was blown inward setting light to her flimsy garments and she was burnt to death. The fate of the hapless Marion had been fulfilled.

The monument—over 100 years old and exceedingly well preserved—is in the form of a stone urn, with a flame on the top—standing on a 15-inch square pillar; the whole being nearly

6 feet high, and is situate a little distance up on the right side of the old graveyard after entering the iron gates.

Another great poet, author and piper was one John Mackenzie who collected and edited the work entitled, *Beauties of Gaelic Poetry*, which contained many of the Gairloch Bard's Gaelic love songs, unequalled for noble sentiments and tender passion to the fair maid who had jilted him. Early in life Mackenzie was apprenticed to a travelling carpenter, and during his travels he carefully noted down all the Gaelic songs and stories he heard and of their origin. At Gairloch he spent much time copying William Ross's poems and then occupied himself to the completion of *The Beauties of Gaelic Poetry* which took him some twelve years. It has all down the years been looked upon as a standard masterpiece of work on Gaelic poetry. He also wrote *The History of Prince Charlie* in Gaelic; and was the author of the English-Gaelic part of MacAlpine's Dictionary.

He translated into Gaelic many religious works.

He died at Poolewe in 1848 whilst he was preparing a new edition of the Gaelic Bible.

On a projecting rock outside the Gairloch churchyard there stands a handsome monument, with the inscription:

> In memory of John Mackenzie, who composed and edited 'The Beauties of Gaelic Poetry' and also compiled, wrote, translated, or edited, under surpassing difficulties, about thirty other works.
> In grateful recognition of his valuable services to Celtic literature, this monument is erected by a number of his fellow countrymen, 1878.

Gairloch and district in its days has seen many worthy men connected with poetry and music; for where there is poetry, there is generally music to be found; and where there is poetry and music, there is generally piety to be found. Gairloch parish has been a religious parish since the days of St. Maelrubha came to Loch Maree and built his first cell there on Isle Maree.

Leaving Flowerdale, and viewing the picture-postcard harbour and pier of Gairloch on the left, with all the fishing boats discharging cod, haddock, herring and such like caught in the Minch, we rise up the brae and pass the bank; the one and only bank here, which opens at 9.30 a.m. as against the common practice of banks in England, 10.0 a.m.

After the bank, the 9-hole, 1975-yard golf course appears

on the left nestling in to the hillside landscape in a picturesque setting. Although but a small course, I consider it to be, as sporting holiday-courses go, one of the most beautiful in the country. The longest hole (the 8th) is only 360 yards long, and the bogey for the nine holes is 31.

The course was planned and laid out by a Captain Burgess, and much ingenuity was displayed in the placing of the greens in the positions they are today. So much has been made out of so little ground available.

The ground on which the course was laid was granted for that purpose by Sir Kenneth Mackenzie, Bart., of Gairloch, and during his lifetime he, as well as his wife, took a keen interest in the Club's welfare and finances.

There is a nicely built wooden club-house with all conveniences, and a wee shop. The greens are beautifully kept because some few years ago the finances enabled the club to purchase a large-size petrol-driven green-cutter; very different from the old days when Angus, the greenkeeper I knew for many a long year, had to cut the long grass with an Old-Father-Time's scythe; he had to pull around a small hand-mower for the greens, up hill and down dale. But he managed to keep it well-nigh perfect. Angus retired in 1950, being greenkeeper since 1923. He used to journey daily from his Strath croft on a bicycle carrying his wee cairn-terrier ('Chappie') in a basket in front of the handle-bars; and the wee fellow would follow him lovingly around the course.

Angus retired to his wee croft to lead a very quiet life, for he was none too strong; from his cottage he could see 'his' golf course a few miles distant, with thoughts of all those good years in which he so carefully tended it. He passed away suddenly on 20th November 1963, beloved by the whole village, for he was such a quiet likeable man, and a great upholder of the Free Kirk; and one of the Precentors in the old days. From the club-house steps one can see the mountains towering in the distance—Boisbhein and Ben Alligin; great landmarks, and from some of the tees (particularly the high one, No. 6, reached by steps cut in the earth) there are magnificent views. You need to go round this small pocket-edition course to appreciate its fascinating attractiveness. In the season naturally it is crowded, but not too crowded; out of season—well it is Heaven. And as you amble round slowly and with no attempt at lowering any records, and look around and admire the majesty of nature, the complete peace—utter and absolute—the stillness of life and of all that is about you, you stand and pause, and if you are religiously inclined you thank God you are alive and able to 'take in' the beauties of the earth; if you are not, well then you can just take off your hat and bow to the almighty Universe.

Yes, to play over the golf course of Gairloch when everything is quiet, is a privilege; a privilege to look upon the firmaments made by One unseen Power. If the poet Omar Khayyám could say, 'There was a Door to which I found no Key; there was a Veil past which I could not see', I would say you need no key to this door opening wide to natural grandeur; and there is no veil hiding this landscape's alluring beauty.

Viewing this wonderful panorama, it may not be out of place to quote the Biblical saying, 'If thou wouldest believe, thou shouldest see', and one feels constrained to bend one's knees in adoration; for the trees, rocks and mountains are before one's eyes—as witnesses.

In mid-August, the Gairloch sheep-dog trials take place on the golf course, along the 'rough' of the 1st hole; and it attracts very many people from near and far.

At the bend of the road opposite the club-house, there is the Church of Scotland, close to the 300-year-old Gairloch burial ground, studded with many trees, now more or less closed, the new cemetery being across the roadway. We carry on up the brae and stop at a lay-by vantage spot near the War Memorial and look down upon the famous golden sandy bay of Gairloch—Gairloch Sands—a stretch of perfectly level, clean sand. It must be one of the finest beaches in Europe. You can wade out in this secluded bay, a hundred yards or so and still only be waist-deep in the clear, blue water washed by the Gulf Stream. The bay is so extensive you feel alone, even during the peak tourist season. The unrestricted beaches here in Gairloch district are so spacious, so *uncluttered*, that a few hundred people or so would hardly be noticed. And there are no deck-chairs with attendants pouncing on you for a 6d. or 1s. hire, as per the English coastal resort beaches!

The War Memorial commemorating the First World War stands silently overlooking the bay, and has sixty-three names inscribed round its sides; men from Gairloch, Strath, Badachro, Red Point, Poolewe, Mellon Charles, Melvaig, Inverasdale, and Kinlochewe. As you mount the twenty steps up from the roadside, you read the inscription facing you:

Erected by
Sir Kenneth and Lady Marjory Mackenzie in memory
of their son Roderick I. Mackenzie, Lieut., Black Watch
and the men of Gairloch
who gave their lives 1914–1919

And on the base is the quotation:

'Be thou faithful unto death, and I will give thee a crown of Life'.

Roderick Ian was buried in a private vault in Beauly Priory. The inscription on the plaque there reads, 'Erected by Sir Kenneth and Lady Marjory Mackenzie, in loving memory of their younger son, Roderick Ian Mackenzie, 2nd Lieut. 1st Bat. Black Watch, died 11th April 1915'.

Passing on, we drop down with the Free Church of Scotland on our left, the manse on the right to Gairloch Hotel, a 3-star 55-room hotel erected in 1872, and enlarged over the years and now equipped with everything of the latest. I have patronised this hotel for nigh on fifty years; it has a most attractive frontage; an unrivalled outlook commanding a beautiful situation 80 feet above and close to the edge of the large horseshoe-shaped bay of Gairloch. Wonderful views are obtained from all the front windows of lounges and bedrooms—the Isle of Skye, the Cuillins and on clear days and nights Stornoway in Lewis and the south end of Harris.

The hotel is superbly decorated; has an attractive cocktail bar and cellar bar; every comfort, with first-class food and most efficiently managed and staffed. In truth an ideal spot for a peaceful and contented stay; you are certainly 'away-from-it-all' here. (During the Second World War it was taken over by the Royal Navy as a hospital; for Aultbea, 15 miles further on was a very important base in those perilous Atlantic convoy-days).

It will not be long before you become acquainted with the Gaelic, viz. 'Gairloch Hotel; Fàilte do Gearrloch' ('welcome to Gairloch Hotel'). Then after blotting your signature in the arrivals' book, you meander along through the spacious, thickly-carpeted lounge to the cocktail bar to see what it's like; and being impressed you say to the smart girl behind the counter, no! *not* 'haven't I seen you before somewhere' technique, but 'Glayva, Slàinte' ... very good, good health. Glayva being also the name of a liqueur, I'd have you know.

Yes, quite a nice restful hotel. A number of the old and faithful servants that I have known for many a long year, are now living in the village, enjoying their well-earned retirement. It is pleasing to see them—links and memories of those good old days—and to talk to them of bygone times, and to wish them all *Slàinte Mhath*. Upstairs to change for dinner; a good meal and then to bed, and looking out on to a perfect bay, completes our journey for today. If you chanced to hear the strains of a guitar playing O *Sole Mio*, you'd say you were in Italy.

*   *   *

Gairloch—the land of the *Fàiltes* and *Slàinte Mhaths*; and mentioned by that great geographer, Ptolemy of Alexandria, Egypt, who lived about A.D. 120. Its name is derived from two Gaelic words, *gearr* (short) and *loch*. It is a typical Highland parish; very large for it covers an area of over 200,000 acres, ranking as the fifth biggest parish in Scotland. It is larger than the county of Rutland in England, and bigger than Clackmannanshire in Scotland; but it has an extremely small population

In 1880 the population was over 5000.

In 1911 it decreased to 3300.

In 1951 the population again dropped to 1990.

In 1961 the census puts the figure as 1763, nearly 50 per cent decrease in fifty years.

The parish has a tremendous coast-line, very indented and possesses innumerable and lovely sandy beaches—all unrestricted as I have said. There are more than twenty-five peaks of over 2000 feet in height; five of them reaching over 3000 feet.

Taken as a whole the people's livelihood may be aptly put as 'one foot in the sea, and one foot on the shore'; in other words, fishing and/or cultivating their bit of land.

In early days it was nothing for the young men to tramp on foot over to the east coast, Fraserburgh and such-like towns, to earn twelve weeks' money for the herring fishing; then tramp all the miles back again in time to fish at this side of the coast.

What a journey! And what stamina was required in those days in order to survive.

The northern-most boundary of Gairloch parish is at the river, Little Gruinard, thence it follows down the centre of that river to Fionn Loch (white loch) and Dubh Loch (black loch) and the mountains to the north-east of Loch Maree, including Letterewe, Loch Maree, Kinlochewe and as far as the eastern end of Loch a' Chroisg, the other side of Glen Docherty, namely almost adjoining Achnasheen. The boundary then follows in a south-westerly direction going across the ridge of Beinn Eighe and Beinn Dearg and coming out at the sea at Diabaig. From there, we have the whole coast-line Red Point, Longa Island, Melvaig, Cove, Inverasdale, Poolewe, Aultbea, Isle of Ewe, Mellon Charles, Mellon Udrigle, Laide and back to Gruinard—our starting-point.

In short, from Gruinard to near Achnasheen, across to Diabaig (near Torridon) up all the coast-line, Red Point round to Gruinard.

The parish is governed by the 'District Council of Gairloch', the District Clerk's office being at Poolewe (he is also the Welfare Officer); and comprises six elected Councillors and two (ex-officio) County Council members. All serve for a term of three years, whereupon an election to the whole Council takes place.

This triennial bloc-election saves the parish much expense.

I have already said the name Gairloch is composed of two Gaelic words. This sea-loch which gives its name to the parish is appropriately called 'short' as compared with Loch Broom, Loch Ewe and other more deeply indented arms of the sea.

As regards postal affairs for this region in the olden days, it is impossible to fix the exact date when a system was established.

Originally a 'post runner'—a man on foot—came from Dingwall by Strath Bran and Glen Docharty to the head of Loch Maree, the same way as we travelled. Thence along the east side of the Loch to Letterewe and on to Poolewe. If necessary he would come on to Flowerdale when the Laird of Gairloch was in residence, which would be the summer and autumn.

Sometimes he might have gone by the west side of the loch to Slattadale, then over the pass by the Kerry falls to Flowerdale.

There was no post at all during the winter months. Even in summer the runner only came to Gairloch once a week, but when a second runner was employed, the post bags were brought twice a week.

After construction of roads the mail came by horse and trap three times a week, and in 1883 the post office authorities granted a daily mail, except, of course, Sundays.

There were no roads in Gairloch until the military roads were made, which took nearly the same course as the present county roads and can still be traced in places. It was all part of the system of military roads constructed under the supervision of General Wade in the first half of the 18th century, *i.e.* around 1745. By the following century these old roads had become virtually impassable by wheeled vehicles.

The potato disease commenced in August 1846, bringing havoc and untold hardships to the crofters of Wester Ross. The road at the upper end of Loch Maree and Slattadale was begun the following spring. Government steamers used to call in at Gairloch enquiring as to the poverty and distress caused by this widespread calamity. A Destitution Committee was set up in Edinburgh with the primary object of 'road making' as a means of helping the out-of-work crofters. Nearly £3500 was spent on the Loch Maree road; and the Committee also assisted in the making of other roads on the north and south sides of Gairloch.

I have already drawn attention to the superstitious characteristics abounding in this part of the country. The Brahan Seer had (as a 'gimmick' we would call it nowadays) the perforated blue divining stone given him as I have stated previously, whereupon he became gifted with second-sight.

Such a stone, charm or spell is called the *sian* and not only can such a charm help predict the future, but it could by means of a certain incantation render any object that it was wished to conceal, invisible either for the time being or for all time, subject then to brief periods of visibility recurring either at the end of every year, or as was more usual, at the end of each succeeding seven years. I may say there are quite a few people around Gairloch who still believe in the *sian*.

There is on record the case of one Alastair of Charleston Gairloch (a wee house situate near the pier, and to this day the name still appears, although the building is not that of centuries ago) who was a dealer in illicit whisky and was frequently engaged in shipping cargoes of it between Gairloch, Skye and

Longa Island. At this time a certain Captain Oliver was commissioned by the government to put an end to this smuggling business, and he cruised up and down the Minch keeping a constant and vigilant watch on any strange craft. Apart from his main vessel he had a smaller one which was utilised mainly for the sea-loch observations, so that Gairloch, and any other loch Captain Oliver might be watching, was veritably blockaded. When our smuggling friend Alastair was afloat and he was approaching a government vessel, he would pronounce the magic words and with the aid of the *sian* his ship would become invisible to anyone else; and so it would seem our Captain Oliver was always thwarted!

Another time, he brought casks of whisky down Loch Maree and when he reached the narrows where the Tollie burn discharges into the river Ewe he landed and hid the casks in the moorland near Tollie farm; and making certain signs with his hands made the casks in their hiding-place invisible. Later on, when requiring the whisky, he sent his men over from Gairloch —those who had been with him when he buried the casks—to collect them and bring them to him. But his men searched high and low, unable to discover their whereabouts, and it was not until our charming charmer Alastair went along himself that the casks made themselves seen to him and his men!

During the rule of the Pictish kings (the Picts was a name given to a race that settled in the Highlands of Scotland, so named because they tattooed themselves) the Norwegian Vikings made continual raids upon the Highlands, at first as lone pirates and later on as followers of Harald Haarfagar, the first king of Norway. These Vikings with their unique and gaily decorated boats used to put in during the wintry months to small islands off the western seaboard, laying up their craft for that stormy period. The Island of Longa, in Gairloch bay, exhibits the Norwegian suffix *a*, meaning an island.

It has been thought that the Danes scarcely ever came across to the west coast, but those Danish invaders who were here were driven out in 1040. There can be little doubt, from records made at the time, that both Norwegian and Danes intermarried with the women of Gairloch. One can discern certain Norwegian, Danish characteristics in some faces of the Gairloch people even to this day.

c

It will no doubt come as a surprise to many that amongst Highland glens and landscape such an industry as ironworks could have existed. But such is the case. Iron ore was worked from very early times (there is evidence as far back as 1500) and the remains of blast furnaces—slag and dross—can still be traced, as well as charcoal deposits. This iron-smelting was known as 'Iron Bloomeries'.

The ancient ironworks of Gairloch were all near burns so that the water could be used to drive the machinery.

Early in the 17th century, about 1605, Sir George Hay worked ironstone on the northern shore of Loch Maree near Letterewe. The furnaces consumed over 100 acres of forest annually and a group of ruined houses marks the village of Furnace near and below Slioch (mentioned earlier). There were also other iron-furnaces at Talladale near Loch Maree Hotel, and near Poolewe.

Many of the workers came from Fife and remained in Gairloch and district for several generations. Deposits of bog iron ore as well as charcoal deposits have been found in many places around the Gairloch parish.

Reverting to 'charm' or the *sian* again, there is another Gairloch belief which is worth recording if only to be read in lighter vein. It concerned one Duncan MacRae who lived near Poolewe and was 'gifted'.

He was a faithful follower of Bonnie Prince Charlie and, after Culloden, assisted in the Prince's escape, always keeping close to his master, using his 'charm' to dumbfound the government pursuers. Funds were often coming over from France to this man Duncan, to be handed over to his Prince at convenient times and places. A small chest of golden sovereigns was given over to him for concealment until there was an opportune moment to deliver it to the Prince in person.

Duncan and his men brought the chest of gold across from near Aultbea to Cove, and from there carried it up the hill to near Loch an Draing, not far from the lighthouse near Melvaig, and there they laid it on the ground. Duncan made use of the *sian* and the magic formula to make the chest invisible.

It is still believed in Gairloch by some that the gold is yet there, visible though, only (as in the previously reported 'Alastair of Charleston' case) once every seven years; and then only for a very brief moment of time. True? Well, it makes for pleasant reading and thoughts!

* * *

Let us now hark back to the hotel, and after a good night's rest (lulled to sleep by O *Sole Mio*), and breakfast, we will carry on to make a tour of Gairloch proper, going up to the hotel garage first to see if Hamish has the car all ready. Hamish took over this garage after his father-in-law (my very old friend Willie Fraser) died on 29th March 1962, aged 82 years. I knew Willie and the family for close on forty years. He was truly a great Highland gentleman, respectful to the last degree; for ever obliging, always lifting his cap whenever he met or left you. Many's a yarn we exchanged in the old days in the public bar, back of the hotel. He used to tell me whisky was grand medicine if taken in moderation—and 82 years seemed to have proved it. He defined the word moderation to me one winter's night over a blazing peat fire in the smoke-filled bar. 'Mr. Bee Jay', he said, 'moderation has aye been my rule. Six or eight doubles is reasonable refreshment, but after that—well it's apt tae degenerate into drinkin'!' Poor Willie has gone, but we shall all mourn and remember him for many a long time. His wife Annie died two years later (22nd November 1964) in her 86th year. The family of four are all married and there are twelve grandchildren. Willie was with the Gairloch Hotel Company for 68 years; a faithful servant unto death.

Well, Hamish has the car all ready; washed down, tyres, petrol, oil and water all checked up, and wishing us a safe journey, we leave the hotel, and a little further along, we pass a small house overlooking—once again—the Minch, Skye, Harris, Lewis, and perhaps Labrador on a clear day!—where one of the most respected and keyman of the village lived until his death in December 1963, Hecky; Hecky MacIntyre. He was the Registrar, and another close friend of mine for many moons. In his capacity he married many a young couple, and in such a setting, I would say it was far more romantic than Gretna Green. He performed the ceremony under the 1939 Marriage (Scotland) Act. All that was needed was fifteen days' residence in Gairloch parish, plus seven days; for he had to put the respective names on a sheet of paper, and stick it up in a window of his general grocery stores in Strath for one week—for all the world to see. Thereafter just two witnesses, and the 'affaire' was over in a matter of minutes. A similar procedure applies to Gretna, to which so many elopers elope! All things being equal then, why not plump for Gairloch, you love-sick lovers, where it is far more difficult for mother to find you 'midst the glens and bracken. It's an idea, surely; for I can recommend both the heather and the bracken!

We next come to the telephone exchange, a very busy centre with underwater cables to the islands, and to Iceland; thereafter to a beautifully arranged cafeteria and shop—'The Wild Cat'. And petrol pumps, too. Sometimes I greet my friend the proprietor there, asking how business is doing at the 'Scalded Cat!'

The Wildcat. When is a wild cat not a Wildcat? When it is a domestic cat running wild! The Wildcat, whose head shows a remarkable resemblance to the tiger, cougar and leopard, is a species, not a way of life, and is largely nocturnal. It breeds twice a year, the gestation period being 63 days compared with 58 days for a domestic cat. An adult tom will weigh, on average, 15 pounds or more. The true Wildcat has broad black stripes on a yellowish-grey background. Its tail is more like a fox's brush, compared to that of the house cat. It has horn-coloured claws; its head is bigger than the ordinary cat; they are easy to trap and are widely looked upon as vermin.

At this restaurant, or landmark, we come to a junction at the main road; straight ahead up the hill and over the moors, to Poolewe and further north-west; to the left is Strath and Mel-vaig, this latter village being the end of the road 9 miles away. Turning down this road to Strath we pass the Police Station, manned by a genial Highlander from the Outer Isles, then come to the village school—Achtercairn School—which in its day has produced many brilliant scholars who travelled far and made their mark; then the Free Presbyterian Kirk, and shortly over a small bridge come to the boundary of Strath village. At this point there is a widely-known weaving shop (Kirk Hand Weaving Store) which deals in all kinds of Highland knitwear—and real good honest knitwear too—from ties, socks, wool 'fore-and-afts', pull-overs, cardigans, to lady's fancy-wear, baby-wear, pictures, pottery (home produced), guide and local books. A real gem of a store, where you can spend both time and money profitably; nothing flashy or trashy such as one finds in many tourist 'trinket' shops; the genuine articles—'From Ewe to you!'

Most, if not all, the knitwear, etc., is the work of local women and some of it very beautifully done. They make a profitable income to their meagre fare during the winter months, and the beginning and continued rise of this 'home industry' can be ascribed to the saying 'sweet are the uses of adversity'. During the years of the potato famine 1846–48, the people were in dire need; large sums were raised to help them, and those in charge of Gairloch parish undertook to support all of them in February 1848 until the following harvest—the able-bodied men working on the roads; the women by knitting. An expert was obtained who supervised the women's work and it was not long before 'Gairloch stockings' obtained a ready market by reason of their superior quality. Other small Highland parishes followed suit; the Scottish Home Industries Association was formed to look after everything concerned and to bring the trade on to a more business-like footing. And so it has continued to this very day. All the crofters those days owned sheep and these yielded wool which was teased, carded, spun and dyed at home from dyes gathered in nearby dykes, ditches and streams. One can see this art of wool being teased, spinning wheels being worked by foot and tartan rugs and scarfs being made by hand today in many parts, particularly in Skye, notably at Portnalong, not far from Talisker distillery on Loch Harport, west of Sligachan.

There is a popular belief in the south that all of us up in the Wild West here, wear plus fours or Harris tweed suits in order to keep us warm in these northern regions! It may well be that going upon the controversial theory of 'Continental Drift', started by one Alfred Wegener over sixty years ago, the north of Scotland may have been in the Arctic Circle 120 million years ago; but not so today. However, such tweed is mainly bought and woven by those who, having come to the Highlands, wish to have something savouring of a Highland garb to sport amongst the gayer places south. (I once had a *real* Harris tweed suit made me just before the Second World War by a local tailor of Badachro, which I simply could *not* wear out. It lasted me for years and years, and in the end I had to give it away!)

All genuine Harris tweed bears the 'Orb' trade mark, over

which (in 1963) there was one of the longest and costliest actions in Scotland's legal history; known as the marathon Harris 'Orb' tweed case versus the competitive 'Shield' tweed mark. The case lasted fourteen weeks, and witnesses came over from the U.S.A., Denmark, the Hebrides and elsewhere to give evidence.

The question was 'What is Harris tweed?'

In July 1964 in the Court of Session, Edinburgh, judgement was given that the only genuine article is tweed processed entirely in the islands of the Outer Hebrides.

The 'Orb' is the trade mark of the Harris Tweed Association Ltd. of London—used by 15 producers; the 'Shield' being the emblem of the independent producers.

At the time of this book going to press—November 1964— appeal made by 'The Shield', has been dismissed in Orb's favour.

It was declared that some of the competitive processes and hand-weaving were not carried out in the Outer Hebrides; in fact some were not even carried out in Scotland, and the wool was not wholly Scottish.

Originally the crofters of Harris made strong cloth for themselves from the fleece of their own sheep, and when it began to have imitators outside the islands, the people of Harris in 1909 secured their stamp from the Board of Trade, which guaranteed that Harris tweed was exclusively tweed hand-spun, hand-dyed, and hand-finished in the Outer Isles. As time went on, and with production so limited, mill-spun yarn became the answer to expansion; and in 1934 the stamp was granted to mill-spun cloth *provided* it was spun, dyed and finished in the Outer Isles, and woven by islanders in their own homes.

After the Court's decision it was a day of rejoicing for weavers, mill-workers and mill-owners in the Outer Hebrides; and many drams went down the hatch in celebration.

Talk about the 'Tangle o' the Isles'; this case was the 'Tangle o' the web'. So Harris Tweed *is* Harris Tweed, produced by islanders.

Onwards past the Swedish-type wooden houses—not very 'Highland'—we pass the one and only bakery; and *what* a bakery to be sure! worth coming all our way even to get the freshly-made rolls each day. The chief baker himself is a veritable master-man; and why not? for his name is Wallace! Whether his Christian name is William, and is related to the famous Scotch hero who defeated the English at Stirling Bridge in 1297, I cannot say. Perhaps not, for he looks upon his 'dough' with far greater affection than the mountains and scenery surrounding his artistry. Maybe he kneads the mountains of dough in the early hours of the mornings with a claymore; who knows ?

Continuing, we pass Kowloon stores, with the name Mackenzie lettered as owner—not 'Hoo Flung High', which one would think to be more appropriate, since Kowloon is across on the mainland of China from Hong Kong. It appears the original store belonged to one who spent some years in Hong Kong and Kowloon, so he adopted that name for his shop. Proceeding, with the bay always beside us, we come to the wee village square, STRATH, where you can park your car all day, all night or all month for nothing; and have a look around. The ironmonger's shop (with an old circular stone embedded in the ground in front of the door, where in those good old days, cart wheel iron tyres were heated over a peat fire outside on the bank, then carried across and put on the stone's rim and shrunk to correct size by throwing water over same), the post office and the general stores which Hecky (mentioned a page or so earlier) had until a year before he died. The stores had been in his family about 110 years—MacIntyre's Store; now owned by George Leask of Glasgow, and managed by his son Robin. In this store, so far away, one may say, from 'civilisation' in this wild-west country, you can get anything—groceries, frozen foods, fruit, papers, milk, tobacco, books, post-cards, electric blankets, face powder, lip-stick and all the usual cosmetics, stockings, shoes, bras, baby's outfits, bikinis, Andrews' Liver Salts—the lot!

Then we mustn't forget Angus Mackenzie's tailoring shop in this square—a Court tailor, who for thirty-six years had a most distinguished tailoring establishment in Knightsbridge, London, where he made dresses and uniforms for most of the Crowned heads of Europe and the Near East. To name but a few, the King of Norway, Prince Bernhardt of the Netherlands and Queen Juliana; King Peter of Jugo-Slavia; the late King George of Greece, and the late King of Albania; as well as our own late King George and most members of our Royal family ; statesmen and their wives, too. Angus came to settle down here in the quiet of Gairloch two years ago, and has a fine display of tweeds and tartans, and carries on making dresses and suits for all and sundry; and is kept constantly busy. Hecky's wife is Angus' sister; he was the son of Donald Mackenzie, who used to have a tailor's shop in Gairloch years ago. Yes, we may be quiet, ordinary folk in Gairloch, but you see we have 'Royal connections'. Yes, sir!

Further along, there is Dan the butcher's shop; so one will realise there is everything at hand here. And what a hive of buzzing activity there is during the 'season'—a brief fourteen or fifteen weeks maybe. Oh! and I mustn't forget the wee boot-repairer, a MacLeod of MacLeod's, who incidentally makes a fine Precentor at the Free Kirk on the Sabbath. All told, and being so far afield, it is wonderful what goodly stores can be found here; far superior to any within miles. It would be very convenient to have a lady's hairdressing shop. We men can get a clip from a local here and there, who may happen to have a pair of clippers and scissors; and we don't really mind if it's not a five shilling posh town hair-cut. But the ladies ? For myself, when I'm looking more like a poet than a quiet, retired Colonial, I call on my good neighbour, Hector, up the hill at the back of 'Skye View', and he gives me a trim in a real professional manner, for he learnt the art from a German when he was a prisoner of war for five years in Germany in World World II. How thankful I am to Hector in this and many other ways; a grand fellow, a grand neighbour, a grand family—grandpa and all!

I have mentioned the post office at Strath. This is a very busy place even out of the season. But in the season, Kenny— another MacLeod of MacLeod's—is run off his feet, although his courteous wife Cathey assists him at times. Both are helpfulness and cheerfulness personified; so different from the austere, couldn't-care-less attitude of post offices in towns as a rule, where, just as you're going to one grille for a stamp or your old-age pension, you find a board marked CLOSED suddenly slammed down, nearly taking off your finger-tips! I have often said to myself in English post offices when this so often happens, why the notice doesn't only say 'closed', but 'gone to lunch, back tomorrow'! However, as a nation we are long-suffering; but for how long ? The amount of business put through by these Highland sub-post-offices would stagger any equivalent in an English village. You need all your wits about you to run a post-office; to know all about licences, pensions, money-orders, transfers, savings books, remittances, dog and radio licences, telephone accounts, and a hundred and one other minor matters —to say nothing of the large amount of clerical work that the head office at Dingwall requires to be done; weekly summaries of each and every item, even to the sale of stamps. They'll be assisting you in your income tax returns one day! 'That'll be the day', as one man said to the other. 'What'll be the day?' his friend asked. 'Why', said he, 'from dawn to dusk!' . . . Slàinte.

These sub-postmasters (and there are very many up in the Highlands) provide an essential service in every village and hamlet. Their income from H.M. Government is small, so most—if not all—depend on selling confectionery, tobacco, post cards of the place, and groceries to make life worth while.

Talking of post offices, the villagers seldom buy more than one or two stamps at a time. Should they have to write a letter and have no stamps, and the P.O. is closed, they merely push their correspondence in the box and three pennies—or more as needs be—so that in the morning when the postmaster is making up the outgoing mails, he has to put stamps on those unstamped letters, to the extent of the money found in the bottom of the box, and he says to himself, I'm sure many a time, 'och chrupelan', a sort of 'oh dear' or 'fancy that' meaning, in English! Or maybe he'll mutter, 'that's old Andra' again out of stamps; why on earth can't he buy a few more at a time and save me all this trouble just as I have to pack the mail bags up for transit! Then, as this is strictly a Sabbatarian country, strangers may care to know that it is not considered at all proper to post any letters on the Sabbath, even though they might have been written on Saturday night; and even though the post box is not cleared till Monday morning's outgoing mail. 'Summer-time' always takes effect at 2.0 a.m. on a Sunday and clocks put forward or back as the case may be. But up here, clocks are *not* altered until the Monday. One needs remember that, should you wish to attend any Church service.

Not only post-office work, but 'visiting' work as well, falls on these Highland P.O.'s. Trying to soothe agitated, neurotic women who want accommodation at the height of the season in August; those arriving about eight or nine o'clock at night 'chapping' at the P.O. house door, asking for a bed, when every

C2

place is on tenter-hooks as to the factory inspector coming round complaining of over-crowding! These 'lovelies' arrive with no place booked—just a blank innocent (?) expression as to 'where can we sleep tonight, baby!' My post office friends here, and all the others dotted around Wester Ross, will have to carry larger stocks of paper handkerchiefs to help mop up the tears of distress shed by all these many lovelies; and smelling-salts, too, to keep them from fainting! But what can Kenny do? He's married, with a wife and two children, and their house is full up. Life is difficult! And of course during office hours there are heaps of queries to answer. I remember one day an old visiting lady was bewildered in filling in a claim form for a missing parcel. 'You just put your name where it states "name of sender"', said Kenny. 'But I didn't send it', the old dear replied, 'I just gave it to you, and *you* sent it!' Truly the P.O. in the Highlands provides many a service not in the regulations. We must not overlook mention of Tommy, the cheery 'postie' who, until May 1964, when he retired, went merrily on his rounds in a nippy little van. Day in and day out for well over fifty years, he was on the 'beat'; icy roads or pouring rain, he would carry on plodding through snow at times to some outlying croft or other; the post must get through, being the motto. When Tommy first commenced service in the post office in his 'teens, the mails were horse-drawn, and he took letters round on his pony, as well as on a push-bike.

The chief-postmaster at Dingwall presented him with an Imperial Long-service Medal on 10th March 1962 at the Gairloch post office. His place has been taken now by his son Donald, nearing twenty years of age; and all, I am sure, wish him 'good posting'.

Verily the postmaster is one of the most important figures in a Highland village. He knows to put your letters and parcels aside if you make it a habit to collect them yourself; and should he look out of his scratched piece of painted window and see your car in the square, jalousing you are in the near-by stores getting your milk and messages, you will find your mail on your driving seat, all ready for you. Service with a capital S; and miles away from 'nowhere' too! Tell me where else in all Britain you get the same privileges, the same attention, the same individualism, as here? I think echo will answer 'where?'

For you see this is Gairloch, a place in a million, but by no means a million in the place, unless it be a million *fàiltes*—a million welcomes—and that, I will grant you.

Up through the village passing the ever-pleasing, spotlessly clean butcher's shop on the left, with, up till recently, the part-time 'butcheress' in charge thumbing over her ready-reckoner (the leaves crumbling to pieces with so much over-work), for you need remember in her day there was no such thing as the 11-plus, and therefore so many pounds and ounces at so much a pound confuses one's brain after 'sixty glorious years'! Then we come to the small bridge over the burn flowing down from the two hill lochs, Badnachran and An Skeroch. The Old Folk's Home is at this point. Continuing (the bay always on one's left), there are only a few small houses, and 'Skye View'— the last house. Nothing between here and the youth hostel CAIRN DEARG, a mile or so distant. Still hugging the bay, comes Little Sands—a glorious clean, fine, sandy beach stretching unreservedly as far as the eye can see, with desolate Longa Island in the foreground.

Thereafter comes North Erradale—just a hamlet—and finally Melvaig, the end of the road, nine miles as I have said from the Wild Cat. Melvaig, a post office and a few houses, and from here one can carry on three miles to lonely Rudha Reidh (Rue Ray)—the lighthouse.

The journey to Melvaig is somewhat twisty, brightened in many places by the views one gets of the Minch. Out of season you seldom pass anything or anybody on the road; unless it be a few sheep or Ian Bain driving the mail bus. There is one deep cave *en route*, into which, legend has it, a piper is said to have led a band of men in search of gold; and never returned. The sound of his pipes was heard in the neighbourhood for many a year after his disappearance. This kind of story is common in many parts of Europe—so similar to the 'Pied Piper of Hamelin'.

As we have reached the end of the road, we must retrace our wheel marks back to Strath, and then take the other road, near the Wild Cat, to Poolewe and Ullapool, and beyond.

In the Second World War, Gairloch and all along the north-western coast line was a restricted area, for much secret naval and military activity was always afoot, and everybody, young or old, no matter whether they had lived here all their lives or not,

needed a permit to pass the barriers; even though it were only
to do some shopping or to go to church.

One good old lady lived near the pier head, and one Sabbath,
walking along to the Free Presbyterian Kirk and reaching the
barrier, found she had forgotten her pass. The sentry on guard
stopped her going through, albeit she looked innocent enough.
He was adamant; much altercation took place, and finally the
old dear, waving her Bible in the corporal's face, shouted, 'This
is the Lord's Book that is taking me to Heaven, and this is the
Book that is going to take me past your barrier to the kirk right
now'. And with that she brushed him aside and stamped along
the road to worship, leaving him—to say the least—taken aback!
For he, poor fellow, had little idea about religion and the
religious feelings of these great people here. This is a true story,
for I happen to have known the old lady herself.

So we come to the end of Gairloch and Strath (Lonemore,
where I write these lines). In the Gaelic, Lonemore is AN LÒN
MÓR, the great damp meadow; though it is by no means that
today. Melvaig, in Gaelic is MEALABHAIG; Norse MELAR-VÍK;
MELR denotes bent grass or a sandy hillock overgrown with
bent grass; VÍK, a bay. AN RUDHA RÉIDH, the smooth point,
the north-westerly point of the peninsula.

Gairloch; the Gairloch of Wester Ross, in the land of restful
quietness ... the country of Shangri-La, where for the most
part you meet with Gaelic folk that seem to have discovered,
as I have hinted, the secret of Everlasting Youth, living in a land
where luxury (as cherished by city dwellers) is not known; for
'tis not their way of life—the REAL Highlands—dwelling as they
do in the houses of their fathers and their fathers' fathers; non-
agenarians, octogenarians, and many youthful septuagenarians.
One old crofter told me he was an *octogeranium*! They seem to
die when their bodies wear out, and their hearts stop beating—
'well-stricken in years'. How do they keep so fit, and live to
such ripe old age? Maybe it is their diet, or maybe more, their
environment in this land of peace and quiet. And there is no
word for 'hurry' in the Gaelic dictionary! Here, Time dissolves
itself in the clear air and scenic beauty.

If Wester Ross had nothing to show but Loch Maree, it is
doubtful if any who have visited and seen it can ever forget the
great expanse of scenery; for by many it *is* considered far and

away to be the most beautiful in Britain in its wildness and in its
gentleness. As I have said before, this is no tourist propaganda
... IT IS FACT.

*   *   *

This chapter is headed GAIRLOCH; and Gairloch is more or
less the centre-piece of this embroidered table-cloth of Wester
Ross, ironed and pressed into some 300 pages and stoutly bound
so no odd patterns can escape. A wild country famous for its
black-faced sheep. The Highlander; the crofter; the villager. A
great religious folk, and half the charm of living here is in one's
dealing with them. Should you endear yourself to them, they
will endear themselves to you. How absurd it is to come or go
amongst any people, anywhere, with any degree of superiority.
Up in the Highlands they are quick to sense this.

I came to live here some years ago after spending almost a
lifetime in searching for *a* particular site, for I considered this
to be so unique a place that I wanted nothing short but a *unique*
site whereon to build a dream house for the 'sunset' years.
'Charlie boy' and a team of skilled workmen took everything
in hand and in due course produced a fitting monument to their
strenuous labours, battling at times 'gainst gales, rain and snow.
In the end it could be likened to George Washington moving
from 'Log cabin to White House'. Then, to make the rough
fields and grass into landscape form; to the making of several
rockeries from the many boulders that lay around the site; to
the planting of trees and shrubs; to bringing along soil, and to
the making of a lawn after digging up rushes, cooch grass and
other coarse vegetation. A five-year plan to be sure in making a
transformation; but when completed and you look out on to
a well-kept garden you have a feeling of real inward joy; a
miniature Inverewe.

There is an old Chinese proverb which says . . .

... If you want a day's happiness, get drunk.
If you want two day's happiness, get married.
If you want a lifetime of happiness, get a garden.

*   *   *

I have remarked upon the charm of living here. And for
the tourist *what* a difference a Highland holiday can be. You go

along to the pier to see all that's going on there, the unloading
of the fish caught during the night in the bay or in the Minch,
and being packed in boxes and taken away by big lorries to
Aberdeen.

You can spend many an hour on a pier; and then you go
down to the village every day making personal contacts in the
general stores for groceries or haberdashery; and to the post
office for your letters. And in all this, if you keep your ears to
the ground, you'll hear some gossip on the way. News and
gossip. Two intriguing subjects!

Although we are far removed from Central Africa and the
land of the tom-toms and bush fires, news travels just as fast—
if not faster. Every whisper overheard in the long grass stam-
pedes someone into action! Many keep a telescope handy, so
that if anything is happening at a body's house a few miles away
up the hill, the lens comes in awfu' handy like! 'Aye, that's
the District Nurse right enough; she's gone into Mistress
Mackenzie's house. I just wonder? Ah! well; and they were
only married last Lammas! Still it's no business o' mine!'
With so many telescopes in the Highlands you need to keep a
watchful eye on yourself and your movements.

Of course the mail van, the carrier's van, the bread van, the
butcher's van, the local bakery van, the traveller's van, and any
other van on the road connecting one village with another is a
grand means of 'conveyance'; and all concerned are not slow
in keeping their eyes and ears open. Still, it all helps to make life
brighter—this 'ever-watchfulness'. For is not variety the spice
of life? And if you are told any gossip the party will tell you
not to mention it for they will say, 'I don't want to put my
tongue in it'. Another Highland idiom.

Gossip indeed! As to the Highlands, a Fleet Street editor
was once reported as saying, 'Oh! those folk; they are all so
blooming inquisitive!' Well, maybe they have reason to be,
for in these parts, everybody's affairs seem to be common
property. Gossip in the long winter nights is as essential as peat
for the fire. Not only their own gossip, but gossip of legend
and of half-truths; gossip as to national policy for the Highlands
and the way in which they've been neglected. The Highlands
seem to be just a picture-postcard affair, whereas by and large
they have been a monument to national indifference. But to

get back to 'gossip'. Personally I am all out for gossip, *but* I put it in the category of 'news'. I like to know what's happening; what's going on; who's having a baby, or who's sick or seriously ill. In short, learning the general day-by-day news of one's fellow beings. As to gossip for gossiping's sake, I have no time and I see red when I know some folk go out of their way to create gossip. It is very necessary to control one's tongue, like learning to play a harmonica. An uncontrolled tongue is a positive danger to society. Think of Hitler and his ribald tirades; and then think of Churchill, the greatness of his speech and tongue which so welded the nation together those dark days of 1939 onwards.

Before listening to, let alone passing on, gossip I think it well to remember this: Is it true; is it wise to repeat it; is it *necessary* to repeat it? News is news; gossip is for those who have time on their hands and whose conscience means little to themselves, let alone to others. In specially writing these lines I would add— 'Where the cap fits'. Love and scandal are the best sweeteners of tea.

At this particular chapter, it may not be out of place to comment upon the roads up north; just for the motorist's aid, not that perhaps he'll pay any attention! For if you tell a person that such and such a road is under construction and really dangerous to travel upon, you can bet your bottom dollar he'll go, despite your genuine advices. However, be that as it may, it is well that those coming to the Highlands should be made acquainted with our conditions.

Many people who plan a tour up north ask, 'What are the roads like? Can we take the car without fear of the back axle being ripped off, or springs being broken, along "those terrible roads" and in such "outlandish places"?' One great name stands out foremost in the matter of Highland roads, and he is General Wade. He was the man who constructed most of the Highland roads after the 1715 Jacobite Rebellion; military roads they were and his little 'hump-back' stone bridges all over the north can be seen to this day. And in some places you pass over them; some 250 years later! Anent this General and these roads, there is a very well-known, cryptic saying, viz.:

if you saw these roads before they were made,
you'd go down on your knees and bless General Wade!

This Major-General Wade was undoubtedly a great man for the Highlands, mending roads, opening up new roads, and generally bringing 'life' to the many isolated villages.

He received his commission as 'Commander-in-Chief of the Forces in North Britain' on 25th December 1724; his immediate objective being to make the roads better between garrisons and barracks—'for the better communication of His Majesty's Troops'; and in the middle of the next year he proceeded from Edinburgh to Inverness. By the end of 1725 he had begun the construction of his great military highway through the Great Glen from Fort William to Inverness; this was followed by the making of the road southwards, Inverness to Dunkeld. In 1731 he commenced another gigantic job, the road from Fort Augustus, over Corrieyairich across country to Dalwhinnie, and thence to Aberfeldy and Crieff. During a period of only eight years he constructed a total of 250 miles of major roadway. He certainly was a great guy!

In 1733 he constructed the Tay bridge at Aberfeldy, whereupon his work as a road and a bridge builder was completed, for he was relieved of his command in 1740, died eight years later (14th March 1748), aged 75, and was buried in Westminster Abbey.

A Major Caulfield was appointed Wade's successor and he continued in office for thirty-five years. Later on, we find the name of Thomas Telford, another great road and bridge builder, looming up in the early 1800's; he opened up a road on the *north* side of the Caledonian Canal from Inverness to Fort Augustus, via Dores and Foyers, which then effected vast changes in the mode of travel throughout the Highlands. Thereafter Telford's name appeared prominently before the public.

In General Wade's day, the pay for masons and special labour was 1s. 6d. a day! The general rough work was done by military parties under their own officer's command, privates getting 1s. a day.

Many of Wade's old military roads can be seen to this very day; and, as I have said, you pass over many of those hump-backed bridges—Wade's bridges; its back arched like a cat stretching itself after a good sleep!

Truly a great pioneer and a prodigious worker.

The roads in the Highlands today are good, very good, *but*

narrow; and for the most part their width does not allow two
cars to pass unless it be at the 'passing places', which are frequent
and clearly marked. This is a peculiarity of the roads up in these
parts. And let it be said, these passing places are what their name
implies—for *passing*, not for 'parking' or admiring the view, or
over-night caravanning. They take the wrinkles out of the
many bends and corners.

I said at the beginning of this book, speed is the last consideration; mostly one cruises along in comfort—and safety—
at 30 miles an hour or less; on some open stretches say 40 as a
maximum, and when that is the case, you are 'travelling some'
as they say in America. In fact you can reconcile yourself in
journeying all through the Highlands and islands to a Victor
Sylvester tempo—slow, slow, quick-quick, slow!

> Such is the way of such roads,
> Such is the way of life here.

*   *   *

I have found these passing places provide much enjoyment
—even excitement—to some visitors in the novelty of waiting
for another on-coming car to pass or for them to pass you. Such
a thing as this never crops up in a town, and some folk—particularly women drivers—give you such a hearty wave of the hand
and a beaming smile, showing a gleaming row of pepsodents
almost blowing you a kiss and doubtless saying to themselves,
'Isn't this fun!'

On the other hand, some don't bother to either give you a
nod of thanks or a toot of their horn in courteous acknowledgement; in fact some can't even wait for you to draw in to a siding.
They are in such a hurry you would think they were bound for
an airport or had a business appointment to keep and were several
hours overdue.

Others may be excused, for they are gripping the wheel with
fixed determination, for they've never been on narrow roads
before, and the dozens of bends and blind corners are a positive
nightmare to the inexperienced. And as for reversing 50 or
100 yards—oh! my. Aweel!

Since a number of visitors are fishing-minded, it may be
useful to make a reference to angling here; for Gairloch and
district has been renowned for years past; as this sport can be

found in loch, river and sea. The Fionn loch (the white loch) and Loch Bad na Sgalaig are but two famed lochs for trout. The Fionn Loch is some six miles in length and runs nearly parallel with Loch Maree, only that it is very much higher—viz. 540 feet above sea-level, whereas Loch Maree is only 32 feet. The Gairloch Angling Club, which has three lochs under its wing, issues permits costing 3/6d. per day for bank fishing, and 15/- a day for boat fishing. Other permits for salmon and trout fishing may be had from Kinlochewe, Loch Maree, Shieldaig Lodge, Gairloch, Poolewe, Pool House, and Aultbea hotels. Fishing in the bay can always be arranged, weather permitting. Over the bay the gannet and solan goose fly constantly in search of fish; and there are eider ducks, drakes, mergansers (a duck-like bird, the goosander), terns, a few puffins, oyster catchers, curlews and sand pipers.

Bird life is always a source of attraction, and such wild life can be found if looked for off the beaten track; golden eagles, goldcrests, buzzards, red grouse and the ptarmigan which turns white in winter to avoid detection in the snow. The first spring migrant to appear is the wheatear.

Then there is the majestic red deer, frequently seen around Loch Maree roaming the hills in small herds, trying to evade stalkers. Roe deer—much smaller than the red deer, may be spotted at times near Slattadale, Loch Maree. Deer of course have the sharpest of nose- and ear-sense; and in stalking, a wind can easily give away one's proximity. Even a frightened bird would instinctively warn the deer of impending danger.

Otters and seals may also be occasionally found.

So in Gairloch and district there is a wealth of 'life'.

Earlier I have said we have everything at hand. However, one thing is lacking—a fire engine. The nearest fire-station is Dingwall, sixty miles away, and over a 2-hour run. By that time a fire would have taken its full toll. At one blaze here, amidst confusion of helpers and buckets of water, the crofter giving orders through the belching smoke, turned to one blackened volunteer saying, 'Where are you from?' 'I'm from Pakistan', he answered. 'My, my, you're here long afore the Dingwall Brigade aren't you?'

CHAPTER 5

TRAGEDY ON THE LOCH

IN the dawn of Sunday 5th June 1960, tragedy struck Gairloch of such a magnitude that no one in living memory can recall its equal. Four Wester Ross men were drowned when their boat capsized in Gairloch bay, off Longa Island, near the village of Strath. Two others of the party of six managed, with superhuman effort, to swim ashore, exhausted and almost lifeless after clinging to their upturned craft for over three hours and watching their companions collapse, lose their holds on the boat and disappear, one by one, into the darkness of the cruel sea.

The Saturday night they set off, around 8 o'clock, for a spot of fishing, was a beautiful, breathless June night in the quiet bay, and the sea as calm as a millpond.

The tragedy was all the greater for the four men who were lost were the four key-men of this little Wester Ross village: the doctor, the veterinary surgeon, the leading grocer and the one and only garage proprietor; Hugh, Robin, Roddie and Angus, all married, and between them seven young children were bereft of their fathers. But for the hand of Fate, the two others, one the Gairloch butcher, the other a brother of the grocer's, might well never have come back.

Four key-men in a small, very small, rural community. The village, and indeed the whole countryside, was stunned and shocked, sad and silent over this devastating blow. All fine men doing fine jobs in the service of the people. In a village such as this everyone more or less depends on everyone else—on each other both professionally and socially. And they were all young men, 40 years of age, down to 32 years.

I knew Angus and Roddie well; in fact I was speaking to the latter a few hours before he went off to fish, and Angus did a small job for me on my car that Saturday afternoon. Everyone and everybody was happy, and contentment was uppermost amongst all, as we joked and passed the usual pleasantries.

I happened to be living, at the time, on the south side, at Badachro, when about 11 o'clock on the Sunday morning word came through of the tragedy. At first I thought there must be some mistake for such a mortal blow to have happened; but no, it was all too real. My Sunday's joint was left untouched. Everybody around was so dazed we just sat, staring blankly, saying inwardly, it can't be true, and thinking also of the stricken widows. Later on we went into Gairloch to hear fuller details, and then quietly and silently motored back.

There was a Great Silence over the bay; a silence conscious to one's very touch; even the waves lapping the shores of Gairloch and Badachro seemed to be lapping them with a gentle reverence. Silence, a Great Silence.

The week opened with the news claiming headlines in all the Scottish and English national papers, with such captions as 'a village mourns'. It became known from north to south, from John o' Groats to Devon and Cornwall, and from east to west. In the village itself little groups of people gathered outside their homes to talk of the tragedy; but all were too shocked to say much. Everyone seemed to be wearing a blank look.

The week opened wet, but somehow or other the heavens brightened on the Tuesday 7th June, the day of the funeral. Not only the whole village, but folk from far and wide—from the Highlands and the Lowlands—came to say farewell at a service held in the open air, and at least 300 people crowded round the 150-year-old sycamore tree at the golf course opposite the Church of Scotland. (This old tree is a landmark for men returning from the sea. There is a natural hollow nearby where the Free Church communion services were held up to 15–20 years ago, at which I had often attended, and where, in the olden days, folk came by bridle-path and boat to attend. It is said to have been scooped out by the giant Fingal for a bed where his white cow might calve, and it is still called Leabaidh-na-bà-Baine, or the 'bed of the white cow').

There was no tolling of a church bell—just silence. In the village the shops had never opened since the disaster occurred. It seemed as though the whole countryside had died too. I have been at many funerals, at home and abroad, but never have I attended such a simple but impressive service, and one which brought so many tears. The service was conducted by the three ministers of the three churches of Gairloch: the Church of Scotland, the Free Church and the Free Presbyterian Church. They shared in the Gaelic and English service. Tourists on the sandy beach below listened in silence as we all sang the 23rd psalm. Across at the little churchyard we gazed sadly at the masses of brightly coloured wreaths and flowers.

This was the end of a chapter in the life of the village of Gairloch. But in this quarter everyone is everyone's friend, a closely knit community, and Time, the great healer, gives new and leading figures to take over where others left off.

I took a Colonial friend across to the funeral, who was staying with me at Badachro, a friend who had travelled greatly but who always appeared to me to be a man that little or nothing could stir. His philosophy of life could be summed up by saying he had yet to meet anyone, or anything, or see any sight to which he would, so to speak, 'take off his hat'. After the funeral we went down to the hollow, lolling reminiscently under the shade of the sycamore. Everything was quiet and peaceful, as the mourners and the cars had all gone. The sky was blue, flecked now and then with white clouds; around us the greens of the tiny golf course, and beyond, the cruel sea—which had struck so harshly three days before in wiping out the community's leading men. We sat on and on; there was no movement anywhere to be seen or heard. A small lady-bird showing its brilliant colours under its beetle-wings alighted on the back of my hand, moved slowly to and fro and then came to rest. Suddenly a more than deep hush appeared to descend upon us; the very atmosphere seemed to be charged, to stand still, waiting, as it were, for something to happen. And then, without any warning, a small brown bird rose above us, and as it rose it sang, and up and up it soared till it vanished as a little speck in the sky; but the sweetness and fittingness of its song seemed to be a symbol. A perfect song, sung perfectly, the same notes as when the world first began; a song that makes the hearts of men of all creeds, colour, speech, or nationality, look up with thanks despite their many sorrows.

We sat motionless, and looked, listened and thought; and turning to my friend I saw him slowly rise, and taking off his hat he stood in reverence and bowed. What a fitting climax to an ever memorable afternoon. We both stood for a while, not speaking. There was no need to speak; there was no need to pass remarks on what we had thought or witnessed both then and at the funeral service previously. *We just took off our hats;* and that was all. And it seemed to be enough.

So ended a never-to-be-forgotten day. In the simplicity of our surroundings, the effect on one was tender and solemn.

The new graveyard, and the 300-year-old one (both restful in their greenness) are not far from the water's edge, surrounded by trees and wild flowers, where the lap of the waves on the golden shore can be heard. We may well describe these sacred plots as 'where the sound of living waters never ceaseth, God's quiet garden by the sea'.

As we wended our way back over the bay I felt if those who had been cut off in the prime of life—those hearts that had been woven of human joys and cares—could yet speak, they would say

> . . . Nerve your hearts and trembling hands, to do
> Something to comfort meaner hearts than ours.
> Complete the tasks we left with all your powers
> And we perchance may therein comfort you . . .

* * *

As I write this chapter, it is nearing five years since the tragedy happened; but this small village still recalls it, and we look upon those who were drowned, with fond remembrances—for the clouds in the sky gather over their place of death, over their homeland; yes, and over their life's work. . . .

Whilst that bird we saw and heard sang but one tune, the song of humanity has infinite variety.

CHAPTER 6

THE SOUTH SIDE

THE other side of Gairloch bay (across from Gairloch, Strath, and the road to Melvaig), is generally known as 'the south side'. In a former book I had loosely termed it as 'Across the Bay'; but any local who was going to, say Badachro, Port Henderson, Opinan, South Erradale or Red Point would tell you he was going 'over to the south side'. So south side it is! as I suppose, opposed to the north side of the bay. From where I live, I look over to Isle Horrisdale, Dry Island, and behind these two small islands, the wee quiet village of Badachro. The remaining small hamlets named are hidden from view, since the bay curls round on its way to Red Point. Over the bay are the hills of Torridon, and further still, the table-topped BEINN BHAN range, 20-odd miles away, towering amidst the Applecross forest.

To reach the south side you turn off the Gairloch main road at Kerrysdale bridge, about a mile from seeing the Gairloch boundary sign in large letters just near the Factor's house. The signpost merely says, Port Henderson 5 miles; Red Point 8 miles. No mention of the important village of Badachro, that you first come to on your journey 'south', 4 miles from the bridge. The County Council should make good this omission. It is a tortuous, narrow road, but very pleasant to travel.

There were, as I have said before, no roads to Gairloch and district until the military road was made. At the time of the potato disease and widespread famine, money was received from the Destitution Committee's Fund (set up in Edinburgh to make more roads) to carry on the road to Badachro; and, of course, today the tarred roadway goes right to Red Point where, looking across the sea, the lighthouse at Rona's tip is clearly seen. It is but 6 miles from Red Point (along the high cliffs looking down on Loch Torridon) to Diabaig, the last hamlet reached by road from Torridon village. If ever there is a road made linking these two points it would indeed form a magnificent circular tour: Gairloch, Diabaig, Torridon, Kinlochewe, Loch Maree and Gairloch.

Turning off then, at the Kerry bridge, you wander on and on as though you were driving up and through a tree-lined approach avenue to an English country manor house. Should you take the journey on an early autumn morning you will find the sun gradually melting away the mists hanging over the landscape, and see the bracken coloured red, yellow and brown; yellow birches and larches a burnished old gold. Everything is still, even quieter than usual, and you pass nothing that hurries. The former Shieldaig Lodge—now an hotel—comes suddenly to view, with its pre-possessing lawn rolling lazily down to the water's edge; another touch of English (Thames) countryside. From thence you carefully negotiate the many bends and come to the wee cluster of bungalows at Leacnasaide ('slab of the arrows') hemmed in with trees and bracken; a very haven for midges! All still, and the road gives no distant vistas of hills or mountains until you start to rise further on, when you catch a glimpse of Gairloch bay and the mainland across, with perhaps the wee village of Strath bathed in a limpid light; and pale and gentle waves lapping the seaweed round the shore you are following.

Eventually swinging high, swinging low, you come to the top of the brae leading down to the village signposted Badachro; and immediately you are—as a familiar radio programme is called—'In Town Tonight'; within a stone's throw of the post office, inn and school, the latter now closed until such time as more babies are born!

In days of yore, Badachro had a large fishing station where curers purchased the herring, cod, ling, etc., from the fisherfolk, and exported their catches in their own boats. It was said the cod fishery of Gairloch was historical. It was carried on by two firms who had curing houses at Badachro, Dry Island and Isle Horrisdale—isle of happiness. These curing houses no longer exist.

During the winter months there is, of course, little or nothing doing in all these wee villages in the north-west. But as spring approaches, the houses are freshened up by a dab of paint here and there, the accommodation signs put up and preparations are made for visitors. In due season there is a general air of restlessness; all on account of the foreign invasion! Cars and their human loads arrive, cooking carries on around the clock, and when these families leave after a week or so's holiday in the peace and quiet of these REAL Highlands—and it is exactly the same in all these wee villages up north—the rustle of pound notes can be heard changing hands. Sweet music! Yes, there is a deal to be done in these out-of-the-way places in looking after all the tourists' needs. The secret of cooking to them is anticipation!

Cooking, baking and preparing meals, washing plates, cutlery and linen; peeling potatoes, clearing and setting of tables, besides attending to their own particular work in the cutting of peat, milking cows, collecting eggs, feeding hens, geese and maybe ducks; getting in the hay, looking after the cats and dogs and a hundred and one odd jobs connected with a croft/boarding house; late teas and cake, and then to bed for say a few hours only. Comes the dawn, then up again to this catering-cum-croft cycle. Feeding becomes the password, for they tell you that part of a Highland holiday is Food, with a capital F. And should you refuse a second helping, you are thought to be off colour! Surely Scotland is the best place to take an appetite—or to obtain one! Seldom have I seen so much put on so many plates so often and so willingly anywhere else in Britain. My! my! this is the life, you can hear the visitors saying to each other. If only we could stay up here all the year! God's own country indeed; fishing and feeding 'midst gorgeous scenery surrounded by lofty mountains, pierced by glens and lochs ... relaxation to the full, and no worries at all. Could one ask for more? The breathing in of air that so refreshes the body, and the sight of the eyes that makes glad the heart. It is all so true; so real. There are no commercial fakes in the Highlands; it is just as Nature made it. And Nature knew what it was about in Wester Ross.

But we are digressing somewhat, for you will recall we have only just entered Badachro, noticing the post office, the old tin-roofed school and the Inn. The latter is situated right on the edge of the little jetty, the sea almost lapping in at the front door. This picturesque old inn has a beer-only licence, and the locals will tell you proudly there is no other such licence in the whole of Scotland.

The post office is one of the busiest sub-offices around here, and has a well-stocked shop too, where you can buy almost

anything from a needle to an elephant—so long as you don't
ask for an Indian, Ceylon or African elephant! It is said elephants
never forget—the reason being because nobody ever tells them
anything! My great friend Willie, full of Highland humour
and charm, is always kept busy coping with everything on both
sides of the P.O. grille, with his ever pleasurable manner; and
many a visitor is beholden to him in answering their queries as
to local information. He also acts as meteorologist to the Gairloch area, the rain-gauge apparatus being located in the garden
of his house further along the road. Yes, Willie and Badachro
are synonymous.

Passing through this tiny village unspoilt by Time, and giving
a glance to the right is the promontory known as Aird, where
the few houses there look down on Isle Horrisdale and Dry
Island. Whilst this latter word 'Dry' has nothing connected
with alcohol, it seemingly takes its name from olden times;
and from the fact that when the tide goes out one can walk
across the stones or causeway to it; not always needing to take
a boat to the one house there. To get across to the two or
three small houses on Isle Horrisdale (official postal address,
Main Street, Horrisdale!) you require to row over from the
jetty at the Inn; in stormy weather one may easily be mar-
ooned 'at home' for a few days. But these little retreats—
away from it all again—are only used as summer houses by their
city owners.

Continuing along, we pass open moorland and a pretty loch
abutting the roadside—Loch Badnahachlish—and soon reach
Port Henderson, where there is a farm, small stores, petrol pump
and a telephone kiosk. Port Henderson is called by the natives
PORTIGIL; Norse, port-gil (gate gulley); by others PORT AN
SGÙMAIN (Haven of the stack). There is no 'port' now, but long
years ago there was one Roderick Mackenzie, an elderly and
much respected boat-builder. When young he went one day to
a rocky part of the shore, and, whilst gathering bait, he suddenly
saw a mermaid asleep among the rocks. He got near her and
managed to seize her by the hair. She, in great embarrassment,
cried out that if he would let her go she would grant him whatever wish he might ask. 'Rorie' requested a pledge that no one
should ever be drowned from any boat he might build. On his
releasing her, the mermaid promised this should be so. I am

told by one living in the district that this is a true story—or at
any rate the essence of it is true, for there is much superstition
around these parts—that the promise was kept throughout
Roderick's long life and his boats continued to defy the storms
and seas; in fact I believe one or two of his boats are still afloat
this very day; eighty years or so old.

From here, another mile or so brings us to Opinan ('little
bays') where the sandy beach and sand dunes stretch for miles,
and you always find yourself alone, or nearly so, looking right
across to Skye with the tip of Rona Island and lighthouse showing.
A post office and telephone, and another phone box further on
near Red Point, completes the last link with the outside world.
Opinan is a wee village which the stage-coach seldom visits!
It boasted a school also, but that has now closed down, and scholars go over by bus to the Gairloch school.

The next small hamlet is SOUTH ERRADALE, a mile or so
onwards; then comes the end of the road, Red Point, which has
but a few crofts. In Gaelic, Red Point, AN RUDHA DEARG, means
the dun or swarthy point. High up on the cliffs of Red Point
one looks down on Loch Torridon, the islands of Rona and
Raasay, and over them, Skye which seems so close at hand. On
the far side of Loch Torridon, the Applecross Forest mainland,
one can see the pebble-whiteness of scattered cottages glistening
in the sun in the various small villages of Fearmore, Fearnbeg,
Kenmore and Ardheslaig. Further down Loch Torridon, but
out of view, is Loch Shieldaig and Upper Loch Torridon,
wherein nestle two other wee villages of Annat and Torridon,
where the Torridon mountains begin.

And it is of Torridon now that I would tell you; of the
Torridon Hills I look upon and see every day I waken at Strath;
and every day they seem to look different by reason of the angle
the morning light and cloud falls on them, a veritable peacock-
parade of colours. There they are, every day of every week of
every year; and yet no two days the same. And this has been
the case for millions of years, for they are considered to be the
oldest hills in creation; they were old before the Himalayas even
started. They are indeed rich in impact value; muscat-purple
mountains against a sky of rose, crimson and gold.

Torridon lies at the western end of Glen Torridon, perhaps
the finest and wildest of the Wester Ross glens. The road to

Torridon is overshadowed by the might and majesty of Liathach ('the Gray one') 3456 feet above sea-level, a terraced mass of Torridonian sandstone topped with white quartzite (frequently mistaken for snow). Beinn Eighe ('The File Mountain', 3300 feet) and Beinn Alligin (3021 feet) also tower upwards, keeping the monarch of these hills, Liathach, company. Liathach is composed of more than three miles of steep terraces of red sandstone, most difficult to climb.

These mountains are of immense interest to geologists, who come from all quarters of the world to study them, for this Torridonian sandstone is some of the oldest rock in the world, so old in fact that no fossils have been found in it, an indication that the rock was laid down before life first appeared on this earth. This chocolate-coloured sandstone is about 4000 feet in thickness. Above this, the Torridon Red, lies a thick-bedded whitish rock referred to above, composed of quartz-grains plus a highly metamorphosed fine sandstone.

The Torridon mountains are known as 'sedimentary' rocks, as opposed to 'metamorphic' rocks, the product of alteration by various geological processes of rocks of diverse origin.

The phenomena of the glacial period are truly shown in this Loch Maree-Torridon area. The strata in general run parallel to the loch's axis, proving the existence of an immense glacier that moved to the sea down the deep hollow now filled with water. Further evidence of glaciation is the number of terraced thrust-planes which must have been borne by the ice sheet dropped from the parent rock in the line of the ice movement.

These hills of Torridon make a striking picture in the varying glows of sunset; in short, as I have said, this precipitous range, as well as many other mountains in the north-west Highlands, provide a wealth of attraction to everyone, especially to geologists in studying so many of the geological problems which still remain unsolved. Torridon for them has a unique interest.

Torridon and Annat villages practically adjoin one another at the head of Upper Loch Torridon, which is part of Loch Torridon itself—a big arm of the sea—which also has Loch Shieldaig in its fold, as I have said. The loch is broad, deep and lone-looking, crowned with these mountains of sandstone that glow like liquid gold in summer sunsets; and in winter present an eerie wildness. The loch also embraces the great Ben Damph forest.

To reach Torridon you turn off at Kinlochewe and travel some 12 miles of good roadway, comparatively wide and straight, through Glen Torridon, to the head of the loch. The area between Kinlochewe, Loch Maree and Glen Torridon is partly a national forest park, though a fair area of old forest has been cut away some years ago.

This journey of 12 miles takes you through wild scenery unsurpassed in grandeur (and again I stress) of loneliness. This utter wildness surely gives us a lesson in humility? No sea-loch in Wester Ross is encircled by such terrifying 'massiveness'.

About 4 miles along the road, Loch Clair is passed on the left; near-by one can see the seat used by St. Maelrubha when he journeyed between his two cells at Applecross and Loch Maree (Isle Maree). Further along this roadside heaps of stones can be seen at times, made by passing funeral parties in the olden days; for here one is in the midst of—

> A land of wayside cairns—the place
> Of resting for the biers of death,
> And tokens of a fading race
> And relics of forgotten faith.

When you are about halfway to Torridon you will not fail to see on the left side of the glen an extraordinary array of hillocks close together, rounded off; and this little fascinating area is called the 'Corrie of 100 Hillocks', or sometimes as the 'Valley of 100 Fairies'. These singular mounds are due to the natural action of ice and water in prehistoric times; the streamlets depositing a series of hummocks of debris, which gradually covered the ground as the ice retreated, leaving these corries behind.

Coming to the head of the loch, the road forks; left to Annat, a quaint-like village (or hamlet I should rightly call it) where a new 18-foot carriage-way road has been made connecting Torridon and Annat villages with Shieldaig, Loch Carron, and onwards to Strome Ferry. This new road some seven-and-a-half miles long enables tourists to cut out at least thirty miles in having to journey from Strome to Achnasheen and then on to Kinlochewe, where if you took this new road you would eventually come to Kinlochewe by a nice, fairly straight, tar-surfaced road.

The new road was opened on 9th September 1963, by Mr. Michael Noble, the then Scottish Secretary of State, with torrential—straight up-and-down—Highland rain falling; however after the ceremony, the sun came out in full glory. County councillors from all over the Highlands, crofters, villagers and many others attended. The new road cost about £400,000 and opens up much captivating Highland scenery which was previously hidden to the tourist. For over two years roadmen struggled against heavy odds in two rain-drenched summers and two Arctic-like winters to complete this highway; and it is bringing new life to villages struggling for survival. Previously there was only a bridle path—a hiker's path—between Torridon and Shieldaig. On a clear day the Outer Hebrides are visible; then, as you continue on the road, the majestic Torridon mountains come into view followed by a dramatic panorama with Ben Alligin to the left and mighty Liathach on the right. With the road sweeping onwards magnificent views of the Ben Damph Estate are at hand; and then Skye and Harris can be seen in the distance. In the midst of these Torridon mountains, and with a darkening sky, it is no uncommon experience sometimes to hear coming from the depths of the many corries, the roaring of stags and the bellowing of deer. Finally the road rolls down to Annat, a wee village, then Torridon village, then linking up with the Kinlochewe-Gairloch main road. The contractor's chairman confessed at the opening ceremony, that the weather was their biggest obstacle, and that they had made a heavy loss on the project, but he went on to say that though they had done the work at a loss they felt they had helped to create something of real and lasting value, something that would bring great benefit to Wester Ross in enabling thousands of tourists to enjoy the real breath-taking beauty of this particular landscape. Very noble of him, I'm sure. This new road is best known as the Balgy Gap road (pronounced Balgee).

So much for the road; so much for the old-world villages of Torridon and Annat. Whenever I have been in these two hamlets it has seemed to me to be siesta-time! Either that, or fast week and communion, for no one seems to be out of doors!

Mr. Duncan Darroch was the original proprietor of Torridon Estate since 1872. An elegant mansion house was built on the shore, 2 miles beyond the village, and near the road turn-off to

Diabaig. This estate, and that on the opposite side, Beinn Damph (the mansion there now being an hotel), was owned, until his death on 4th December 1964, by the fourth Earl of Lovelace, who was the ultimate heir of philosopher John Locke (1632 1704) whose writings influenced the drafting of the American constitution.

I have mentioned Shieldaig, the start of the new road, and in doing so would like to take readers to the nearby Applecross area (to the mountainous region of Applecross Forest, which I have said earlier I look out upon, with Beinn Bhan looming on the far horizon from my windows) and to the wee villages already named—for apart from the scenery, this district has been very much in the news. Throughout this scattered area, live some 55 old folks in the 12 townships. They have no roads, save the roughest of tracks and one is, to all intents and purposes, cut off from the outside world; and in case of sickness or urgent hospital attention, patients have to be taken by stretcher up and down these rough tracks to be put into a small boat at Applecross, then away to Kyle and Inverness. What a journey, what a detour, what a hardship, and any one acutely ill could well die before reaching hospital aid. The County Council consider it would cost nearly £900,000 to make the necessary 22 miles of roadway, and a County Officer airily suggested all these folk be evacuated to another area—picked up and dumped down in some strange unknown locality—where more facilities would be at hand! Does it never occur to authority that these people have been born and bred there? One can picture their distress at thoughts of being evacuated. It savours once again of the 'Clearances', and at the turn of the 20th century, too! Evacuation (a word well-known during the last World War), the alternative to providing even a minor road for these souls. Can you beat it? it is incredible. Sherlock Holmes would call it 'The Applecross Affair, or the case of the non-existent road'. Strung around this northern coast of the magnificent Applecross peninsula are, as mentioned, 12 villages or hamlets, some consisting only of one single occupied house; the whole with 55 people, and of these, twenty are over 65 years of age. Oh! blessèd peace surely. No road though, only tracks more suited to scrambling. There is no doubt in the minds of those who live on that coastal strip, that it is a case of un-Christian neglect, and that whilst others take roads, piped water and electricity for granted, they are being deliberately cut off to save expense, doomed to dwindle into extinction; doomed to wither like a Goldsmith's *Deserted Village*. When £400,000 was spent on the new 8-mile stretch of road Shieldaig-Torridon, crofters in Applecross area were annoyed. The County Council no doubt has its own order of priorities. I knew of a good minor road in the Highlands that served only a few houses and wide enough for large vans to traverse, with passing places provided, yet it was widened and a major job made of it, forsooth, at a cost running, I would say, into five figures. But who am I to pass censure, being merely a lone individual; but sometimes some lone individuals *do* have a sense of business acumen. But when it comes to spending other people's money ? 'A'weel'. Economy ? What an astonishing word. Experts prove that all is well; then all is not well; so the truth lies somewhere in between. Unemployment and falling production brings on a depression. Employment and production rise; then the cry is 'inflation'. Wild and unproductive government spending results in increased taxation to provide the government of the day with more money for wilder and more unproductive spending. And so it goes on. But the poor folk of Applecross, what of them ? Oh! they are up in the Wild West; leave them alone to their loneliness. However, I must not make this into a political tirade! It is good to think, though, in March 1964 the County Council decided to try and prevent this 'Clearance', by proposing to make an unorthodox road—a narrow, twisting path, I suppose—and spend £5,000 on just *one mile*. As this road is to be made fit for a Land-Rover to jog over, there appears to be no possibility of a grant under the Congested Districts Act. This area *could* be largely developed from many an angle if a Government grant under the Township Road Scheme were obtained. How long are these good old folk to wait for the breaking down of red-tape ? And Echo answers 'How long indeed ? The humble crofters of Applecross area may know there is one person in Gairloch who wishes them well in their trials; and if any suitable occasion arose, I for one, would not maintain a Trappist silence with the authorities, as some councillors do. Good roads are as necessary as decent houses if you want people to be happy.

There is one strong big-hearted man though who tackles this

rough Klondyke track daily—in fact he *has* to—and that is the postman, 'Kenny the post', not to be confused with 'Tommy the post' of Gairloch renown. Kenny, who has been a postman for nearly twenty years, has been on this 'beat'—the toughest in Britain—some five years. He makes the perilous journey all the year round by motor bike; he would surely make a first-class dirt-track rider? At times, the path is only about twice the width of the tyres; he would seem to have been born a tight-rope walker to keep on his saddle. In this back-of-beyond country, the only living creatures on his way at times, seem to be the wild deer. But despite storms, blinding sleet and heavy drifts of snow, the post must get through—even though it be only a circular he carries in the bag across his shoulder.

Applecross, as I have said, is on the coast, and the approach to this sweet wee place is off the Loch Carron/Shieldaig road at Tornapress, about ten miles of adventure if ever there was one; the road curling up and around the formidable mountainside—the highest road and the nearest approach to any Alpine climb in the British Isles, over the old BEALACH NAM BO ('Pass of the cows'). A hair-raising experience, with hairpin bends of a vengeance, apart from steep gradients, 1-in-4, to the summit, 2050 feet. Then you come to a wilderness of rock, boulders and moorland, finally dropping down to the sea—and Applecross. It is nothing unusual for this road to be blanketed out in the summer by swirling mist; and in winter it may be blocked by snow for many weeks. Yes, life can be hard in the Highlands, and you need to be tough, mighty tough. At Applecross, the patron saint Maelrubha founded a monastery in A.D. 673 and was buried in the little church north of the village.

What then a better place for the first West Highland School of Adventure? This school is to be run on Outward Bound lines financed by the Dockland Settlements, whose chairman, Major John Wills (of the tobacco family) is the laird of Apple-cross, owner of the whole peninsula. This school is his brain-child. The object is to foster the spirit of adventure whereby boys (between the ages of 16 and 20, who will come from industry, clubs, colleges and schools) may achieve strength of character through the pursuit of tough experiences. The course will last for three weeks, and the boys will get a chance to take part in outdoor pursuits, such as small-boat sailing, canoeing in

D

the Inner Sound of Raasay which is just west of Applecross, canoe construction, rock climbing, trekking, life-saving and seamanship. There will also be cultural classes, discussion groups, educational films, library, pottery and sketching. There will be a warden in charge, Lt.-Cdr. Shelton, who will have a team of three skilled instructors assisting him. The pupils will also tackle a formidable army-type assault course. Yes, they'll get it tough down Applecross and the 'Pass of the cows' way. We never had such schools or instruction in our days, say we of the 1900's. Ah! well, it all makes for progress.

And now let us leave Bealach, the summit of Tornapress Hill before we get too dizzy, and come down to earth; back to Torridon village once more. Passing through this quiet village, we come to the 8-mile run to Diabaig over a fine macadamised road, but with many hairpin bends, such as you encounter at Applecross and in the Alps and which no one but an expert driver should attempt. I rate this 8-mile journey, passing Alligin village 1 mile away down on the shore, as one of the most—if not *the* most—spectacular in Scotland, with superb views going and coming back. Perhaps you could call it the most fascinating, and one that many a driver mayhap would offer up thanks upon arriving back in little Torridon village again, safe and sound!

A few years ago I travelled the road with the county's road engineer—a skilful driver if ever there was one—which was fortunate, for high up in the mountain pass (and sometimes you come to the crest of a rise where you cannot see—until you are *on* the crest—whether the road goes straight on, turns right, or veers left) we suddenly came upon a funeral party (the road foreman's mother) complete with several cars, the coffin being on a lorry; looking neither to the right nor left we managed to steer clear of each other by inches; but to anyone but an expert handler of cars, I felt we would have joined that funeral party! Either that, or suffered nothing short of a nervous breakdown for years to come!

So ended my first memorable ride to Diabaig; and believe me I would not have missed it for all the corn in Egypt, let alone the tea in China, or all the oatmeal eaten west of Garve! There is a sweet old-world jetty when you get down to the village nestling on the seashore; shades of the past when 'puffers', of the Para Handy age, called in with supplies of coal—and whisky. You can easily turn round there for the journey back—after taking a large neat brandy, of course!

A marvellous journey of but 8 miles—a mileage of sheer delight. Diabaig is wee (pop. 40). But so big in majesty.

Diabaig is a Norse name, its meaning unknown, but possibly connected with *Dia* (God) and *aig* (a small bay), so that it may reasonably be interpreted as 'the small bay of God'. This reference may well be by reason of religious infiltrations from the neighbouring monastery at Applecross. On an old map of 1662, *Diabaig* is spelt *Typack*.

In the autumn of 1964, I had occasion to visit Diabaig again. It was a perfect mid-October morning ; the Torridons looked at their awesome best, and in going over the mountain pass, the various golden autumnal colourings of the bracken, moorland, trees and lochans were beyond description ; and one could liken the sea to a Mediterranean blue. The whole journey was a sight and an atmosphere given to few.

I did not meet a single car or human being on the pass, and dropping down to Diabaig, walked along to the end of the little jetty. It was unusually quiet ; not a soul to be seen save an old woman taking in a few peats stacked at the side of her small cottage for her fire ; and two collie dogs. Along the jetty there were fishing baskets, ropes and nets thrown about in a haphazard fashion ; and in the small, almost land-locked bay, two outboard-motor boats rode idly at anchor. The sea was dead calm—not even a ripple—and like a mirror reflected the mellowed autumn sun. I felt I could almost walk across that stilled water, just as He did on the Sea of Galilee ; in fact the whole hushed atmosphere, the rocks and little hills standing out so vividly, gave me a picture of what those ancient days in Palestine must have been like. I was so moved, I could not hold the world close enough.

Everywhere a breathless silence, but not a Silence such as was caused by that tragedy written of in Chapter 5 ; but of one enacted nearly 2000 years ago.

As I stood spellbound on that jetty, Time and Eternity, the Here and the Hereafter seemed to mingle. It was all so real and over-powering . . . like picking up a champagne glass and taking the first sip.

After solemnly drinking in all the beauty and the deep thoughts of Life that swelled within me, I went back to the car. The old woman met me, and after my saying how quiet and ravishingly peaceful everything was, I asked 'where *was* everybody?' 'Oh', she said, 'they've all left hurriedly as you would see from the way in which the boats and fishing gear have been strewn around'. 'Left?' I queried; 'Yes, they have left and followed Him' was her reply, quietly adding 'I see you were there also, and that you, too, were wrapped in emotion'.

I knew then, this old and gentle woman was referring to Matthew, chapter 27, verse 35, where 'they parted my garments amongst them, and upon my vesture did they cast lots'. The robe was woven, she told me, without a seam; all in one portion, Galilean homespun in fact.

I went back again along the jetty and stood, for what seemed an eternity, at the clear water's edge. After a while, I felt a touch at my elbow. I turned, but there was no one there—at least no one I could see. I looked up and out to sea, Loch Torridon and the Minch, and saw a rainbow. Yet there was no rain falling and everything was crystal clear in the autumn rays. It was then I realised I was seeing *this* rainbow through tear-stained eyes.

Yes, there was no question—not the slightest doubt—'I was there'.

Returning to the car, I sped upwards over the pass giving one glance over my shoulder to Diabaig and its superb bay; then dropped down into Torridon village . . . where I woke up.

Whilst the Norse equivalent of Diabaig is so apt, so significant ('the small bay of God'), I came away with an even better name for it in Arabic, ROHALBI . . . 'soul of my heart'.

*   *   *

I make bold to say that if there was only a minor tarred-macadam road from Applecross, round the northern peninsula, to Shieldaig, thence by the magnificent carriage-way—the Balgy Gap road—to Torridon, and a new road made from Diabaig to Red Point connecting with Gairloch, the whole would open up undreamed of possibilities, resulting in one of the *greatest* panoramic views in all Europe; and should there be a good-sized decent hotel built either by private enterprise or Government at the tip of the Applecross area, say at Fearmore, the whole area would be visited by thousands during the summer. The result in tourist potential would be enormous. There is

already the superb mansion hotel at Torridon; with one at
Applecross point, the most spectacular district of all Britain—
yes, and I would say of all Europe—the area would be inundated,
not only with our own folk, but with our ever-welcomed
overseas cousins.

No longer would the operative word be 'Clearances'.
Those associated with the areas should go all-out to achieve a
Pyrrhic victory.

Why *should'nt* the beauty of our own land be laid bare to
travel? Why not? A million pounds or so would be money
well spent. To accumulate one needs to speculate. It would be
no gamble in this case. And what is a million or so to a Government now spending to the tune or symphony of £3½ million
a day alone on Education? Just think of that; £150,000 an
hour, £2,500 a minute. A gargantuan expenditure. Britain's
annual education bill has soared by £797 million to £1276
million in ten years; and now takes up five per cent of the
national income. Such a circular roadway would be *true* education from every aspect and from every standpoint.

Make no mistake about this, Mr. Secretary of State for
Scotland, whoever you may be!

There is yet another link that could, and should, be made
to 'open-up' Scotland's beauty, and that is a roadway from
Royal Deeside to stately Speyside—from Braemar across the
22 miles to Aviemore; instead of which, from Deeside one
needs to travel south down the Devil's Elbow, through Spittal
of Glenshee, branching off via Kirkmichael to Pitlochry, thence
north to Blair Atholl, Dalwhinnie and so to Aviemore and
Inverness—about 100 miles all told in this devious route. As an
alternative, but via a tricky road, one could turn back from
Braemar going via Cockbridge, Tomintoul (the highest village
in Scotland), thence to Grantown, Carrbridge, and Aviemore or
Inverness. This would clock up about 60 miles.

Such a new venture as I have indicated of some twenty-five
miles at the outside, would open-up new and exciting landscapes
through the mountains, the Grampians and the Cairngorms,
the land of the eagle and of the osprey, the land of the ancient
Caledonian forest; the backbone of Scotland. Only ten years
ago, or so, the cost of this spectacular roadway was about ½
million pounds; now it will be five or six times that sum

perhaps. But, again, what is *that* cost compared to the 'draw' in this wonderland discovery. We hear so much nowadays of wanting to boost tourism in Scotland; well, I have given two practical expositions for those who sit in State. Will they take heed?

The Scottish Tourist Board, and those who may be dealing with Scotland's publicity, and have Scotland's welfare at heart, seem to me to miss the bus in not striking out bravely and boldly. In another ten years' time, the Applecross and Grampian/Cairngorm costs, will doubtless be beyond all dreams.

We shall have then lost it all. '*Quel domage*'; and Government's will have no one to blame but themselves. Have those in power, and directly concerned with Scotland's needs and welfare, no more than a school-boy's vision? I often wonder!

Sometimes I think we are plodding along at a pace set by centralised planning, red tape, rules without responsibility and regimentation without recourse. Government is never an end in itself. We should say 'No' to apathy; 'No' to convenience, but 'Yes' to our consciences. Every form of public control is but a means toward human purpose. St. Andrew's House should be more of a Scottish bureaucracy; not a Whitehall bureaucracy. Verily, promises are *not* performances. He who goes in search of mountains does not stop to pick up stones in the road.

CHAPTER 7

GAIRLOCH—ULLAPOOL—LOCHINVER

BACK again, in the scalded cat country ('Wild Cat' restaurant to you!) that we saw as we turned left at that landmark for the Strath and Melvaig district earlier on.

There are no wild cats to be seen in this area nowadays; though a year or so ago, on the south side, a so-called wild cat was shot; but it was found to be—sad to relate—a lovely ginger-coloured house cat—a pet; *fi donc*! There is a certain amount of wild life—deer, eagles, and that rare animal the pine martin—in the Kinlochewe forest and Beinn Eighe 10,000-acre National Nature Reserve heritage.

At the restaurant junction, taking the main road up over the hill and across moorland, brings us to Poolewe, Aultbea, Laide Gruinard, Dundonnell, Braemore; then up Loch Broom to Ullapool. From there we are going further on to a delightful little spot, Achiltibuie where the road, four miles further along at Culnacraig, ends; thence retracing those miles, we cross the border to Sutherland (*not*, let it be noted Sutherland*shire*) via Inchnadamph and Loch Assynt to another charming wee village, Lochinver. Home again then to Gairloch, going straight from Braemore along the fine broad highway to Garve; and from there, Achnasheen, Kinlochewe, Loch Maree and 'destination Gairloch'—having cut out Dundonnell, Gruinard, Aultbea and Poolewe.

Starting the journey then, *en route* to Poolewe we pass Loch Tollie (Tollie meaning 'a place of holes') and then get a charming view of this—the western—end of Loch Maree, with Beinn Airidh Charr in the background, and which, on a bright sunny day, almost rivals the other view of Loch Maree from the top of Glen Docherty and before dropping down to Kinlochewe, you will remember. It was from somewhere near Loch Tollie that Horatio MacCulloch's great painting of Loch Maree was made.

There is a very nice, sheltered, secluded spot down the side road leading to Tollie farm and, a little beyond, which brings you right down to the water's edge of the loch, pebbly, but very lovely and restful.

On the side of the main road to Poolewe, barely a mile from 'Wild Cat' junction, there is a big boulder on the right called 'The Shoestone' (Clach nam Brog) which derives its name from the fact that in olden days the women walking over the hills barefooted on their way to church at Gairloch, carrying their shoes and stockings, rested at this boulder for a while and put on their footwear here so as to present a proper, neat and dignified appearance upon arriving at the Kirk; and on the return journey, off came their shoes and stockings again at this spot.

There are many other legends *en route* at almost every tarn and rock. One tarn, into which the defeated warriors in local feuds were compelled to throw away their arms; a rock where two lads were killed and buried by their ruffian uncles, who brought the blood-stained shirts, to show they had done this foul deed, to the one who had enlisted their services in the murder; but a friend of the two youths stole the shirts, used them in evidence before the Crown and obtained just retribution (*vide* chapter on Gairloch); a cairn where coffins were laid down when the bearers needed refreshment; and the 'Field of Blood' where cattle used to be herded together and bled, as blood and oatmeal were the ingredients of 'black puddings' then, even as we know them today.

From Tollie Farm (side road) we drop down the steep Croft Brae to the short river Ewe, to Poolewe lying at the head of Loch Ewe—a big sea loch. Poolewe is just another small village with the usual post office and store. The District Welfare Officer —who lives in Strath—has his office here. He is assuredly one of the key-men of Gairloch parish. As mentioned earlier, since he is clerk to the District Council as well, he is a very busy man; for with his dual duties, his work takes him throughout the length and breadth of this extensive, 200,000 acres, parish. A District Nurse is also stationed here. There are two hotels of fishing renown, excellently managed and where one can relax in the full enjoyment of peace, good food and, above all, moderate charges.

The village and district around Poolewe, enters into the

journeyings of Bonnie Prince Charlie, which episode of the '45 rebellion is given in the chapter 'Skye and Flora'. Poolewe (or as it was spelt in those days, Pollieu or Polliew) was in Seaforth's country and was visited towards the end of July 1746 to early August by Major Macdonald of Glenaladale and Lieut. John Macdonald, son of Angus Macdonald of Boradale, as envoys of the Prince, for they had heard some French vessels had been seen in the bay of Loch Ewe. Should there happen to be any such craft it would have enabled the Prince to sail back to France. They arrived only to find there had been one a few days previous, but it had sailed off again; so their journey, fraught with difficulties in avoiding the few government troops stationed in Poolewe, was of no avail, and they returned, reporting to the Prince, whereupon it was resolved to change their course, and all went back south to Glenmoriston.

At Poolewe, and before going further on to Inverewe Gardens, Aultbea, Ullapool and beyond, there is a most delightful run through the village, skirting the southern side of Loch Ewe, to Inverasdale and terminating at Cove, where you see relics of masonry work of dug-outs, and gun emplacements built during the Second World War period. The road is good, though narrow. From the point at Cove, one looks across the boom to Aultbea.

The village of Inverasdale holds close association with the 'Stone of Destiny' (Lia à Fàil) which was daringly removed from underneath the Coronation Chair in Westminster Abbey on Christmas Day 1950. And why? Because one of the inhabitants of that small village (then 21-year-old Kay Matheson) happened to be one of the 'partners-in-crime'. Kay lives with her mother in a house, 'Firemore', at Inverasdale, overlooking Loch Ewe; and today teaches domestic science at Achtercairn School—not far from where these lines are written. She is still a most ardent upholder of the Gaelic language and is convener to the executive council of An Comunn Gaidhealach, which deals with Gaelic Youth; and it is in these hands that lie the future of Gaelic as a living language, and the whole Gaelic culture and way of life.

This 'exploit' was fully and vividly described in *And it Came to Pass*, but perhaps a few details here may not be out of place. Kay Matheson at that time (1950) had strong Scottish Nationalistic views. She had gone to study at Glasgow University, later becoming a domestic science teacher at Eastpark School, Maryhill, Glasgow. There were four members in this 'raid', Kay being the lone woman; and they were all friends of Dr. John Mac-Cormick—one of Scotland's most fervent advocates of Home Rule—a lawyer by profession and one of the greatest orators Scotland has produced this century. He was nicknamed 'King John', and might conceivably have become Prime Minister of Scotland had his dreams come true. Unfortunately he died at the early age of fifty-six, in October 1961.

The plot to remove the Stone was hatched on Friday evening, 15th December 1950, whilst the Glasgow University undergraduates were celebrating 'Daft Friday' at the traditional ball in the Students' Union; the plan being to bring the Stone of Destiny up to Scotland on Christmas Day. The weather was wintry in the extreme, the roads snowed up and icy. However, they made it, and the Stone was removed, but in doing so, it broke into two parts. Kay took the smaller portion in her car, but whilst travelling through London, the Stone fell out of the boot at Hyde Park Corner of all places, but she managed to lift the one hundredweight load back again. The other piece of the Stone was taken and hidden in a grass field near Rochester. In due course both portions reached Scotland safely and were successfully joined together in a Bearsden (Glasgow) mason's yard. Later it was taken to Arbroath Abbey, for it was there that the original 'Declaration of Independence' was signed. The Stone was carried through the Abbey gates, across what is now a carpet of green turf, and it was placed in front of the High Altar and covered with the blue and white of the St. Andrew's Cross. As they turned away, the leader of the party seemed to hear the voice of Scotland speak as clearly as it spoke in 1320:

> ... 'For so long as there shall be but one hundred of us remain alive we will never give consent to subject ourselves to the dominion of the English. For it is not glory; it is not riches, neither is it honour, but it is liberty alone that we fight and contend for, which no honest man will lose but with his life.' ...

This exploit and its many other episodes duly came to an end, and the Stone returned to Westminster Abbey.

To end in humorous Glasgow vein:

The King sits doon in London Toon, and sair he racks his brain,
'Whaur will I get a wise-like chiel tae bring me back ma Stane?'
His guid wife Liz laid down her broom, says 'George, man, it's
   no' canny,
The man that pinched that Stone wid tak the pension aff his
   granny.'

There were no prosecutions as the Government of the day
had no desire to make martyrs who might bring more signatures
to the petition for a Scottish Parliament. It is the only instance
in modern Scottish legal history where clear proof has existed
and no prosecution has followed; though the maximum penalty
for sacrilege is fourteen years.

Today, Kay teaches nearby where I live in Strath; the
remaining members of that 'Christmas party' have long since
scattered.

This removal of the Coronation Stone stirred few Scottish
hearts. It was described in the press as a shabby exploit. Scottish
necks, it was said, grew red at the thought that the thieves were
Scots! Extremist demonstrations of any kind shock the canny
Scots' mind. When shame is added to shock, the damage is
complete.

On the 25th June 1963, a statement signed 'The Guardians',
arrived by post at most newspaper offices in London, claiming
that the Coronation Stone was still in the possession of 'the
Scottish Guardians of the Stone'. However, a Westminster
Abbey spokesman said at the time the Abbey authorities were
quite satisfied when the Stone came back 109 days after its
disappearance that Christmas of 1950, that it *was* the same Stone.
With 'the Guardians'' statement was a photograph showing a
large stone, an iron ring at either end embedded in a grassy
hollow. Since the Stone's return from Arbroath in April 1951,
it has been subjected to quite a lot of technical investigation;
and there can be no doubt but that this *is* the original.

A mile beyond Poolewe is Inverewe Gardens, famed for its
rare plants and superb background of loch and mountain. Some
70,000 visitors a year pay to view these gardens, which 100 years
ago was but a barren promontory which the late Osgood
Mackenzie purchased in 1862 and which today is a veritable
tribute to all who were engaged in the task.

The peninsula (known in Gaelic as *Àm Ploc Ard*—the high

lump) is a mass of red Torridonian sandstone, and was then devoid of vegetation apart from a few stunted heather and willows. With the exception of the thin low line of the north end of Lewis, 40 miles away, there was nothing between its top and Labrador, and it was continually soused with salt spray. Mr. Mackenzie planted trees and waited for 20 years. He cut clearings and to their shelter carried earth and peat to make these gardens. He filled them with rare and lovely things; trees, shrubs and plants from China, Tasmania, Tibet, Central America, Chile, South Africa, New Zealand, the Himalayas, Australia and Japan. His daughter, Mrs. Mairi Sawyer, carried on her father's work until she died in 1953, shortly after formally handing over the Gardens the year before to the National Trust for Scotland, with an endowment for its upkeep. (It was only in 1950 that this N.T. for Scotland set up a Scottish Gardens Committee to act as an advisory body to the Trust and to guide policy concerning the administration of gardens connected with properties owned by the Trust.)

Mr. Osgood Mackenzie believed that the proximity of the Gulf Stream would provide the warmth for a garden at Inverewe and would be virtually free from frost.

There are exotic plants by the hundreds, and its charm lies in its naturalness and true magnificence of its setting.

In 1954 Dr. J. Macqueen Cowan, C.B.E., V.M.H., F.L.S., F.R.S.E., retired from the office of Assistant Regius Keeper of the Royal Botanic Garden, Edinburgh, and took up residence at Inverewe House to look after the gardens for the Trust, and when he died in 1960, his widow, Mrs. Cowan, carried on her husband's work.

The centenary of Inverewe Gardens was celebrated on 7th April 1962. When Mrs. Cowan relinquished charge of the gardens, the National Trust—early in 1962—appointed Mr. Allan F. A. Lamb, O.B.E., B.Sc. (Forestry) Edin., their representative. Mr. Lamb was previously in the Colonial Forest Service in Nigeria, Sierra Leone and British Honduras. He only held the position for a short time, for early in 1963, Miss Alice Maconochie, who had been general organiser of Scotland's Gardens Scheme since 1954, was appointed the National Trust's representative. She and her mother, Lady Maconochie, reside in the big white house at Inverewe.

The question is often asked, 'What is the best time to see Inverewe?' Conditions vary from year to year, and so no definite answer can be given; but there is plenty of interest to be seen at every season.

In a good rhododendron year the display of colour reaches its height *late April–early May*. The early rhododendrons flower in *February* and *March*, and towards the *end of March* daffodils are coming into bloom.

Azaleas enhance the coloured glory towards the *end of May*.

The Rock Garden is at its best *late May–early June*, apart from a host of other plants flowering throughout the whole season.

By the *middle of June* most rhododendrons have finished flowering.

All through *June* and *July*, colour is to be seen in the massed plantings of primulas and meconopsis.

The herbaceous border is at its best in *July* and *August*.

Hydrangeas begin to flower in *August* continuing through *September*, *October*, *November* and even into *December*.

In *September* heaths and heathers are at their best; and in *October* and early *November* the leaves of maples and other trees and shrubs have turned to yellow, red or russet brown. Even in *December*, *January* and *February* a few plants will always be found in flower.

Just before reaching the garden entrance gate, you pass on the seaward side a carefully made conical cairn to which a plaque has been fixed with the following inscription cast in bold lettering:

In memory of Alexander Cameron
The Tournaig Bard, 1848–1933
Who lived all his long, useful and highly respected life on the shores of Loch Ewe and whose Gaelic poems and songs earned for him a wide and an honoured reputation throughout the North.

Here follows another eulogy to his memory in Gaelic. (*Tournaig* is a large house with a croft or two around, a mile out from Inverewe on the Aultbea road.)

These gardens are a veritable tribute to those who undertook such a task. It clearly demonstrates that the labour put into any worthy conception is never wasted; and after a thorough tour you cannot but come away, closing the gates, thinking of those words written on Sir Christopher Wren's tomb in St. Paul's Cathedral:

SI MONUMENTUM REQUIRIS CIRCUMSPICE
'if you seek his monument, look around'

Such words are so appropriate to Osgood Mackenzie and his daughter, who carried on her father's wealth of fortitude.

Proceeding northwards, the road rises high, very high, and precipitous in some parts above Loch Ewe, to Aultbea ('Awlt-bay'). This is a really beautiful run and a magnificent drop down to sea-level into the village, with Isle of Ewe in the middle of the loch, literally beaming at you. Here again, there is in Aultbea a fine medium-size hotel situated at the water's edge, perfectly managed and well renowned for fishing and good food. Aultbea is a fresh, pleasant village.

Isle Ewe, legend has it, is believed to be a haunt of fairies; and the folk of Aultbea often said, long ago they saw strange moving lights on the little island and even heard soft fairy music wafting across the bay. The tale is told of a whale smelling the tar of a new boat lying at anchor off the island, came in from the Minch, struck and broke the boat, resulting in the drowning of three men; and so the belief sprang up from this that whales attack newly-tarred craft.

The pier and tracks of the 'boom' across the mouth of the sea-loch (for Aultbea was a naval base in the Second World War) are about all there is of note here—except perhaps the large community hall (built out of a Nissen hut by the navy) which is complete in every detail; has a large stage, tea-room, cloak-rooms and is capable of seating many hundreds of people. The weekly dances there are widely known and patronised, and often a B.B.C. small orchestra comes through to officiate. Conviviality is greatly in evidence; the very pretty local girls, the Isobel's, the Bella's, the Cathie's and others lending the necessary glamour; and for repairs and improvements this small village can easily raise several hundreds of pounds. Yes, much joviality and *slàinte mhath's* prevail each week here.

Aultbea is extremely busy with the building of new oil-tanks, pier and so forth; so the village is now a 'boom-town' in more senses than one.

From here we carry on across another peninsula—or shall

we say, neck of land—to Laide, a very tiny hamlet at the southern
end of Gruinard Bay, with Gruinard Island facing us and the
Summer Isles afar off. There are thirty-two isles which make up
what is known as the Summer Isles; and the whole provides
an enchanting panorama. It was thought they were given this
name because the sun was often shining on them, when it was
not shining elsewhere. These Summer Isles were the scene of
much smuggling in the good old days!

Near by on the shore of Laide district, is the ruined Chapel
of Sand of Udrigle, with the tide gently lapping at its walls.
This Chapel is reputed to be one of the earliest Christian churches
on the west coast, erected by St. Columba of Iona fame. There
now remains only the four walls. The evening sun, streaming
through the empty shells of windows alights on two graves:
John Maclaren and Andrew Urquhart, both of Aultbea, who
after years of war service, are laid to rest in the shadow of that
little isolated church.

There is a lovely little sandy beach and bay a little over two
miles down from Laide named Mellon Udrigle; a nice cooling
name too! On the way you pass Loch na Beiste which long
years ago was haunted and inhabited by a monster (the devil)
and no pedestrian would ever venture past this evil loch. In
order to allay the fears which this legendary beast had upon the
local folk, and which the local Free Presbyterian minister failed
to exorcise, it was decided to drain the loch. This, however,
was found to be too formidable a task, so they resorted to kill
the water Kelpie by emptying barrels of lime into the loch; and
nothing further was heard of this 'beastie', only the name of the
loch reminds us now of this legend.

Still another piece of legend which is recorded as taking place
as late as 1826, and connected with Mellon Udrigle.

It was Communion week, miles distant at Clachan Church,
Loch Broom. All the men-folk of Mellon Udrigle were there,
but it was too much of a journey for their women-folk to undertake. These latter witnessed a remarkable sight. The whole sea
near Priest Island, situated almost in the middle of Loch Broom,
appeared to be filled with warships, and everyone was greatly
excited.

They saw the galleys being filled with soldiers and arms and
were rowing to the shore as fast as their oars could bring them.

One of the women left the crowd and made for her house to bury her jewels and money in the sand out of harm's way. The young girls were told by their elders to take to the hills, to Greenstone Point—which is the tip of the peninsula—as the Redcoats' reputation was very questionable regards women.

For a long time everyone watched the galleys pulling shorewards, but strange to relate no boat reached the shore and no soldier landed. It was undoubtedly a vision corroborated by hundreds of witnesses; possibly it was a mirage that accounted for this phenomenon.

In 1914, eighty-eight years later, the Grand Fleet under Lord Jellicoe at the outbreak of the First World War, used this and other near-by bays and lochs for his bases. Possibly what the inhabitants of Mellon Udrigle saw in 1826 was the forerunner of things to come.

Priest Island, one of the Summer Isles aforementioned, is reported to have got its name in a peculiar manner. An Excise officer had been sent to investigate smuggling which was believed to be taking place near Laide. To avoid and throw off detection, he disguised himself as a priest and asked to be ferried across Loch Broom to Achiltibuie; but the boatman, being suspicious, left him on Eilean a' Churich (this island under review) instead, and thereafter returned to the mainland to market the brew. When the illicit spirit had been safely disposed of, the boatman returned to the island to collect the angry 'priest', and that is how this island was called Priest Island, or Cleric Island, to this day.

There is another little turning—a run of about three miles by a narrow rough road—halfway on the left between Laide and Mellon, to Slaggan, which is on the coast. Quiet and peaceful and nobody around. A mile or so further on from Mellon, and the end of the road, is another lovely little bay, Obinan. All these beaches have silvery sands, very like those at Morar and Arisaig, near Mallaig.

From Laide and winding our way with the sea just at hand and below us, we come to the little croft-villages of First Coast and Second Coast, *Bad an T'Sluig* and *An T'Oirthir Donn*, to quote the Gaelic; strange names, but this comes of the bygone days when there existed the custom of numbering the compass from the sun's position, viz. 1st, East; 2nd, West; 3rd, North;

and 4th, South. This part of the journey is called the Gaza Strip, for there always seems to be a battle going on 'mongst the dwellers there!

From here, we soon reach Gruinard Hill (Cabeg Hill) which has now been greatly widened, affording easy passage, and there we view the wonderful beach of white sand and blue water which on a warm sunny day resembles a tropical lagoon. Further along via Little Loch Broom we arrive at Dundonnell with An Teallach ('The Forge') (3483 feet) towering in the distance. An eminent geologist left on record, nearly 100 years ago, that Dundonnell was unsurpassed as a field for geological research. Quantities of rose quartz, moss agate, topaz and amethyst quartz can be found in this region; and when duly cut and polished by lapidaries, they appear beautiful.

After Dundonnell we leave the sea, and the road we travel is one of the several destitution roads in the Highlands which were built to provide relief during the famine in 1851, the Gairloch-Loch Maree road as previously stated was one of the first schemes to be really effective as a measure to provide work, food and money for the practically starving Highlanders. The Dundonnell section to Bracmore (at which junction we meet the road from Garve-Ullapool) was achieved through the efforts of Mr. Hugh Mackenzie of Dundonnell, but great difficulty was experienced going through peat-bogs, deep gorges and the like, and the track is today still known as Destitution Road. Dundonnell is a popular climbing centre to which climbers come from all parts of Britain.

At Braemore junction, where there was a prisoner of war camp in the First World War, turning left we commence the road up by Loch Broom itself, to Ullapool. A footpath near Braemore Lodge leads to a wooded gorge (now belonging to the National Trust) where you look down 300 feet to the Falls of Measach, also known as the Corrieshalloch Falls ('the dirty corry or hollow'); a most remarkable defile, the water tumbling over like the 'graceful drapery of a Shetland shawl'. The differing colours of the rocky walls, combining with the silver of the cascade and being themselves in the wooded canyon and chasm below is a spectacle you cannot afford to miss—awe-inspiring in its depth. The extensive Lael deer forest that one passes *en route* here adds a softer note to this wild country. From

1865–1916 the whole of this valley was thickly wooded with larch and spruce, but much was cut during the 1914–18 war: and has now been reafforested.

Close to Braemore House, are four large stones placed, it is said, to mark the 'leap of Rory'. Rory was born nearby in Strathnacalg, and when as a child he was sent by his parents to keep the bull from the croft, he struck the animal such a blow that it fell dead. Later on in life he became mixed up in smuggling and was outlawed, finding himself eventually confined in Edinburgh Castle. At this time there happened to be an English outlaw at Perth, and someone was needed to give him a sound thrashing. The Governor of Perth jail, hearing of Rory's strength, got in touch with Edinburgh. Rory was granted freedom and a sum of money if he would beat up this Englishman. The encounter took place in Holyrood Palace of all places! Rory hit his adversary over the heart with a terrific blow, and the Englishman fell dead. Rory was then a free man, and made for home. He first caught sight of Loch Broom from a spot to the north of Braemore House, whereupon he gave three terrific leaps of joy which are marked by these stones. So much for legend!

A little over 12 miles further along Loch Broom ('Loch of Showers') we are in Ullapool standing at the entrance to Greater Loch Broom with, let us hope, the striking view of the fishing fleet in the bay. This 12 miles of road is very beautiful, being flanked, for the most part by masses of rhododendron bushes on each side.

The beauty and splendour of Wester Ross is still to be seen in this village of white-washed cottages and countryside. It is the largest village north of Gairloch, and out to sea like a fleet at anchor lie the Summer Isles, already named, and a sunset over these islands can be impressed on one's mind for many a year.

Ullapool, once entirely a fishing village, is first mentioned in the Fishing Acts of 1587, but fishing did not really flourish until the late 1700's. In 1788 the British Fishery Society proceeded to lay out and build Ullapool village as one of their chief stations. They erected a pier and large stores and the village those days was presided over by a Provost, John Mackenzie. In 1847 it was all sold to James Matheson of Lewis for just over £5000; and the fishing flourished for many years bringing many benefits to the inhabitants. Ice was an unknown quantity in this area in those days, so boiler houses were built and the fish partially cooked to preserve it for transport. They were called 'boil houses'.

Herring fishing during the winter months then brought prosperity to Ullapool. In its train came gutters, packers and curers, all requiring accommodation taxing the resources of the village to the utmost.

It was recently thought Ullapool would become quite a busy village in that there was a proposal to operate a big ferry service, capable of taking 600 passengers and 70 cars at a time across the Minch to Stornoway, a trip of only three hours, which would cut out the long journey by the *Loch Seaforth*, which daily plies from Kyle to Stornoway, and the inconvenience of having to book so much in advance for your car, for at the most that vessel can only take about six cars at a time; an insignificant number really. Unfortunately at the last moment, this most useful service, sponsored by Stornoway business men, fell through. No doubt as time goes on, MacBrayne's may come to the rescue in this very necessary ferry service.

An interesting though sad affair took place in January 1905, and I quote from a local paper of that date:

. . . The worst storm within living memory fell upon the village. During the previous six weeks a very intensive fishing had been in progress and never in the history of Loch Broom were such high hopes entertained for a prosperous season. The fishing fleet dropped anchor in the harbour and the crews settled down to enjoy a well-earned Sunday's rest. On Sunday morning a south-east wind sprang up and the crews could be seen putting on extra anchors and chains. By midnight the boats seemed to be riding the storm and the inhabitants of the village went to bed. At 5 a.m. the wind increased to hurricane force—one boat furthest windward dragged her anchor, she came down on her neighbour—and so on shorewards until every boat in the fleet was mixed hopelessly with each other. All with one exception, the 'Isabella' which sank, came ashore on the beach. When daylight broke such a sight met the eye as one never desires to see again; wrecks everywhere, boats, nets, men, buoys, masts in confusion. At the end of Point Street, 'Lizzie' and 'Dragon' of Ardrossan and Glasgow could be seen lying broadside on the sea, waves dashing over them 100 feet high. Next came four fishing boats, then the Pier intervened; again ten fishing boats, curing smacks, small craft—twenty-five in all, breaking up rapidly.

A sorry sight miraculously attended by no loss of life. Towards afternoon five crews signalled they were in danger and must get ashore. Mr Mackenzie, fishery office, assisted by John Maclean, mason; R. Mackenzie, merchant; Macdonald, carpenter; and A. Macdonald, who constituted the rocket crew, rose nobly to the occasion. The boats' bush rope floated ashore on a hawser while the sea anchor supplied a breeches buoy and two men were taken off in this manner. The coastguard boat was the only one safe and suitable to use in such a sea, but some regulations bound with red tape prevented it being used. Messrs Mackenzie and Macdonald undaunted jumped into the boat and were preparing to effect a rescue when the coastguards, risking a breach of regulations, gallantly took over the boat and proceeded to the scene of disaster. Toole, Scott, and Saunders worked hard and, with spray and sea dashing over their boat, succeeded in saving thirty-six souls; a very plucky piece of work.

The hardest part of the work now fell on the inhabitants—to house and feed 150 men within a few hours is no easy task even in a village. Mr Kenneth Cameron was equal to the occasion and within a very short time, had board and lodgings and food ready to supply to these men who, tossed all night in a terrific sea, were worn out and soaked to the skin. From Rhidorrach came two hinds, from Inverbroom two sheep and half a cart-load of rabbits, and these helped materially to supply a good meal for the destitute seamen. The damage to boats and nets was estimated at £5,000. The Royal Lifeboat Society awarded 30 shillings each and a vellum of thanks to coastguardmen Scott and Saunders . . .

Today the pleasant little white-washed-cottaged-village of Ullapool is no longer historic as it was fifty years ago; indeed none of these Wester Ross fishing villages are; the fish seem to be lessening.

So we leave Ullapool down Loch Broom again to Braemore junction, taking, this time, the main road straight on to Garve, 19 miles away. But before finally saying adieu to Ullapool, I would recount the story of an Ullapool worthy who was trudging one wintry day to Laide. In order to remove a lump of snow from the sole of his boot, he kicked his foot against a boulder which became dislodged and started to roll down the steep hillside near Dundonnell. As it gathered speed it collected snow to such an extent that an exceedingly large snowball—an outsize really!—landed on the shore of Little Loch Broom. Some weeks later, when the snow melted, two fine stags and a hare were found lying dead beside the stone! caught in the boulder's rapid descent. Strange the Highlanders with their legendary flair and taste have not called that boulder by some fairy name, but just left it lying by the roadside, unnamed and unsung?

Another traditional story connected with the sea and Loch Broom is concerning one Mackenzie, a native of Gairloch, who lived in Ullapool. He was known in the Gaelic as Murdo the son of Murdo (MURCHADH MACMHURACHAIDH); handsome and tall. He had a fishing boat and spent his time going round the villages with his herring. One day he put into the island of Luing, south of Oban, near Loch Melfort. Going ashore that night he found there was a fashionable ball in progress, and the daughter of Lord Breadalbane was there. She saw this handsome fellow, and fell in love with him at once. He took her off in his boat, and they were married when they arrived back at Ullapool.

In those days no boat had any name or number, and Lord Breadalbane offered much money to anyone who could find his daughter. When Murdo heard that money was forthcoming he dressed himself up, and visited the lord at Taymouth Castle, near Aberfeldy in Perthshire. At the interview, Breadalbane said: 'You'll get the reward if you tell me where my daughter is'. Murdo replied: 'When I get the money I will tell you', and he got the money and then said 'if I get another £300 I will tell you where the man is who stole her'. He got his £300, whereupon Murdo, holding out his hand, said 'there is the hand that stole her from the Isle of Luing!' Lord Breadalbane was so amazed at his courage that he accepted him as his son-in-law, and gave his daughter a substantial dowry. Prior to all this, and at the time Breadalbane knew his daughter had eloped in a fishing smack, he went to the King and a law was duly made that all boats should have their name on them; and that is how such boats are named and numbered to this very day.

A few miles south of Braemore which we are leaving and off the wayside is Loch-a-Bhraoin, a fresh-water loch four miles long. Here are the graves of Lochaber men who had been cattle-raiding in the strath; yes, these Highlanders were aggressors, even as there are aggressors today. They were followed by an Ullapool man in the guise of a beggar. When the raiders had supped well and were sound asleep, he snatched a sword which he had hidden under his rags and slew them all but one, the sentry, whom he spared so that he might tell the tale when he got back home to Lochaber.

To Garve again then, along a fine wide macadamised roadway made for travelling at 70 or 80 miles an hour; across open country passing hydro-electric power stations. Across this wide expanse may be seen, over Direadh Mor, the remains of the old fir forest of Caledonia; gnarled, bleached and twisted tree trunks, roots and branches showing white in the peat dykes where they have been bleached by wind and rain. Another legendary story is that the dense fir forest which in effect covered the whole North of Scotland years ago, and was a shelter and habitation for wolves and all manner of wild beast, was destroyed by fire, for many of the tree roots and trunks which have worked themselves through the peat show signs of charring by fire. The tale goes that the forest was destroyed by a Danish princess, named Donan, who was sent by the King of Denmark to destroy all these pine forests so that he, the King, would have the sole, and of course bigger, market for himself and his own grown timber.

We stop for a while at Aultguish Hotel for a nice homely tea; then pass the great Strathvaich deer forests, into Garve.

*   *   *

We will now come back to Ullapool, for early in this chapter I said we were to 'take in' Achiltibuie and Lochinver. We will take the Lochinver journey first.

From Ullapool on Loch Broom (this loch is in three parts; Loch Broom proper 15 miles long, Little Loch Broom about half that length, and Gruinard Bay a wide inlet some six miles across by seven miles long), taking the main road north-west we journey through a rugged picturesque stretch of road skirting the shores of Loch Kanaird, turning inland through Strath Kanaird making towards Ledmore. About four miles out of Ullapool in the sheltered Kanaird bay lies the sacred St. Martin's Isle which you see to advantage from the village of Ardmair. At one time St. Columba ministered on this small isle where he left an impression of peace and sanctity. As to its name, there is doubt whether it was called after the famous St. Martin of Iona, or from the actual cleric who built his cell upon the isle, and who had been banished as a student from Iona, for his general manner appeared distasteful to St. Columba; and he was debarred from Iona until he had given proof of changing his mode of life. It is thought he first went to one of the other Summer Isles—to Priest's Isle. Howbeit, St. Martin died on St. Martin's Isle and over his grave there is a large stone on which the cross is seen covered with hieroglyphics. The ruins of his chapel are at the west corner of the isle; close by are the graves of his followers.

Onwards then through Strath Kanaird, we come to Drumrunie Lodge where one obtains an open panoramic view westwards seeing Ben More Coigach (2348 feet), south of Achiltibuie —a wall of sheer rock and scree. Thence we cross into Sutherland by Knockan and Elphin, and skirting Càm Loch, arrive at Ledmore, having travelled twenty miles.

Ledmore is on the main road from Lairg (county town of Sutherland), 27 miles distant. Sutherland is really 'The South Land'; strange, for it is one of Scotland's two most northerly mainland counties. The name comes from the Norse, as in early days this area was ruled by Scandinavians. It is the most sparsely-inhabited area of Britain.

From Ledmore we go due north to Inchnadamph (8 miles), a beautiful run with expansive views on all sides; Ben More Assynt (3273 feet) on the right, and on the left Canisp (2779 feet) and Suilven (2399 feet) standing well out against the sky line. Suilven is generally known as the Sugarloaf, from its shape when seen from east to west. Owing to the great variety of rock here, it is a classic ground for geologists and botanists. Inchnadamph is at the head of Loch Assynt, which grand loch is about seven miles long; a perfect loch in its wild setting, and within short range we see, off the north bank, Gl'asven (or Glas Bheinn) 2541 feet, and jagged Quinag (2653 feet). There is an historic castle, now in ruins, near the edge of Loch Assynt, Ardvreck Castle built by the MacLeod's of Assynt in the late sixteenth century. After the Marquis of Montrose was defeated at the battle of Carbisdale he fled into the mountains, but was captured and betrayed by his old friend Neil MacLeod, imprisoned in Ardvreck Castle, then sent down south to be beheaded. (This betrayal has gone down in history as a 'deed of deathless shame.') Assynt Council are now to preserve the castle ruins.

Inchnadamph is but twelve miles from Lochinver and the sea, travelling most of the way alongside Loch Assynt. Lochinver

is ideal for the sea angler, for it has been said by experts to be
one of the best venues for that sport in Europe; indeed it has
been recommended for the European Sea Angling Champion-
ships. It is really a charming little fishing village with a 'white
fish' pier which is to be enlarged at a cost of some £50,000.
Looking out westwards, Lewis can easily be seen, and Stornoway
on a clear day. At Lochinver there is a narrow, winding switch-
back run along the coast road to Stoer and Drumbeg viewing
lovely Loch Nedd, and carrying on with care and adventurous
spirit come to the main road north of Inchnadamph at Unapool
descending steeply to Kylesku ferry crossing the sea-loch to
Kylestrome, at the point where Loch Glencoul and Loch Glendhu
unite to form Loch A Chairn Bhain (Loch Cairnbawn). Thence
onwards to Scourie, Laxford Bridge (where turning south you
are on to the main road to Lairg, 40 miles), Kinlochbervie and
other small intriguing spots, a paradise for fishers. Near Scourie
is Handa Isle, a sanctuary for literally thousands of sea-birds—
guillemots, razor bills, puffins, terns, cormorants—and seals.

Handa cliffs, some 300 feet sheer, being of a rusty-looking
sandstone, stratified in horizontal beds, have eroded into tier
upon tier of shelves and balconies, all packed with vociferous
fowl. All the common cliff colonists are there (a snow-storm
of flying sea fowl, the noise striking one like a blast), each making
a noise after its own kind. Throughout the day, tumult reigns
uppermost; birds whizzing to and from their ledges, crannies
and holes; and when one disturbs them 'tis like a feather-
mattress being shaken. There are seals, porpoises and basking
sharks—some 30 or 40 feet in length.

In this journey across the Sutherland border to Lochinver
and a little beyond, we have taken in scenery of great variety;
hill lochs and fantastically indented sandy bays; roadways
bordered by heather, bog myrtle and wild roses. In fact we have
been an ideal trip, and certainly 'got-away-from-it-all'.

* * *

Now we had better return to Ullapool for our detour there
to Achiltibuie. One turns off at Drumrunie (about eight miles
out of Ullapool on the main road to Ledmore) travelling along
the side of Lochs Lurgainn and Baddagyle viewing Cul Beag
(2525 feet) a weird-looking mountain and An Stac (Stac Polly)

2009 feet.   Carrying on, we skirt Loch Osgaig and then turning southwards via Loch Vatachan we soon come to Achiltibuie, charmingly situated on Badentarbet Bay in which lie the delightful Summer Isles.   The largest of these is Tanera Mor and a little to the south-east is Horse Island, renamed Elizabeth Island by the inhabitants, after the Queen's visit to Achiltibuie a year or so ago.   On Tanera island there are to be seen the ruins of an old fish-curing station.   All these Summer Isles can be conveniently visited from Achiltibuie.   A little further down from Achiltibuie (4 miles) is Culnacraig, another small village (and the end of the road) where an easy ascent of Ben More Coigach may be made (2438 feet); a splendid viewpoint resulting.   Altogether this is a most beautiful run, passing lochs, sandy bays and beaches, and where—once again—bog myrtle, wild roses, heather and gorse all grow in wild profusion.   In this area large quantities of homespun wool and tweed are made, and distributed far and wide.

Achiltibuie ('field of the yellow flowers' in Gaelic) hit the headlines in the national press in March 1964 in respect of a baby porpoise, 'Puffy'.   This one-year-old male baby of 40 lbs. weight, was caught on 1st March in a salmon net in the bay. In the Flamingo Park Zoo near Pickering, Yorkshire, there was 'Flipper', a frisky porpoise that had gone into a fretful decline, pining there since her 2-year-old baby daughter 'Cookie' had died two months previously in January; and it was at once thought, and hoped, that she might adopt Puffy.   The newly-found babe was transported the 550-mile journey south with utmost care, wrapped in wet blankets and foam rubber in a specially constructed crate.   Two Zoo experts travelled with him, giving him pain-killing and vitamin injections *en route*; and they took turns in crouching in the back of their station-wagon car, to pour water on Puffy's sensitive skin.   At the Zoo, Puffy was placed in the charge of a pretty young attendant; at least Puffy said she was as pretty as a porpoise that he had played around with, off the Inner Hebrides back in Scotland!   The V.I.P. was given over to his foster-mum, Flipper, after two days, and Flipper took on a new interest in life, starting to do all her playful tricks again with rubber rings and toys.   This typical fairy-tale story, however, had a sad end, for poor Puffy took ill suddenly after being six weeks at the Zoo: and although attendants kept vigil over him night and day giving him anti-biotic injections, he died. Poor Puffy; poor Flipper.

*   *   *

So we come to the end of our journeying around Ullapool, and into the boundary of Sutherland. There is little more to travel in this vicinity hinging on Gairloch; no more to be said, unless it be 'will ye no' come back again' to this majestic country, which, though solid in character, alters its shape and scenery so frequently every day in consort with the weather's mood; and to those who venture the long journey here, above latitude 57° and between longitude 5° and 6° I would say we have plenty of weather! It can rain in deluges (Highland up-and-down rain as I have said before) in the north-west; but this, combined with our mild climate makes fuchsias, hydrangeas, buddleias grow like weeds; and rhododendrons flourish.

I would tell all readers, that the surest indication of a good Scottish summer is when, throughout spring, soft clouds of mist hug and kiss the hillsides in the early part of the day. To be a witness of this, you need of course to begin living here before spring; and so carry on being here most of the summer! *Slàinte*.

CHAPTER 8

AFLOAT TO THE ISLES

I FIRST came to know of Gairloch—in 1914—through travel-ling on David MacBrayne's steamer, the old *Claymore*, a vessel of only 726 gross tonnage, built in 1881 and sold in May 1931 at Bo'ness for breaking up. The present-day *Claymore* (1024 tonnage) is a very different ship from the old one; a beauti-fully lined, sea-worthy vessel, spacious cabins in polished wood-work, and one's morning tea brought in by a very chic stewardess.

> The earth unto the Lord belongs
> And all that it contains;
> Except the Western Highlands,
> Which belong to the MacBraynes!

The *Claymore* (a screw-steamer), the first ship built for the fleet after the business was being carried on in Mr. MacBrayne's own name, was for the Glasgow/Stornoway run.

To get to the isles in those days, one *had* to go by this steamer; there was no air service to the Outer Hebrides as there is now, i.e. Inverness to Stornoway, or Glasgow to Barra or Benbecula; in addition to this there are now car-ferries (operated by Mac-Brayne's and Government-chartered) from Mallaig to Armadale (south Skye); and from Uig (north Skye) across to Tarbert (Harris) and Lochmaddy (north Uist); and from Oban to Craignure (Mull) and Lochaline (on the Morvern-Ardnamurchan mainland). These ferries, as I have indicated earlier in this book, can deal with 52 cars and 600 passengers, and travel at $14\frac{1}{2}$ knots.

The reason for this chapter, is that many people coming to Gairloch, feel they would like to visit other parts of the Western Highlands and Islands; and now these car-ferries operate, it is a very simple matter, whereas before, one had to book up many months in advance to get one's car on to any of the passenger steamers. Now you just drive on; nae bother! If only, as I have said in chapter 7, we had a similar car-ferry from

Ullapool to Stornoway, this route would be a tremendous boon, and open-up untold fields of pleasure.

The name of MacBrayne runs like a slogan throughout the Western Highlands of Scotland. There is nobody else! and the little ditty given a few lines earlier is very significant. There are MacBrayne steamers, buses, lorries, piers, and so forth; and a MacBrayne tartan. In the whole range of world transport, *Wells Fargo*, of the Western States of America fame, is the only other title which can compete with it as a personal name applied to transport tradition. Good old Well's Fargo, often depicted on television; good old MacBrayne!

These days, the number of passengers carried is well over half a million, and freight some 100,000 tons. Cars galore, and mails colossal.

MacBrayne's never operate any of their steamers or ferries on the Sabbath. Recently there has been much trenchant criticism by both the kirk and the people of Skye, as to the suggestion to work the ferry across from Kyle to Kyleakin, Skye, on Sundays, run by the Caledonian Steamship Coy. (you will remember I have mentioned both this and the Strome ferry do not function on the seventh day).

I am in full agreement with those who object to Sunday running. Visitors should come to share in the life of the community here, in respecting the 'keeping of the Sabbath'. Their money or their desire to do anything they please, should coincide with the community's way of life *in extenso*. No more, no less. The islanders, as well as those on the mainland, can surely decide for themselves.

David MacBrayne himself was an outstanding example of the perfect association of circumstances which bring together the man and the opportunity.

The company held its centenary in 1951.

Travel in the good old days at the beginning of the 19th century was an adventure, and there were few 'goings and comings' to and from the Western Highlands and Islands. Very few.

*   *   *

Henry Bell's *Comet* of 1812 was the first steamer to sail regularly between Glasgow and Fort William making calls on the way. This vessel was wrecked in Loch Craignish in 1820.

Her successor, *Comet II*, started sailing in 1821 but had a short life, for she sank in 1825 after being in collision on the Clyde, between Gourock and the Cloch lighthouse.

Sailings on the Caledonian Canal, although incomplete, were started in 1820 by the *Stirling Castle*, from Inverness to Fort Augustus. The Canal was completed in 1822, and the sailings extended to Banavie and round to Glasgow.

In 1824 G. & J. Burns was one of the companies operating the West Highland trade. The year 1847 was a landmark in the history of the Highlands, for in that year Her Majesty, Queen Victoria, travelled through the Crinan Canal from Ardrishaig to Crinan, and there joined the royal yacht *Victoria and Albert*. The passage through this wee Canal was made in a track-boat (barge), the track-horses being ridden by postillions clad in brilliant scarlet uniforms. In 1873, after staying at Inverlochy Castle, Her Majesty sailed in the *Gondolier* from Banavie to Inverness. The lochs and waterways leading to the Highlands traversed by the Queen became known as 'The Royal Route' and the name clings to this day.

With Messrs. Burns's many other interests taking up more and more of their time, they handed over their West Highland trade in 1851 to David Hutcheson, their chief clerk, on condition that their nephew, David MacBrayne, became one of the partners.

The firm, David Hutcheson & Co., was founded, and the partners were David and his brother Alexander, and David MacBrayne.

That was the beginning of the Company as it is known today—David MacBrayne Ltd.

The new Company, inaugurated on 10th February 1851, started off with a promising building programme. New tourist routes were gradually opened up throughout the Highlands. The railway line from Callander to Oban was completed in 1880, and it was thought by many that this would be the end of tourist traffic so far as David MacBrayne was concerned; but it turned out to be the reverse. Traffic expanded year by year, and Oban —the Charing Cross of the Highlands as it was known—also grew to be a favourite tourist centre.

In 1876 David Hutcheson's operated a steamer service between Glasgow and Islay. The company's *Iona*, 174 gross tons, was the crack vessel on the Clyde until 1877 when a competitor launched the *Lord of the Isles*. This compelled the company to build the *Columba* in 1878, and it was a vessel far ahead, in every respect, of any river steamer then in being, second to none in comfort and design and almost as fast as Clyde river steamers today. Its gross tonnage was 602 tons, a paddle-steamer. It was probably the best known river steamer in the world. There were several features about the vessel which were unique. She was the first floating post office in the kingdom and probably the world. It was the first of the Company's ships to be built of steel, which at that time (1878) was still in the experimental stage. She was then the largest of all the Clyde steamers and to this day there has never been a river steamer of greater length; it is not so long ago since she was exceeded in tonnage.

The *Columba* became a household name and many a trip I have taken on her. She was only employed during the summer months on the Glasgow–Ardrishaig run. During the winter she was carefully docked and closeted in cotton wool! She continued in service until 1936 when she was broken up (nearly sixty years of service); a great steamer to be sure. The name of the *Columba*—symbolic of Scottish history—is appropriately continued in her successor the *Saint Columba*—the former *Queen Alexandra*.

The two brothers Hutcheson retired, one in 1877, the other in 1879, leaving David MacBrayne as the sole partner and owner of the fleet, and the name of the Company was changed to David MacBrayne.

In 1880 MacBrayne took over many steamer and mail contracts from the Highland Railway Company, and in 1888 steamers of the Highland Fisheries Company on the Island routes were taken over, and so the ramifications of the Company extended. By then they had over 100 ports of call throughout the West Coast and the Islands.

In 1902 Mr. MacBrayne's two sons, David and Laurence, who had spent all their business lives in the service, relieved their father of the more burdensome details of management, although Mr. MacBrayne always made a daily appearance at the office. He died at his Glasgow residence in January 1907, aged 93. Truly a wonderful man and a man to whom the Western Highlands and Islands owe most.

The firm was then converted into a Private Limited Liability

Company in 1906, and it then commenced operating bus services. The first service was between Fort William and North Balla-chulish with one bus. Today the fleet numbers about 120.

During 1929 the mail steamer operating between Inverness and Fort Augustus was withdrawn and road services substituted, satisfactorily catering for passengers, mails and parcels traffic. Goods and livestock were conveyed by goods vehicles. Parcels traffic has been conveyed by the buses since their inauguration, but as the volume of traffic expanded considerably, goods lorry services were started. Such services also operate on some of the Islands, their function being the collection and delivery of traffic for the Company's steamers.

A major change in the Company came in 1928 when Sir Alfred Read, Chairman and Managing Director of Coast Lines Ltd., and the late Lord Stamp, President of the L. M. & S. Railway Company acquired the fleet and business of David MacBrayne Ltd. and entered into a contract with the government for conveyance of mails to the Western Isles. The name of the new Company was David MacBrayne (1928) Ltd.

The next few years saw expansions and improvements equal to those which had taken place under the old régime, as routes were being opened by linking road and water transport in order to open up still more of the Highlands to the outside world.

In 1929 the *Lochness*, 777 tons, was launched for the Stornoway–Kyle–Mallaig mail service, and in the same year the cargo vessel *Lochshiel* was built, 208 tons.

In 1930 the building of the motor-vessels *Lochearn* and *Lochmor*, both 542 tons, furnished the Inner and Outer Hebrides with ships exceeding in comfort and convenience all previous mail boats.

Shipping history was made in 1931 with the building of the *Lochfyne*, 754 tons. She was the first diesel-electric coastal passenger vessel in the United Kingdom. In addition to the propulsion by electric power, all deck and auxiliary machinery, cooking and other services were operated by electricity.

This vessel proved so satisfactory that a ship with similar propulsion and machinery, the *Lochnevis*, 568 tons, was built in 1934 for the Mallaig–Kyle–Portree mail route.

During 1935 negotiations were completed for the taking over of the Turbine Steamers Ltd. fleet, the grand old ships *Columba* and *Iona* had made their last voyages in the MacBrayne fleet and were replaced by two turbines, the *King George V* and the *Queen Alexandra*.

In 1935 the *Queen Alexandra*, 851 tons, was renamed *Saint Columba* and underwent vast alterations. The boat deck extended well aft, two funnels replaced by three smaller ones and a main mast added. As such she is now the only passenger coastal vessel in the U.K. with three funnels. Two years later she was converted to oil-fuel burning, with result that today, although nearly fifty years old, she is still amongst the fastest vessels operating in the Clyde estuary.

At the outbreak of the Second World War the MacBrayne fleet again began to play its part in war as in peace. The Western Isles now depended entirely upon MacBraynes; and so it does unto this very day.

Many ships, including the old *Queen Alexandra*, were requisitioned or acquired for government service. Two of their fleet were at Dunkirk, and one of the ferry-boats in the Normandy D-day landings. The *King George V*, conveyed, on two occasions, Mr. Winston Churchill to the battleship when he was on his way to the other side of the Atlantic.

The war over, all the vessels emerged from their battleship-grey to their familiar livery—black hull, white superstructure and red funnel with black top.

There were no ships built or acquired during the war and so deficiencies had now to be made up.

The *Loch Seaforth* was built in 1947 for the Stornoway–Kyle–Mallaig route and is now *the* ship in the fleet, with the greatest tonnage (1090). She was also the first to be fitted with radar; really a beautiful ship.

David MacBrayne Ltd. of Clyde House, Glasgow, C.2, are now the sole operators of regular steamer services, both passenger and cargo, to the Western Isles and Islands, and they receive an annual subsidy from the government for so doing.

From the foregoing, readers will have realised the tremendous part 'MacBrayne's' have played (and are still playing) in the far-off Highlands and Islands.

*   *   *

As to the isles themselves—the Outer Hebrides, the long stretch of the Outer Isles—they extend from Barra Head in the south to the Butt of Lewis in the north; a total of some 120 miles. Originally, millions of years ago, all these islands would be one long stretch of territory; so the name 'Long Island' may still be talked of today by the older generations. Now, with the passing of centuries, the Atlantic seas have made inroads of the low-lying grounds, thus forming the chain of islands, from south to north; Berneray, Mingulay (where thousands of sea birds abound in the glory of the sheer cliffs), Pabbay, Sandray, Vatersay, Barra (Castlebay), Eriskay, South Uist (Lochboisdale), Benbecula (Creagorry), North Uist (Lochmaddy), North Berneray, North Pabbay, South Harris (Leverburgh and Tarbert), North Harris and Lewis (Stornoway).

The island of Lewis in the north is somewhat odd, in that it is only half an island, for the island of Harris (*i.e.* north Harris) is the southern half of the island proper. The island, however, is solidly joined on to Lewis, and the two form one geographic unit, though in different counties. Lewis is in Ross-shire, Harris in Inverness-shire; indeed all the other Outer Hebridean isles are part of Inverness-shire. The population of all the southern small islands is very small. Stornoway is the largest town in all the long chain, with a population of around 6000. To deal with these various places therefore . . .

BARRA, lies due west of Mallaig (some 65 miles across the sea) and takes its name after St. Barr, a saint of the old Scottish church long before the Roman religion spread to the island.

VATERSAY (pop. 100) situated south of Barra by a narrow sound, was the scene of a tragedy of the lamentable 'Clearance' days. An emigrant ship from Liverpool in a sudden gale was driven against its rocks and wrecked in 1858, and four hundred people were drowned. These poor, wretched folk lie buried in the sand dunes north of the stone obelisk monument erected on the west bay. In Vatersay, there are vast deposits of fine shell sand all there to be dug and used as an A.1 agricultural lime product—millions of tons, in fact. Its analysis reveals a calcium carbonate of some 80 per cent. Limestone for the shoveling ! There is untold wealth in Vatersay, which belongs to the Department of Agriculture and Fisheries for Scotland.

I refer to MINGULAY (long evacuated). Mingulay's records are housed in Vatersay, as clear as they were written in the year 1870, with the visiting school-board members' and inspectors'

E

names. Their comments are there; but Mingulay is dead. ERISKAY, that familiar name in a very romantic, lilting, love song, lies just north-east of Barra across the Sound of Barra. It was on this island that Bonnie Prince Charlie landed on 23rd July 1745; and to this romantic island there still come folk from far and wide in memory of this event.

SOUTH UIST is almost joined to Eriskay, being separated only by a narrow strait, the Sound of Eriskay. The only town and port of any importance is Lochboisdale. There is only one main road running up the island on the west side; many small townships have no road approach at all, and any stores, fuel or household goods need to be carried by hand or shoulder or wheelbarrow. Another village of memory is Milton (five miles north-west of Lochboisdale), the birthplace of Flora Macdonald. The centre of the island is mountainous; two peaks, Beinn Mhor and Hecla, rising to 2000 feet. It was in a shore-cave below Hecla that the Prince hid for several days in 1746.

BENBECULA—pronounced in the Highlands as BEN-BECK-you-LAH—joins South Uist by a causeway, over which one can motor to the north of this small island to Gramisdale, where there is an airport. About three miles to the right of this road and shortly before reaching Gramisdale, is Loch Uskavagh, renowned as the spot where the Prince and Flora embarked on their journey 'over the sea to Skye'. On this island there are to be found the remains of some Danish forts—circular duns as they are termed; one being called the Tower of Elvina, named after the daughter of Rory, a renowned Danish chieftain. It is not possible to motor from Benbecula to North Uist, but at low tide, one can walk across the three-mile north ford sands, which separates the two isles. What fun!

NORTH UIST, with Lochmaddy as its chief port of call on the east side, has a fairly level roadway circling the island. Here again, there are a few Danish forts. Much seaweed is washed ashore by the Atlantic on the western coastline, and a seaweed factory exists here. Deep seaweed—callish—contains a large percentage of iodine.

We now come to HARRIS, the southern portion of the island of Lewis; known really as South Harris, being separated by some ten sea-miles from North Uist by the Sound of Harris, the nearest port being Rodel, which is linked by road to Lever-

burgh, named after Lord Leverhulme, who set up a large oil/soap
refinery there some years ago, but which did not prosper. Carrying up the island road, the next village of any size is Tarbert—
which I think is the nicest of all the Outer Hebridean places—
thence on through the deer forest of Ardvourlie. The road is
dreary, with the two mountains of Beinn Mhor (1800 feet) and
Clisham (2600 feet). Continuing, we are soon in Stornoway,
the largest town, as I have said, in all, the Hebrides. It has a
sheriff's court, provost and town council—and an airport connected with Inverness. It possesses a fine sheltered harbour.
Stornoway (in Ross-shire, you will remember) is an old town,
and its name dates back to the Viking times—maybe earlier.
The old Stornoway Castle was reduced to ruins in Cromwell's
time. The island of Lewis is the largest of the British Isles,
Ireland excepted. The northernmost tip of Lewis is called the
Butt of Lewis. Eastwards from Stornoway, across a narrow
isthmus is the Eye Peninsula. At one of the villages there,
Knock, in the ruined church, is a stone, presumed to mark the
grave of the 'last of the MacLeods'. How untrue this is! This
northern part of the island is uninteresting, being mainly a flat
peaty moorland. Sixteen miles due west of Stornoway is
Callernish, famed for its Druidical Circle (sixty-two feet in diameter) or Standing Stones as it is generally called, supposed to
be over 4000 years old, and regarded—after Stonehenge, near
Salisbury, in Wiltshire—as being the most important Bronze
Age Monument in Britain. From Callernish, southwards, the
minor narrow road brings us via Little Loch Roag westward to
Uig (not to be confused with Uig in Skye). It was here that the
celebrated Brahan Seer was born. Away, some fifty miles in
the bleak Atlantic, is the deserted isle of St. Kilda. Isolated as
the French Legionaire outposts in Africa.

   The long chain of these Outer Hebrides—from which you
can see many startling 'Sunsets on the Lochs', form a fitting
breakwater against the relentless Atlantic storms and swells, if
not the crossing of the Minch here would be a real hazard. There
is not much beauty really in visiting these 'outposts of Empire'.
There is a sad lack of vegetation and greenery; merely naked
rocks and brown flat moors. Nevertheless it makes for grand
seafaring cruising enthusiasts, given a stout boat with powerful
engines. There is plenty of clear, deep water, and few tidal

streams; very different from other seas which may require far more skilled navigation going through buoyed channels and the like. The prevailing winds up in this area are south-west, which more often than not, veer west to north-west according to the 'depressions' which so often visit us here from the Atlantic.

Of course, with these new drive-on car ferries I have mentioned earlier, they are encouraging far more tourists than ever; thousands of cars, buses, heavy lorries and so forth. In fact a visitor can now drive from Land's End to Lochmaddy in North Uist, without getting his feet wet once! With all this, there is naturally much congestion on these islands' roads; much wear and tear, and it would seem the local authorities are in for a fair amount of headaches and expense in the repairs, for the Government says that trunk roads, which get 100 per cent grant, *end* on the shores of the *mainland*. Island roads get only classified road grants, the maximum of which is 75 per cent. None of these roads are thought suitable to be upgraded to trunk-class roads. Now that island traffic is stepping up so sharply, it would appear time for government to consider this unjustified distinction? There are many hours' delay even on the Kyle of Lochalsh ferry system on account of the greater number of lorries going across Skye to Uig and thence to the Outer Isles. In fact it may be argued, all these ferries are in effect a bridge between the mainland trunk roads and the Hebridean roads; none of this heavy passenger and freight traffic makes any direct contribution to the local rates for maintenance and/or upkeep of their roads. Sooner or later—most likely the latter!—there will be some 'extras' dished out to these worried, back-of-beyond, island councillors by the Government of the day. Who knows?

In the above, I have dealt with the Outer Isles.

The so-called Inner Hebrides, Skye, Canna, Rhum, Eigg, Muck (all in the county of Inverness-shire), Coll, Tiree, Mull, Iona, Colonsay, Oronsay, Jura, Islay, Gigha—all in Argyllshire —are far more accessible, and have much more to attract, being more fertile. Mull is a particularly lovely island, and was the subject of my love story in *The End of the Rainbow*.

GIGHA, a small green island of six square miles, with silver sands, is three miles across the Sound of Gigha from the western seaboard of the Mull of Kintyre; and you take the small ferry boat from the village of Tayinloan. The gardens of Achamore

House, often open to the public, are well worth seeing at the season when azaleas and rhododendrons, in yellow, mauve and white are blazing. The island belongs to Sir James Horlick—of 'Horlick's' fame.

ISLAY, is a biggish island about 230 square miles in extent with a population of some 4000 people. It lies further west of Gigha, has good roads and is easily reached by steamer from West Loch Tarbert (Kintyre) to Port Askaig or Port Ellen, or by air from Renfrew. It is a very fertile island, which is almost cut into two on the western side by the sea lochs Indaal and Gruinart. Long years ago it was a stronghold of Somerled, Lord of the Isles. Islay whisky is renowned and has a peaty flavour since the water there travels through peat and gravel. There is also quite an important creamery on the island; and we must not forget the noted 18-hole golf course. At Bowmore, the capital of the island, eleven miles north of Port Ellen, there is a round church built in 1767 by the then Lord of the Island (Campbell), designed as such, so 'tis said, the devil would find no corners in which to lurk! Islay is owned by Major Morrison.

JURA, separated from Islay by a narrow stretch of sea, is wilder and hillier, and is the third largest island in Argyll. The Paps of Jura (all over 2000 feet high) are well-known. There is only one main road round the south of the island and three-quarters up the eastern shore. There are lots of deer and eagles in Jura. At the northern tip of Jura, between there and the small island of Scarba, is the whirlpool of Corrievrechan, which was the 'centrepiece' of a dramatic film many years ago, 'I know where I'm going', with Celia Johnson as the star.

COLONSAY, a small island of 15 square miles west of Jura, also reached by steamer from Tarbert, is attractive in its small way, with a golf course and sub-tropical gardens.

ORONSAY, south of Colonsay, is linked to Colonsay by an isthmus at low tide; and there are the ruins of an old priory, supposed to have been visited by St. Columba on his joirney to Iona; and it is recorded he consecrated the island as a sanctuary.

COLL (28 square miles), and TIREE (30 square miles, and said to have a high sunshine and low rainfall record) about seven miles off the west coast of Mull, can be reached from Oban.

There is also a direct air service from Renfrew to Tiree. Both are crofting, medium sized, islands—but flat and treeless.

Tiree is devoting itself nowadays to the growing of daffodil and tulip bulbs as I mention later. This venture is doing well. The bulbs are sent in attractive cartons. There are two 18-hole golf courses on Tiree.

In all these islands there are many sandy beaches, coves, and caves. All form restful places; and the grand *Sunsets on the Lochs*, need to be seen to be believed, as well as the *Sunrises*, for you'll always want to be up early in the mornings—very early.

There are mountains, wide horizons and sea in plenty. Lying amongst the heather, you will get sun-tanned with salt spray; you will feel the touch of isolation and contentment alongside you. You will wish to live on the juicy, fatty herring. If herring were equal in price to salmon, there would be little salmon eaten. In olden days the herring was looked upon as *the* food up in the North; herring and oatmeal. And in all this, you will many times think of the toast:

> Here's tae us
> Wha's like us ?
> De'il the yin.

Herring and freedom, both in plentiful supply; and it will be thus you will remember the Isles, and have no worries. You will certainly not feel like Atlas, groaning beneath the Hemispheres.

Scotland in the *autumn* in the isles and on the mainland of Wester Ross, can be enchanting. At no time is the heather so rich in colour, or the mountains more striking. A short vacation after your usual summer holiday, in such a season of the year, affords a final break before the onset of winter; and on average it is a drier time of the year than midsummer up here. The hotels and guest houses are not so choc-a-bloc, and you get more individual attention—there seems to be much more time to spare. The angler, too, has a surfeit of lochs, rivers and tidal pools more or less to himself; there is now a special angling course at Loch Maree, during the first fortnight of October.

Yes, autumn around Gairloch in particular will hold many happy memories for you. You will return home from this 'outpost', not failing to notice the looks of envy on your friends' faces; those who have never thought to visit these parts ... And envy can be two-ways; sorrow at another's joy, and joy at another's sorrow.

CHAPTER 9

EASTERN INTERLUDE

As this is the half-way house, midway in this book, I would now venture to take readers back through the Corridors of Time, to certain incidents in that poignant romance recorded in *The End of the Rainbow*—a romance that ultimately anchored in Gairloch, where we now are.

Apart from Fiona, whom I met in Mull and whom I subsequently married, bringing her to the dream house in Strath, there were two other 'heroines'. *Marcelle* in Ceylon, and *Tháfne* in Egypt. The former married another, a Ceylonese; the latter was killed by a stray bomb dropped on Alexandria during the time of Mussolini's invasion of Ethiopia just before World War No. II. That story was brimful of anguish, pathos and the like; heart-rending if ever a true story was—a story that *could happen to any one of us*. And although those episodes happened nearly thirty years ago, I still recall the incidents.

At the time I was, like David of old, greatly afflicted, and became as a hart that finds no pasture. The break with Marcelle, to most readers, I think, would be most touching; the sympathy and sorrow intense, for parting is even worse than death (as the French say, *partir c'est mourir en peu*, 'to leave is to die a little'). Nature decrees death must come to each one of us sooner or later, and one has then to put death in the background. But a parting—never! It crops up even when the past is a dream. And so at that time my heart was heavy. But Time is a great healer, and one's heaviness blows away with the winds. . . .

Heaviest the heart is
In a heavy air;
Yet every wind that rises
Blows away despair . . .

Quite often, vanished love evokes inspiration, and so frequently out of sorrow there comes gladness. If one be sad,
one's prayers do not rise up to the altar of God—for sadness is
still in the heart; and so one therefore needs put sadness from
one's soul. To everything there is a season and a time to every
purpose; a time to weep and a time to laugh; a time to mourn,
and a time to dance. At that sad time, I looked upwards and
onwards. In the end I found Fiona; and she found me. For
many years I had been searching; searching at times for the truth
within myself, and in the end I found it—not in myself, but in
another, Fiona. When one finds *that* in someone else, then one
instinctively gives everything one has got; everything. That
makes for enduring happiness. Christianity tells us there was
nothing in the beginning, only thought; and so our lives are
what our thoughts make them.

*   *   *

After we had been married a few years, Fiona said to me
as the wintry months approached, 'What about us going to
sunny climes, and journeying to Ceylon which was your former
home—and Egypt as well, visiting the places you wrote about
and seeing how Marcelle was getting along?' Fiona knew that
those days, those 'loves' were truly forgotten. Fiona was a
woman in a million. Love tipped our tongues, winged our
feet, opened our hearts, permeating every thought and act. She
was a woman who, in *her* life too, had had romances, but they
—like mine—were obliterated by Time. Both of us knew full
well that 'whatever *had* been, *had* been'. She had a motivating
power and guiding influence in my later life, and both of us
knew that one could not go through life without a certain amount
of heart and love pangs, and that in the end one met one's true
mate on this earth. In earlier years one *thought* one had come
across one's counterpart; but in the end it invariably resolved
itself into finding and into knowing who one's *real* life-partner
was. For years both of us were searching, and it came to pass
in our coming together, and in realising the tremendous love we

found in each other. I am thankful to say, *that* love continues to grow and to be uppermost in our 'togetherness'. In fact we still read the many love-letters we wrote each other during those waiting years; love-letters have the power to enable one to live again the happy hours which they invoked; they make of enforced absence, a more perfect and a sweeter presence.

And so we went East for three months, out to Ceylon first; that lovely island, the Isle of Delight, where as the hymn says ... 'Every prospect pleases, and only man is vile' ... Even that Venetian traveller Marco Polo in the 14th century A.D. said it was undoubtedly the finest island of its size in all the world; and I had lived there close on 25 years. We went just to see the place once again, where I had earned my living, toiling, as ran the Commandment to Adam, 'in the sweat of my brow'. We went by air, flying out from London one dark December day about Christmas time, and reached Ceylon after seemingly only a few hours in this age of SPACE, touching down on the air-strip outside Colombo.

The morning sun was brilliant as it generally is in the clear Oriental sky, and Colombo looked at its best in those early hours of daybreak, with a few clouds floating high. The ancient Egyptians called the dawn clouds that cradle the sun 'wings of morning'; and surely no one could ever improve on that saying. Ceylon is a Buddhist country at heart, and as such does not believe in celebrating Christmas. However, I heard myself saying 'in my Father's house there are many mansions', so who are we to criticise? Instead they celebrate the birth of the Lord Buddha, and at Kandy which is the spiritual home of Buddhists the world over, in August they pay homage to Him in the *Esala Perahera*—a magnificent festival, the most spectacular in Asia—where millions of pilgrims from many thousands of miles congregate to pay obeisances, shouting and chanting their reverent 'sadhu's'. This Kandy *perahera* is in the form of a procession consisting of drummers (tom-toms), exotic dancing by the far-famed Kandyan dancers—males, whip crackers, and as many as a hundred caparisoned elephants; temple chiefs in all their oriental regalia, torch bearers, and so forth. A magnificent tusker elephant, gorgeously bedecked and jewelled, bears on its back a jewelled casket used for enshrining the Sacred Relic of the Lord Buddha himself; the great Hindu

E2

sage who proclaimed his doctrine in the sixth century B.C.
Ceylon indeed is a country of relaxation and loveliness. After
Adam and Eve were cast out of heaven—so says Moslem tradition
—they had the choice of all the world's loveliest places for their
earthly Garden of Eden; and chose Ceylon. Adam's Peak is
literally the holiest mountain in the world, revered by countless
millions because of the foot-shaped impression in the rock at its
summit. To hundreds of millions of Moslems and Chinese, this
is held to be Adam's footprint. To 400 million Buddhists, the
print is said to have been made by Buddha on his last visit to
Ceylon. Then again, as to Hindus, they claim it to be the footprint of their god, Siva. So there are a number of theories!
At the top, Buddhist priests, in their saffron-coloured robes,
officiate at a tiny temple—one of Buddhism's proudest titles
'High Priest of the Peak'. The Holy Footprint, the Sri Pada, is
some five feet long and three feet wide.

Typically depicting the life and soul of Ceylon and its villagers
is that which the great sage wrote over 2000 years ago, 'yet a
little sleep, a little slumber, a little folding of the hands to sleep'.

We arrived, as I have said, just before Christmas Day. In
going through the city later on I thought Colombo was shabby
and dirty compared to the days when I was there, 1914–1937;
the main European shops which in my time were big, portentous,
and crammed with Western goods, seemed much reduced in
size and had little to sell, and little to attract the European visitor;
for since 4th February 1948, Ceylon ceased to be a Crown Colony
as it then became an independent member of the British Commonwealth, running its own affairs. However, it was a joy to see the
old familiar landmarks, and to relive one's earlier life.

After taking Fiona to Kandy, we went to the city of gems,
Ratnapura (rat-na-purer). From this ancient town came fabulous
gems that have for the last 3000 years filled the treasure-vaults
of Sultans and Shahs, and decked the crowns of King's and
Emperors. Sheba's queen at the height of her glory drew her
jewels from Ceylon; and King Solomon's argosies made
hazardous journeys in quest of them. Zircons, amethysts, moon-
stones, sapphires, tourmalines and rubies are mined there. From
here we went to the buried cities of Ceylon, Anuradhapura and
Polonnaruwa (*Anna-rajah-purer* and *Pollar-na-rue-er*); the former
founded in 437 B.C. when the Parthenon of Athens was being

built, the latter being 1700 years younger. In its hey-day, Anuradhapura was larger than London and it lasted longer than either Rome or Carthage, or mighty Thebes. The jungle tide crept over both these cities.

We also went up-country, to the hill-station Nuwara Eliya (*new-rail-ia*), 6250 feet above sea level; a wonderful journey by car with *real* hairpin bends to negotiate. Fiona was holding on to her seat like grim death! Nuwara Eliya has a climate and scenery akin to Scotland's Wester Ross—minus the lochs, of course. A startling paradox in the tropics. It has also the flowers of spring; a variety of species, a variety of colour. The town has a fine golf course, said to be the best in the East, and a most picturesque racecourse. The small town is free of the din of traffic; a most restful place nestling 'mongst the hills. As one would say in the Gaelic GU ROBH SÌTH AN SO ('peace is here').

Upon our return to the renowned Galle Face Hotel in Colombo, I made enquiries of Marcelle, and she came and had tea with us sitting on the hotel terrace looking on to the swaying coconut palm trees, with the waves of the Indian Ocean tumbling up against the coral reef. It was a great surprise to her, for I had not written of our coming out. Poor Marcelle; although she still looked pretty, there was a touch of sadness in her eyes, and in her general make-up. She was more than thrilled to see me and to meet Fiona, and to know that after the long years I had found Love and was truly happy. As for herself, she told us that after only a few years her husband had died and she was left a young widow with one son, Dennis, who was now twenty-seven years of age. Fancy that! a son of nearing thirty, and when I had left Ceylon she was but a young girl. The years had certainly slipped by. As she was stricken down so young in marriage she was barely managing to exist, and had had to work day in and day out ever since, at a job with the Y.W.C.A. Her husband, only young too, had left her at his passing but scant gear with which to face the trials of widowhood. But she was cheerful, full of courage, rich in faith and indomitable in spirit; and naturally full of Dennis who had recently passed out as a B.Sc., and had a good post with a local textile firm. She was— indeed she had to be—content with her lot, and said my theme *Que Sera, Sera* ('whatever will be, will be') in *The End of the*

Rainbow, was, oh! so very true to life. We talked over the good
old days in Colombo, and I praised her once again as being the
greatest private secretary I had ever known. Such reminiscences
brought tears to her eyes. As Shakespeare says, 'Praising what
is lost, makes the remembrance dear'. Then she quoted the
Singhalese version of 'whatever will be', namely *Wentà Thiyanà
Deyà Wenawamayà*—again with tears overflowing. However,
she had a son whom she idolised; without him she would have
been completely shattered. And so she meant to carry on, and
to live on. Dennis came to collect her later in the evening;
he was a fine strapping fellow despite a serious illness he had had
when he was young.

She had outstanding memories of me, and when feeling lonely
or disheartened, thought of those many years she was by my
side in business, and so close to me in pleasure; all of which
terminated by her sudden marriage in 1937. It made sad history;
sad thoughts, she said, half whispering, and I was deeply moved
by her touching glances. However, she added, life had to flow
on, and all of us must take the rough with the smooth, for so
it is ordained. I told her that sorrow truly accepted can be the
seed of a rich harvest, and that Dennis was now *that* harvest—
an abiding inspiration in her fading light. Choking back further
teardrops she softly answered, 'Yes, Stanley, you are right'.
When one loses one so dear to you, I said, you never really say
goodbye to them. You try to press on after them, hoping they
may not win too far ahead for you to overtake them and resume
the companionship broken meantime here. Indistinctly she
murmured in Singhalese '*ow*' (yes). Yesterday is no more, and
tomorrow will soon be today. 'You may be poor financially',
but looking at Dennis I said, 'you are rich in other ways'. That
comforted her greatly, and she understood.

We both kissed her a fond goodbye, knowing we should
never meet again. Our paths which at one time might have
merged as one, had branched into two opposite directions in
1937. Shadow and sun, so too our lives are made . . . We cannot
control our destinies; we can only see beforehand, afterwards,
say the Irish.

Dennis whisked her away in his small car; and as they drove
out of sight of the hotel steps, she was waving and smiling
bravely. Bless her! I prayed our meeting out of the blue,

had not caused her pain; for up till then, I had had no knowledge of the tragedy in her young life.

Fiona and I left Ceylon by air early in January for Egypt, landing at Cairo. It was a fine cool morning, and we made straight for the world-renowned Shepheard's Hotel. This hotel was started in 1845 by Samuel Shepheard, an Englishman born in Northumberland; and many notable people have stayed there during its 120 years. In the early years they included H. M. Stanley, the African explorer and journalist; General Gordon, known as 'Gordon Pasha', who was sent by the British Government to help the Khedive against the Mahdi, and who in 1885 was killed during the storming of Khartoum; and the French novelist Gautier. Shepheard's had been burnt down since I was there before, but had been rebuilt near the Nile, on the most ultra-modern lines; its former site in the city was now a car park. After breakfast we had a casual look round; there is both old and new Cairo, and we gazed at the many starch-white onion-shaped domes and minarets of the various mosques. The whole place had altered considerably since 1937; everything was smartened up, big buildings and wider streets. There was much evidence of modern planning, showing great credit to Egypt's President, Gamal Abdel Nasser, whose presidential palace was not far away. Nasser; Egypt's jet-age Pharaoh.

Yes, things had changed with Nasser as a tenacious leader. Few of the natives now donned the little red fez; the beggars no longer harass tourists, and a serious attempt to oust the loose long-flowing ankle-length cotton *galabiyas* (that were such a familiar sight with the peasants and townsman, and which looked like the nightshirts our fathers used to wear) is being made at Government level; for the state-operated co-operative stores, had put about 500,000 cotton suits, consisting of trousers and jackets in grey, blue and red on sale at half the cost of the *galabiyas*. But as these flowing gowns have been worn since the days of the Pharaohs, it will be a difficult matter to persuade the 'FELLAHS' to change their dress to 20th century habits. It is on record that an ardent Nasser journalist wrote, 'the *galabiya* is quite unsuited to this age of "space travel". If you rise above the earth, its ends will fly also, unless you put them between your teeth'. He had something there ?

The new Cairo tower, whose base is built from rosy finished

Aswan granite, is a very spectacular affair. It is about 600 feet high (150 feet taller than the Great Pyramid) and one obtains a wonderful panoramic view of all Cairo. The decorations in the entrance are most attractive and represent the new industrial and social life in the U.A.R. (United Arab Republic). It was completely designed and constructed by Egyptian technicians and materials. There is a roof-restaurant, consisting of three Halls, Harroon El-Rasheed, Al-Dawar, and the open-air garden; the cafeteria above consists of the Arabic Hall and the Pharaonic Hall.

We also spent some time in the Cairo Museum, where most of the Tut-an-Khamen relics lie, unearthed from over 4000 years ago; and which were profoundly interesting. Some of the ancient enamelling of pottery in such a richness of colour even today was astounding. They must have been a great people in those far-off days—a great nation.

And, of course, we went out to the fabulous Mena House Hotel, built on the edge of the Nile, and took camels to see the Pyramids which are a wondrous, stupendous sight rising to such great heights in the spaceless, silent desert—standing as landmarks and sentinels, built thousands of years before Christ, even before the Children of Israel had ever seen Egypt. They are tombs, the greatest tombs in the world; tombs of mighty, wealthy kings who believed themselves gods and prepared what they thought to be a fitting resting place, and their bodies were meticulously embalmed. The Great Pyramid—the Pyramid of Cheops—is 450 feet high, and each base of this conical structure measures 700 feet and covers an area of 13 acres. Years and years, and tens upon tens of thousands of men were engaged and spent upon these buildings. Fiona and I stood in wonderment at such relics of well over 5000 years; and when we spoke, we spoke in whispers. The limitlessness of Time in the limitless desert. Everything of the past many thousand years stood out before us in bold relief and stamped itself on our minds. It was the attainment of the famous Arabian standard, 'He speaks the best who turns the ear into an eye'.

We returned to Mena House, taking camels as before. The camel always has a supercilious look, contemptuousness personified of any other animal in the world. Legend has it that Allah had entrusted to the camel what the eighth wonder of the world was. But as I looked at this ship of the desert, it remained as inscrutable as ever—ever since Time began. The camel never lets you into his secret. When he bites, nobody knows what is in his mind—but himself!

The view from the verandah of Mena House Hotel facing the Nile is delightful looking through the trees on the embankment to the fairy lights beyond; the water of the Great Nile being of a pale blue, tinted with pink—the whole having a most romantic atmosphere. The dhows sailing silently manned by Arabs in their brightly-coloured turbans and robes, with curved daggers here and there showing at their waistbands. Simple men, holding a firm belief in Allah to whose Will, all good or all evil is attributed. Their tempo of life is full of ease; when Allah made Time, He made plenty of it, they will tell you. Very like the Highlands of Scotland, for patience in the Highlands is not only a virtue; it is an integral part of daily life.

After about a week's sight-seeing, and going the round of all the cosmopolitan night clubs, and Arab quarters, and of course curio-collecting, to say nothing of seeing the many domes aglow at night with the smouldering fire of a desert sunset, we took off from Cairo for Alexandria, where readers of *Rainbow* will remember Tháfne's home was in Rue Ste Julienne, a suburb of Alex. (some four or five miles from the city's centre) where I lingered awhile in the autumn of 1937, falling in love with that fabulous Grecian beauty, whom I then termed ROH-ALBI (roch alpee) 'soul of my heart'; and again in Arabic HABBIBI (Habeebee) 'Darling'. I likened her to the Rose of Sharon.

It was a clear crispy morning when we touched down on the airfield, the Mediterranean sea was its usual blue, and we booked in at the main hotel, Hotel Cecil, on the sea front; had breakfast and a general look around. Alexandria, like Cairo, had altered in its appearance too; clean, tidy, and an air of good living and good money uppermost. Both these towns are now superb cities.

The following day we took a taxi out to Rue Ste Julienne to see what remained of the former place, and to obtain, if we could, first-hand information of what occurred that fateful day when the bomb from an Italian aircraft was accidentally dropped. The taxi driver had still the same old technique as I had experienced before in both Cairo and Alex.—driving haphazardly from right to left (driving in Egypt is on the *Right* side of the road). I asked him why he kept swerving first from one side and then to the other, and he replied there was no right or left, only sun and shade! It seemed to us that we were mixed up in a Z police car dodging in and out of traffic and passing all controls regardless, in an all-out attempt at catching some daring bandit who had escaped from Dartmoor or from Alcatraz Island in San Francisco Bay!

The car eventually drew up with a jerk and screeching brakes, and the driver waving his sweaty hand to the right and left said, 'This is it'.

We got out, and looking around, saw nothing but rubbled heaps of stone which apparently for some reason or other had not been cleared since those days of long ago; grass and weeds were growing in profusion where once stood a noble structure —a structure that had at one time been so closely associated with my own self. My heart skipped a beat, and I was filled with a wistful melancholy. Nothing to be seen really but wilderness, and no one about save a few dirty Arab children playing amongst the débris, and an old wrinkled Egyptian whose age and appearance resembled that of Abraham. His face was leathery and smiling. After a while I went up to this Old Testament figure and found he spoke a little English. He knew of course I was a visitor, and at once began to think of a few piastres that would be coming his way. After remarking upon the day and how we should thank Allah for being alive, I casually mentioned if he had known this place for a while. 'Yes', he said, 'I was born here in Rue Ste Julienne these 85 years ago, and am now passing my days in just sitting, looking and thinking'. 'Did you know this block of flats before a bomb struck it?' 'Oh, yes. That was a sad day; so many innocent people killed in a flash. But that is the Will of Allah, as indeed is everything'. 'Did you know any of the occupants?' 'Oh, yes, I knew them well, for I used to go messages for them, and they were very good, giving me many piastres, praise be to Allah!' 'There was a youngish Greek girl', I said, 'dark with blue eyes and very pretty, named Tháfne'. 'Oh, yes, I can remember her—a Grecian Goddess she was— and her mother was a sweet woman also, a Greek, too; her father was English. A very nice family, and her Greek uncle and cousin lived with them'.

I asked him more about that day a stray bomb dropped. 'Yes, it happened one day at noon, just before siesta-time; a noise as of thunder, and then—nothing. It was as if the earth was opening up, and the world coming to an end, and I felt I would soon be in the presence of the Great One, Allah. Then there was silence—a great silence—and when the dust had cleared, there was nothing to be seen except', as he stretched out his knarled fingers and pointed, 'just what you see now. A ball of death tumbling from the heavens'. He thought there were about sixty people killed. The bells of the nearby cathedral began to toll, and priests ran out to give succour and the last rites to the innocent victims as they were being brought out of the ruins. Church bells indeed! the ringing of same solemnises both marriages and funerals; the carillons ebb and flow with the wind . . . So this ancient Egyptian told us in his own simple way. Death and desolation to be sure; and our eyes were dimmed in tears. I felt myself saying inwardly, 'the fairest pearl within it, was now silent in the grave'. I was moved beyond words, but Fiona gripped my hand, and I felt reassured. 'What happened after all that?' I enquired. He didn't rightly know, but the authorities came along, searched everything, and all were later laid to rest in a mass grave in the Greek cemetery in Alex. My mind went back to 1937 when Tháfne and I had been at Cairo for two weeks, and came back to Alexandria, and the Arab house-boy had greeted her by saying 'the light has returned to Alex.'. The light indeed. Now it was extinguished; darkness just darkness. In soliloquising I heard myself saying in Greek OTI EGEENÉ, EGEENÉ—'whatever has happened, has happened'. I thought of Shelley's lines, 'when the lamp is shattered, the light in the dust lies dead'.

There was nothing more we could ask now, and in silence we moved away. In a moment of mute emotion, I seemed to hear Tháfne's voice say:

> If I should die, and leave you here awhile,
> Be not like others, sore undone, who keep
> Long vigils by the silent dust, and weep;
> Instead, for my sake, live again and smile . . .

Inwardly I thought of the Biblical saying, 'put off thy shoes from off thy feet, for the place whereon thou standest is holy ground'.

And once again I thought, let the past be as it may; let the future come as it will; let us live for the present in the sense of the glorious I AM. Later on we visited the Greek cemetery. 'Live on again and smile', did I hear her say? How can I add more; in fact what more *can* be said, unless

> I'll ne'er forget her happy face
> Her cheering kindly voice;
> So full of life, so full of grace
> So full—must I rejoice?

All perfect things are saddening in effect, since they leave nothing better to expect. So wrote Ella Wheeler Wilcox. 'Love is Enough . . .'

*   *   *

A few days later we took train from Alex. to that cosmopolitan sea-port at the entrance of the Suez Canal, Port Said, for we were booked to sail back to England by Orient liner from there. The rain was falling in gentle drops, but as the sun peered through the early morning clouds, the water-drops glittered like pearls on the leaves; and the birds sang . . . such is Life.

And so, thinking of those far-off days of the Pyramids in Egypt, of Alex., and of Adam's Peak in Ceylon, where from its summit (7360 feet) at sunrise one can see the enormous shadow 'of a man's hand' cast in the sky—the sun appearing apparently *three times as sun* from the peak—we embarked for England and the White Cliffs of Dover, where there happened to be a rainbow encircling the harbour as our boat dropped anchor. Strange, yet true.

A heavily-draped curtain finally hung down on the East of my early life; a life that was tinged with love and sorrow.

ෙවන්ට තියන ෙදය ෙවනවාමය

Wenta   Thiyana   Deya   Wenawamaya

Whilst in Alex., where the Greek community is large, one often heard of the 'Greek Orthodox Church'. I remember it back in 1937, and one sees it appearing in the press these days in connection with Cyprus. I often wondered what this actually meant and involved, and as I learnt more about it when Fiona and I paid this visit, doubtless readers may care to have some details of these Greek churches also.

In Apostolic times the Church was one; but as it grew and spread as far as Rome, there were so-called heresies and divergencies of opinion which in time separated the East from the West. One of the biggest causes was the wording of the 'NICENE Creed', so named for it was drawn up in Nicea in Asia Minor. It will be noticed in the Church of England service of Holy Communion, the 'Holy Ghost proceedeth out of the Father *and* the Son', whereas the Greek Church says only 'From the Father' ... following St. John, chap. 15, v. 26. These three small words, known in Latin as the 'FILIOQUE' clause, practically caused the break or Schism and so east and west went their own way; the western church under the Pope (the Greek bishops refused to acknowledge the Pope as supreme head) the eastern church to the Orthodox faith, held not only by Greeks, but by Russians, some Syrians, Lebanese, Armenians and Copts (Christian Egyptians). The word 'Orthodox' is from the Greek 'orthodoxia', or 'correct worship'. The word 'schism' is also Greek, meaning to split or tear apart; hence *schismatic*, used as a term of contempt by the R.C.'s when referring to the Orthodox.

The Greek Orthodox Church exercised much power in Byzantium, in Alexandria and in Asia Minor in the olden days; and the church comes under four Patriarchs, who have their seats—as in ancient times—in Alexandria, Constantinople (Istanbul), Jerusalem and Antioch. The Patriarch of Antioch is now a Lebanese Orthodox. There are differences in the Roman Catholic churches and the Eastern churches. With the former the child at baptism is not immersed and is confirmed and given Communion when about eight years of age. At Communion, or Mass, only the one element, or 'wafer' is given; no wine, and one may take Communion as often as one wishes. The Sign of the Cross is made by touching the forehead, chest, left shoulder then the right, with the first, second and third fingers of the right hand.

Their church is decorated with statues. There is no divorce, and priests cannot marry.

In the Greek church, the child is totally immersed at baptism, and given Communion either then and there, or a week later.

There is no Confirmation, and Communion is given in both 'elements'; bread is crumbled in wine and water and given to the faithful in a spoon. Communion cannot be taken unless one fasts; that means abstaining from meat, butter and at times, fish and oil; the meals consisting of practically boiled vegetables, at least two days before. The very strong and saintly fast longer; those in poor health only fast one day before. Communion is only taken at Christmas, Easter, and on the Virgin's Day, August 15th—the day both East and Roman Catholics commemorate the death of the 'Mother of God'. Some people in the Greek Church can take Communion forty days after the previous occasion; but this is rare. The Sign of the Cross here is made on entering the church by putting the thumb and the first two fingers of the right hand together and touching the forehead, chest, and firstly the *right* shoulder, then the left; and this is done as often as a prayer is said.

The Greek church is decorated with pictures, 'Ikons', from the Greek 'EEKONNA'—meaning 'picture'. Upon entering the church, a worshipper must make the Sign of the Cross, kiss an Ikon and light a candle. Divorce is allowed; and as in Greece there is no such thing as a register or consular marriage. Permission to marry must come from the church. Divorce is fairly easy, and a marriage can only be dissolved by the church; and as a marriage can only be conducted in church, there are no scruples in re-marrying divorced people. A deacon may marry, and can then be ordained priest; but as a married man, he remains a priest all his life, and rises no further in the hierarchy. Should he wish to attain an exalted position, he must put all thoughts of marriage aside, and devote his life to the church. There is no organ; the chanting is monotonous, and the services interminably long.

The Western churches, including Protestants and Church of England are more inclined to dwell on the Manhood and Cross of our Lord.

The Eastern, tend to think of Him in Glory and Majesty; and many mosaics show Him in Glory and as King on a throne.

There are certain things common to both the Greek Orthodox, and the Roman Catholic churches. Incense is much used; and prayers for the dead. The 'Mariolatry'—or the cult of the Virgin—holds both churches enthralled. To the R.C.'s, she

is the 'Mother of God'; to the Greeks, she is the PANAGHIA
—'the All Holy'—or 'THEOTOKOS', the One who brought forth
God. She is prayed to and invoked, and there is no home
without an ikon of Her, with the Child in Her arms; and on
15th August, feast of The Assumption, all prayers are said in
Her honour.

On one point, the East and West differ. The Orthodox
maintain She died a natural death. ... 'She fell asleep'. The
R.C.'s maintain 'She was carried bodily into Heaven'.

To sum up, Orthodoxy holds on to tradition rather than to
the Bible; and some of their beliefs came in literally years and
years after the Apostolic times; and a great deal of their so-called
religion is merely superstition. For example, a believer will ask
a Saint, or the 'Panaghia' to heal a child, or some other wish,
and if the prayer is answered, a candle is lit, or something is
given to the poor, or a silver or gold ornament is added to the
ikon of the Saint who has answered the prayer. Some of these
ikons are laden with gifts of silver, gold, or even jewels; and in
this respect the Roman church is very similar.

The Greek churches are square; and right across one end is a
screen, with a door at each side and a curtain over an arch in
the middle. This screen is called an 'IKONOSTASSI'— an ikon stand,
pronounced EEKONOSTASSEE—as it is covered with ikons, including
the two doors. The altar behind this arch, and the curtain at
times is drawn back to enable the worshippers to view the altar.
There are innumerable candles in the church, and the priests'
vestments are very rich. Their high hats take on a look like
chimney-pots.

Everything is very ornate to our eyes. As a church, the
Church of England in Alex. has always been on friendly relations
with the Greek Orthodox Church, and at the moment there is
much talk of Unity; to wit 'ecumenism'. Only a few years
ago the word 'ecumenical' meant nothing to the average lay-
man. It was just so much Greek. Now, we are confronted with
these two words in sermons, in literature and in church courts.
Ecumenical means worldwide or universal; and in relation to the
church, implies the oneness of Christians in the faith and all of
which flows therefrom. Ecumenicity is *not* a religion. Rather
it is a fruit or manifestation of Christianity. It is a Christian
unity which crosses all social, racial, denominational or national

barriers. This ecumenical movement is a relatively new phenomenon. With the Reformation there came into being a number
of denominations. The force was centrifugal—*away*, from cen-
tralisation—often independent, and sometimes divisive in effect.
However, in recent years the pervading force has been centri-
petal—*towards* co-operation, union, and unified action.

There is little more to be said on this subject; only the query,
With all this, are we going to bring in a New Earth? We
should remember, Adam was in Paradise when he fell.

As a footnote to the Orthodox Church, perhaps I may
comment on the Russian aspect. The present position of that
church in that country is that it *has* the right to worship in Soviet
Russia, but is forbidden to circulate any religious propaganda,
or even to reply to anti-religious matters. Recently a priest was
sentenced to eight years hard labour for printing tracts to dis-
tribute to his Congregation, which were held to be propaganda.
In many parishes, the churches are refused fuel; and their people
are told they could stay at home, if the church was too cold.
Such—and much more could be said indeed—is the measure
of privilege granted to the compliant Russian Orthodox Church.

*   *   *

Previously in this chapter I have referred to Buddhism and
Anuradhapura. It may be interesting to enlarge on this. Apart
from the August festival, one of the greatest days in Ceylon is
WESAK, 25th May; the actual date Gautama Buddha was born
in Nepal 2527 years ago; and thirty-five years after his birth the
Buddha received enlightenment on that same day, 25th May,
528 B.C. when the world's seven hundred million Buddhists pay
reverence to the Birthday and the Enlightenment. The Sacred
Bo tree at Anuradhapura is the oldest known tree in the world,
said to have grown from a cutting of the tree at GAYA, in India,
under the shade of which the Buddha attained Supreme Enlightenment. The tree was planted in the 3rd century B.C. in this ancient
Ceylon city. Under this tree thousands upon thousands of
pilgrims, clad in white, assemble carrying lotus blossoms and
kneeling, chant the words 'I pay homage to the Supremely
Enlightened One—the Buddha.' They come from East and
West; Nepal and Australia; Japan and Alaska; Burma and
Bolivia.

CHAPTER 10

HIGHLAND LIFE—GAELDOM

THIS is a land of crofts and crofters. The definition of a croft is given by a frustrated crofter as 'a small piece of land surrounded by regulations'. The story is told of an old crofter, who, whilst talking with a visitor, complained of the increasing amount of smoke on the land. 'Smoke?' the visitor asked, looking dumbfounded, for all around him was green grass, heather, valleys and hills. 'Yes', the crofter said, 'too much smoke from the cars of all the government officials that keep coming and going!'

A croft is a little field adjoining a wee dwelling-house; agricultural smallholdings in fact; a land-holding of not more than seventy-five acres for the largest. There are seven crofting counties in Scotland—Argyll, Inverness, Ross and Cromarty, Sutherland, Caithness, Orkney and Zetland; and it can be appreciated this includes a wide variety of ground from the rich land in the east to the peat and bare rocks of the west. There are about 20,000 crofts, of which only 2000 are of more than fifty acres. In the islands and the West Highlands, the majority are about three or four acres only. The land worked may be a small patch among rocks, the soil being scraped into ridges and potatoes planted; or fields reclaimed from the heather and bracken. In the summer many crofters let their cottage to visitors, whilst the crofter and his family live in a make-shift shed at the back. Life doing that is hard with all the croft work to attend to as well. On the land there has been for generations a crippling lack of capital to effect improvements or buy machinery. It is said crofters are making as good use of their land as the men on the bigger upland farms. But they cannot make a living on present-day standards from crofting alone, and the economists say the reason is the majority of crofts are too small, and their resources far too limited to give an adequate volume of output.

Money is still required to be spent constructively, and legislation to accompany same. Hitherto, the central government has generally given but a niggardly amount of money to carry out a 'rebirth' of the land economy of the Highlands.

A Crofters Commission was set up years ago to help them out of their difficulties. A year or so past this Commission set about seeking powers to 'rationalise crofting agriculture', which of course obviously meant dispossessing crofters, who by reason of absence, disability or age, were not working their land to advantage; throwing crofts together and so forth. Throughout the years, the crofting system has survived all these rigours and pitfalls to a remarkable degree. In social terms it is very effective; it gives inner joy and satisfaction to the people in their gaining happiness from the produce of their soil.

A new Crofters Act came into force on 27th August 1961 in which provisions are made for sub-letting, but which will not affect their tenure in any way. The main change provided in this new Act is to get more crofting land under cultivation by re-organising the township and sub-letting crofts to create bigger holdings, but no such re-organising of any township would be attempted without the majority consent of the members.

Much has been blamed on the crofters themselves, such as lacking in initiative and unwilling to help themselves; but such accusations more often than not come from people without intimate understanding of crofting conditions, or of human beings who for generations have experienced depression and poverty and who through such lengthy endurances are not able to surmount difficulties unaided; and many lose heart.

Nothing is really possible without money. In the past the Highlands must have been the most expensive area in Britain from the point of view of money given in Public Assistance, poor relief and unemployment benefits. Unproductive money is money down the drain, and the Highlands have been dubbed 'an area of a receiving character; a subsidised land'.

However, from my experience and knowledge they serve the country well; and they are not ashamed of their heritage. I have yet to meet a crofter who is not a most likeable person and character. A number of them may be poorly off, living in wee cottages through whose doors luxury has never entered. But they still live in *Tìr nan Òg*—the land of the ever-young. There is only one kind of poverty, and that's to have no love in the heart. They are a worthy, if not a wealthy, folk.

The Gaelic communities in the islands and of Wester Ross, are some of the oldest remaining cultures in Europe, possessing the same roots as the Irish Gaels, with whom they used to consider themselves to be one people. Then there is the oral tradition—the folk tales and historical legends from ancient days still on the lips of those in the islands and the north-west.

The Highlander will put forward his whole effort if a reasonable profit is at the end of his labours. If there are no proper roads, no transport, no steamers calling to create life and prosperity—well, he can't build or make them himself; so logically, in the far-away spots, he says, 'I'll let the world go by'.

After all:

> Will the peats dig themselves?
> Will the fish jump ashore?

To his eternal credit, the Highlander has all the virtues of a generous man—a sense of humour, a sense of companionship, a sense of occasion. There are still people of genius and drive in Scotland today; people who can—if they will—achieve distinction. The whole character of the nation is tough and resilient; Scottish labour is acknowledged as second to none; its natural resources in the Highlands, rivers, glens and scenery are hard to outstrip.

It makes gloomy reading, those terrible days when a people were forced by poverty and sometimes by other men's greed to cross the seas to a new home—the 'clearances' after the '45 Jacobite rebellion in which hundreds of thousands of clansmen were banished; the forfeiture of clan estates, and the disintegration of that social system; glens emptied—even the aged and sick being mercilessly ejected, their cottages and furniture burned. 'Prince Charlie's Year' to be sure! All this, 'that a degenerate lord might boast his sheep'. Then the sheep went too. Sheep in place of people!

Years of famine came, unrelieved by any government assistance, when people scratched along the beaches for food; and liable to be evicted at their factor's whim. It was not until the Crofters' Act of 1886, following the Napier Commission's report of 1883, that security of tenure and fair rents came to be established—exactly one hundred and forty years after 'Charlie's Year'.

One may ask why the Highlanders did not offer more resistance to the inhumanity of those clearances? One factor was their God-fearing nature; many of their ministers told them it was the Will of God. And another cause was the young active males were away in the Napoleonic wars, fighting for the very people and government that were clearing them away; and when they returned they found their homes and people gone.

Great strains; great hardships; all making for sad reading. But this, in its stark reality, is the background to crofting; a history founded on mistrust on an exhausted population; a turbulent history. The last of these Highland clearances, occurred as recently as the middle of the nineteenth century. These ruthless evictions are still bitterly termed as barefaced stealing. The crofts that did stand on the land unwanted for sheep remain to this day—standing on the same poor soil that is particularly hard and unrewarding to work.

The news nowadays constantly refers to the closure of the Highland railways, which in the absence of decent roadways would undoubtedly spell more ruin to this countryside. The 'Beeching closures' would assuredly complete the work of the Highland clearances; for if there had been no clearances, there would be no need for closures. There would be population, not desolation.

Since the clearances, crofting in the Highlands has never been the same. Putting it bluntly, to my mind, it 'knocked the stuffing' out of this Highland industry; this, together with the Highlands being so far away from the markets, doesn't help matters either.

Not so long ago, the Chairman of the Crofters Commission said that crofters should take full advantage of the changes and innovations introduced into crofting legislation by the afore-mentioned Crofters (Scotland) Act of 1961. If this were done, so he said, the Act might be seen from a future perspective as a landmark in crofting history almost comparable with the original Crofters Act of 1886—nearly 80 years ago!

Since 1912, the crofter has had a nominal right to erect buildings on his croft for purposes other an agriculture; however, that authority was of no use to him as he could not sell the building or claim compensation for it, at outgo. The 1961 Act changed this, and gives the crofter the right to compensation at outgo for buildings erected for the purpose of his ancillary occupation, always provided they did not interfere substantially with the use of the croft as an agricultural subject. In areas where tourism was increasing, it meant the crofter was no longer regarded purely as an agriculturalist. Legislation for sub-letting approved by the Commission, would allow sub-tenants to qualify for grants; so that a man could get security of tenure for a number of years without disturbing the tenant, which could result in a number of derelict crofts finding their way into the hands of those *really* interested in agriculture. Many of these derelict crofts—and one cannot help but see many as one tours around—are in the hands of elderly folk who are unable to cope with new ideas. Should this new move 'get going', and people saw these derelict crofts coming more into cultivation, it might surely have a goodly effect on the morale of the whole village community. Then there is the question of free access to capital. A crofter cannot borrow money on the security of the buildings on his land, for the simple reason they belong to the laird, which means that all loans on security of buildings available to other people are closed to the crofter except in the case of the Highland Fund, that gives 'character loans'.

I am happy to think—despite all Government red-tape that we know so well exists—the Department of Agriculture and the Government itself are now beginning to realise that the crofter is not purely an agriculturalist, but that he *can* be allowed to augment his income elsewhere. In all this, of course, application for assistance is considered on its merits; and takes time. It is to be hoped assistance to crofters will be in a liberal manner. It does not seem that grants and loan-aid will be increased materially; but what is significant is, that a crofter who has repaid part of his loan can 'top it up' again to the maximum. In 1963, a sum of nearly £300,000 had been paid to crofters in grants; and the acreage of land involved was 32,000.

I am indeed glad to realise that—to those who run the country—it *is* common knowledge that crofters in these parts from where I write, cannot make an adequate living off the agricultural produce of the croft. They *have* to supplement their existence from other sources, such as fishing, weaving and 'bed and breakfast' to tourists, so that it all boils down to the fact that the croft is but a base from which to earn a living. Believe me, 'tis a hard life. Some crofters find the answer to making a few more shillings in caravans, should he have a piece of hard ground near the road; just odd caravans, because for a regular caravan site it is necessary to get a licence from the County Council. And this licence lays down conditions as to their density, amenity, washing and toilet facilities, and so forth; which may be awkward for his particular small field. But no licence is required where no more than three caravans at a time are sited on his croft between 1st April and 30th September, provided the croft is not less than two acres in extent. There is a further provision of significance in that a crofter needs no licence to accommodate a caravan on his croft at any time of the year, for a period not exceeding 48 hours at a time, provided that in the course of any year the total number of days on which a caravan is on the croft does not exceed 28 days—which serves to cover the odd caravan that may come along, wanting to pull in for a day or two. But as I have said before, *once you pass Garve nobody hurries*; and am pretty certain the local official here will not bother himself unduly as to how many days, how many caravans', etc. For up here, I'd have you know, we are a peaceful, easy-going community; always ready to give you a wave and a smile:

> We're friendly people in Wester Ross
> We laugh and chat, and none of us 'posh';
> We share our joys and sorrows too
> And life is richer, because we do.

> Far from the noise and bustle of town
> We live our lives without renown;
> We do our work in a peaceful way
> Helping each other day by day.

> Those from the South say we're dull, I fear
> But *we* find bliss in all that's here;
> And when the tale of our life is told
> Some of the pages may shine like gold.

Yes, we live in a world apart. In a bracing, dust-free air. You only need to clean the windows about every three months or so!

Town life and the street one lives in appear in the Highlands to be an unrealistic background; reality in the Highlands is the scent of the wind, the ripple of the sea, the babbling of the streams ('burns') as they flow towards the sea, chattering away in Gaelic; the sheep and the skipping lambs that one has to be so careful of in motoring, the cows you suddenly come across at the many blind corners, chewing their cud as if it were chewing-gum, looking aimlessly at you and your car, and just—thinking! hearing the call of the owl—the 'old woman of the night', as it is termed in the Gaelic; and the overwhelming significance of the starry heavens.

In the towns and cities, man measures himself by his constructional works, of the improvements he makes, of scientific advancement and so on; and boastfully prides himself on his greatness in such achievements. But up in the Highlands, man is completely dwarfed in his own importance by the mountains and scenic wonders constantly surrounding him, and must humbly stand aside in admitting the greatness of nature and of an unseen architect . . .

I have dwelt more than a little on crofting. The Crofters Commission, however, born of good intentions and phrased in flowery language, appears to me, not to have the zip, the compelling force, the impetus so desperately needed to current times, to current needs. It would seem to me—as an outsider—to be just another branch of St. Andrew's House. These crofters up here don't know how to formulate an arresting, pointed letter or demand; they need personal visitation, personal guidance, personal assistance in the drafting of their requirements. They are not Oxford dons! There are several bodies and organisations of one sort or another interested in land in Scotland. It would be better for more unification of interests. No government or body can expect to stem several hundrd years of deterioration, putting it on a solid foundation in a matter of a year or so; and a far greater comprehensive land commission—freed from all political pressure, and *personally* conducted—would, to my knowledge of local politics, be the ideal set-up. The personal touch is the one that counts, and pays handsome dividends. The integration of forestry and agriculture, as would seem to be the trend nowadays, would take another hundred years— and more—to fructify. For years the Highlander has been the self-imposed concern of industrial magnates turned lairds. Whilst the lairds have largely disappeared, they have left the Highlander as 'naebody's bairn'. Transport charges are extortionate in the Highlands, and thereby strangle a lot of trade and folk, where ancillary employment is not at hand. It has been proved that small local light industries are economic; the labour is there, the choice of siting unlimited . . . so what?

The tourism harvest is but seasonal—and a short season at that. Many visitors see and appreciate the crofter's problems in making a living. They have told me so. It is up to those in authority to act and move; and to adopt a more personal attitude. The Highlander needs a heart-to-heart talk; not just forms beyond number sent him to fill up. Each croft has its own problems; each crofter needs the personal touch of government, and to know and to see he *is* being thought of as an individual, and not as a herd like his sheep in a widespread community away up in the Wild West. The Government employs plenty of officials. They could surely spare a few to pay personal visits, and to make impersonal approaches, personal. It is the only way—and I draw such reasoning from experiences both at home and abroad—to obtain, not only the esteem, but the valued co-operation of these worthy folk. The Highlands must not be allowed to go forward, backwards. The north-west must not be encouraged to go coasting along in neutral; it is high time it got into gear. No one ever did anything well to which he did not give the whole bent of his mind. The Highlander does that; but like all of us, he needs encouragement; a few pats on the back. Seeking to satisfy a hungry man by feeding him with air-bubbles and fanning him with peacock's feathers, leads to nowhere. Unless the crofter is guided, helped personally, and made to know he *is* a figure of some importance and value to this 'good earth' of ours, he will become like a squirrel imprisoned in a revolving cage; his thoughts and his poor neglected way of life turning over in a never-ending gyration. All this is so very true. I live here, and I know.

The crofter must not be forgotten. If he is—albeit Crofters Commissions may be good up to a point—then Heaven help this land of ours. No more, no less. And I am not a Highlander; but I do know human nature; I *do* know the call of the pipes, and the sough of the wind o'er the Hebrides.

Surely 'tis a truism . . .

> When plenty flows, we good advice despise,
> 'Tis want, that sharpens thought and makes us wise.

At times one has to lean backwards to support the common cause; otherwise we are apt to get nowhere—fast.

I have seen it reported that many absurd questions are asked of crofters, such as 'What is your yield of silage per acre?' where silage is not grown. Again, 'What are your suggestions for the manure needed?'—in a rainfall where any application of consequence would be washed out in a matter of weeks! I think I have made these points clear enough.

In some of the Western Isles, a grow–more–bulbs drive started in 1961. Scotland's 'little Holland' has plots of bulbs in Lewis, Harris, Barra, North and South Uist, Tiree, Coll, Mull and Islay. The growers—mostly crofters—have their own concern, The Hebridean Bulb Growers Ltd. ; a large number of bulbs are graded and packed in Tiree. In my Gairloch garden I have scores of such daffodil bulbs from Tiree; and they do wonderfully well, their finely-shaped trumpets blowing fanfares heralding Spring. It is thought Oban, as a centre, would suit the majority of growers. Undoubtedly there is a big future for Hebridean bulbs, and it could well be great help to the Western Isles, if the crofters developed this line of business in all earnestness, for it is reckoned a net profit of some £300 an acre could be expected from bulb growing; and an acre is not much for a crofter to handle along with the running of his own croft. The sale is for bulbs—not flowers.

There is a phenomenal re-seeding of moorland on the island of Lewis. In Shetland there is a lobster-marketing board; and the crofter-fishermen from around there have increased the value of such fish handed in to the storage tanks at Scalloway by nearly 800 per cent in seven years. There is, too, a thriving marketing arrangement for eggs, in South Uist.

A crofter in Bunessan, Mull, has recently succeeded in growing grass which it is thought may revolutionise livestock-rearing in the Highlands. The grass is a kind of tussock, found almost exclusively in the Falkland Islands; the grass keeps green all the year round. In the Falklands, even poor cattle put on this grass come into fine fettle within two months; and sheep achieve top condition in just over three weeks.

*   *   *

In connection with this north-west area, the County Surveyor has a big task, covering not only roadworks but bridges, piers, coast protection, cemeteries, and ferry slips. The work on highways falls into three categories: maintenance, minor improvements and major improvements. The total expenditure of the Surveyor's department in 1963 came to some £1,200,000. For work carried out on trunk roads a hundred per cent grant is given by the Government. Class I roads receive a grant of 75 per cent; Class II, 60 per cent; Class III, 50 per cent; and unclassified, nil. There are 130 miles of trunk roads in the County of Ross-shire; 300 miles of Class I roads; 170 miles of Class II roads; 270 miles of Class III roads. In dealing with snow clearing and gritting, the County has 40 snow ploughs and four snow blowers. In 1963 an experiment was made in treating the roads with a mixture of sand and salt and has proved successful. Just before the first snows fall, salt is sprayed on the road at the rate of two ounces per square yard. The first snow to fall melts quickly and subsequent falls do not stick to the road; this makes for greater road safety.

As I have said, this is not a land of luxury living by any manner of means. There is an old Chinese saying, 'Possessions are like a drug; the more you have the more you want'.

There is no luxury in the world that can be said to be the last; each new gadget breeds another new gadget; and no money can buy enduring contentment and happiness. That comes only from within; and that 'within' can be abundantly satisfied by the glory of nature seen here in its ever-changing moods across the bay and to the mountains far beyond—and with the people who inhabit this great corner of Scotland, Wester Ross, all of whom have deep religious feelings. Every household up in this area is wrapt in Faith; faith the substance of things hoped for; the evidence of things not seen. By faith, Abel offered unto God a more excellent sacrifice than Cain. By faith, Noah, moving with fear, prepared an ark to the saving of his house; by faith, Abraham went out, not knowing whither he went, to a far place which he was to inherit; he sojourned in the land of promise;

through faith his wife Sarah received strength to conceive when she was long past age; by faith, Moses refused to be called the son of Pharaoh's daughter, and by faith he led the children of Israel through the Red Sea as by dry land, which the Egyptians assaying to do, were drowned. By faith, the walls of Jericho fell, after being encompassed seven days.

Scotland as a whole is a Church-minded nation to a far greater extent than England, so that in such a context the Church of England is relatively the junior partner. Church membership in Scotland is 2½ times what it is in England. It will appear galling to some devout Scots ministers when the Church of England is projected as 'the National Church in Britain'. In fact, only about 10 per cent of the English adult population can lay claim to full Church membership; whereas the Church in Scotland can claim 66 per cent of the adult population to Church membership. Rather staggering figures, surely? It is predominately Protestant; and the smaller the religious denominations, the more loyal the members. On a normal Sunday one million adults in Scotland attend at least one service; sometimes two services.

The lonely, barren, treeless Island of Iona, situated about one mile off the south-west extremity of Mull, is the cradle of Scottish Christianity, for in the year A.D. 563 St. Columba landed here from Ireland with twelve companions (disciples), established a monastery, and used the island as a base for his evangelistic journeys.

He was then 42 years of age. When he died on 9th June A.D. 597, aged 76 years, he turned to those around him urging them that they 'preserve with each other sincere charity and peace'.

St. Columba built his church on family lines; prayers and study mingled with their outdoor labours; for he believed that, to live a balanced life, a man must have work for the hand as well as work for the mind.

Iona is an island of peace and reverence; and a place of pilgrimage even to this day.

*   *   *

The crofting community—the Highland life in fact—looks upon religion as of paramount importance. Every Sabbath you will see families walking along the road to the kirk; and all

F

types of cars conveying folk. In the week-days, crofters and road workers may be dressed in torn and shabby clothes—their work-a-day suits—but on the Sabbath, all are dressed smartly in dark suits, black shoes highly polished. The women, walking with, or behind them, exchange casual hushed conversation. The children in their Sunday best and respecting Sabbath behaviour to the full, walk quietly under their grown-ups' eyes; their pockets full of 'pan-drops', which they had bought from the sweetie-shop on Saturday!

In the Free, and Free Presbyterian Churches, one stands during prayers and remains seated whilst singing the Psalms to metre. There is no organ or musical instrument of any form in these churches. The Psalter without any instrumental accompaniment is used in praise in accordance with the pattern of worship set in the Apostolic Church and revived by the Reformers. The praise is led by a precentor, and is of a depth that one rarely comes across in an English church; and Psalms sung in Gaelic are profoundly impressive and heart-moving like the voice of many waters, or the roll of thunder. Certainly there is no need for an organ or harmonium, for such would not be heard in the loud swell of so many living human voices.

Just below the pulpit is a closed pew, where the precentor sits, along with the elders of the congregation—the men of gracious light and leading. The elders and minister have an equal voice in the management of the church—a democratic arrangement learned from the New Testament.

In a Gaelic service, the precentor sings one line of the Psalm, which is then taken up by the congregation; then another line, so the singing of a verse takes a proportionately longer time than in an English service. It is not uncommon for a service to take the best part of two hours; the sermon alone may well take an hour and a quarter. All the same, the children sit through everything quietly. There is never a sign of any rustling or fidgetiness, such as I can well remember when I was taken to church as a young child. I seemed to long for the service to end —particularly the heavy, ponderous sermon, that was far and away 'above my head'.

But up here, all is so different, and one can sense this present life is but the preparation for the Future; for there is nothing luke-warm in the Highlanders' religion—nothing. At Communion time (twice a year) very many will travel miles from their own village to attend the communion at another township. At Gairloch, the Communion is held the fourth Sabbath in June, and the second Sabbath in October; and practically everybody provides accommodation and meals for all these visitors from afar. Their religious hospitality is unbounded; it is part of the Highlander's life. These communion or 'fast-weeks' start on the Thursday and carry on through till the Monday forenoon. The shops close, schools are on holiday, and generally everything is at a standstill. Yes, their religion gleams with a neon sharpness. They accept the Bible in its entirety, as the inspired and inerrant Word of God, and so as the only rule of teaching and conduct. In the past—in the 'Clearance' days—the Presbyterian way of life in the Highlands cost the Highlanders blood and suffering; and never, even to this day, will they throw away their form of life unconcernedly.

In the old days I remember witnessing these communions which were held in the open in the famous hollow at the Gairloch Golf Course, the *Leabaidh na bà Baine* (Bed of the White Cow), and thousands from near and far (50 or 60 miles even) came to join in the service. Days before the fast days every spare hole and corner was got ready to accommodate the throng of folk; every hut or shed with a roof over it was got ready by strewing it with straw to act as beds during the five or six nights of their stay. Undressing or washing was never thought of. This hollow, a deep oval, was ideal for such a gathering and at one end was the preacher's 'box' affording him shelter from wind, sun and rain, so that his voice could be heard distinctly. It was never rain-sogged, for the soil was of pure, porous drifted sand; and the sheep saw to it that the grass was short. This hollow accommodated as many as 2000 people; and any stranger passing by, hearing these voices floating up out of the deep, chanting beautiful and ancient Gaelic psalms, could not fail to be moved with such utter solemnity; purely reminiscent of our Lord's time. Unhappily this practice has ceased these many years, the services now being held indoors in the respective churches.

When the communion is held at Shieldaig—near Applecross—some 15 miles as the crow flies, but nearly four times that distance by road via Loch Carron, a party from Gairloch will hire a motor-launch and set out from the pier in the early hours of the

Sabbath for the long sea-journey, worship there, getting back again about 10 o'clock that self-same night. Others will go by car the sixty-odd miles, early; also returning late. And it is not to say those who make the journey are young. There are many elderly folk who insist on participating in the Faith at such times. They even travel as far afield as Staffin—near the northern tip of Skye—taking the mail-bus from Gairloch (a day or so before the Sabbath) to Achnasheen; then train to Kyle of Lochalsh; thence by boat from Kyle to Portree and then finally by bus to Staffin. Many hours and many miles of a journey.

This devoutness is a time-honoured custom the crofters and villagers believe in keeping; a custom as old as the hills; a traditional way of life that neither time nor age will alter. Where else would one come across such devotion? And echo answers 'where?' In their homes the Grace is said at the beginning and end of each meal. The Sabbath is not deemed to be a 'visiting' day either, excepting communion times. And here I should add, one must *not* arrive or depart at a guest or bed/breakfast house on a Sunday (with hotels it is different); in fact the B.-and-B. signs come down on Saturday nights and go up again on Monday mornings—for this, as I have said, is a staunch Presbyterian land.

Faith indeed. The stars pursue an honest, sensible and orderly plan. It is difficult to account for this world without believing in a Creator. The people one meets in these islands and High-lands of Scotland are all humble. As the lark that soars the highest builds her nest the lowest; as the nightingale that sings so sweetly sings in the shade when all things rest; as the branches that are most laden with fruit bend lowest; as the ship most laden sinks deepest in the water—so those most holy are the humblest. There is an old saying, 'some people are so heavenly-minded they are no earthly use'. But this can never be levied at the Highlander; for they are all of immense value in a variety of ways, not only to each other, but to the entire community in which they live and serve. You can trust a Highlander. The consequence of Trust is steadfastness. The fruit of TRUST is Peace; and peace is not only serenity of mind but of every kind of happiness.

John Knox's work for the Scottish church and nation will bear every investigation; and the reformer emerges as the greatest Scotsman of his time, whose service to Scotland remains unsurpassed. The year 1964 was the 400th Centenary of John Calvin—the great French reformer—who died 27th May 1564. He was born 10th July 1509 at Noyon in Picardy, a city which had been under ecclesiastical domination from the 6th century, and which from the 8th century when Charlemagne was consecrated in its great cathedral, had been the most important religious centre in the north of France. Just about the time of this event, so significant for the history of the Reformation— and for the whole world—there took place in the Augustinian Convent at Erfurt, another equally significant event. Martin Luther, then in his mid-twenties had, through the reading of St. Paul's Epistle to the Galatians, made the great personal discovery of Peace with God, and had at the same time rediscovered the great Biblical doctrine of Justification by Faith ... the prime watchword of the Reformation movement.

The Highlanders hold on fast to their religion, as did their fathers and their fathers before them. They do not attempt to shout it out, at all and sundry from the house-tops, nor force it upon strangers nor even defend it; they just *live* and *work* in it, so that the truth they uphold is loosed around and about them. You don't defend a lion; you just turn him loose, and he will defend himself. So it is with their religious beliefs; it defends itself. You can never win anything or anyone by compromise. It is said in many quarters today, that religion cannot be defined; that you must just *experience* it. It is true you cannot 'hold fast' a mist or a fog; you cannot harpoon a jelly-fish. But you *can* hold fast to religion; the Highlander shows it to you, and not only for ONE day in the week; and I know—for I live amongst them. Their religion gives them a generous heart, and in their opinion there is nothing meaner than a mean gift. The worst thing a man can do to himself or his fellow-creature, is to bestow a grudged gift. It is not in the Highlander's character to give away something that should be *thrown* away. Oh! no. And I hold that the basis of religion is Love.

Up here in Wester Ross, the Sabbath takes on a totally different sense and feeling to that experienced in England. Everyone and everybody is keeping the day Holy. *That*, I think is the key—the answer—to the difference down south, where people make Sunday a holiday outing in the car, or cut the grass; buses run, and coaches make up so-called Sunday 'mystery tours'. There is none of that here. There is no *movement* to be seen or heard; save the going to and from the Kirk. It is a custom, not a code; a day of supreme peace. The Sunday paper-van from Inverness that supplies the various hotels *en route* to Aultbea, is barred from entering into some areas on its 'Wells-Fargo' dash through! A complete day of rest, relaxation and thought *does* enable one to start the week with a calm confidence and renewed vigour.

Through the many centuries, of course, Christianity has had many blows given it; but it has more than weathered all such storms. It can be likened to the anvil in a blacksmith's shop, where if one looks in, one sees many worn-out old hammers lying around the floor. But peculiarly enough, the anvil never wears; it is the other way about; the anvil wears the hammers out. And so it is, the anvil of THE WORD which has been battered upon is unharmed. 'Tis the hammers that have perished. The Bible and its teachings has lost nothing of its value with the passing millenniums—nothing. Other books fade and die, but THE BOOK, and its message—so amply borne out by the High-lander—lives on. People are rated higher than possessions with the true Highlander; and such good friends make the latitude and longitude of life. You can't sustain life by eating pound notes; what really matters at all levels is not the money one earns, but what goods and services can be obtained in exchange for them; what 'good-living' can be assimilated thereby. Up in these parts, before every verse of Holy Scripture, we might write the rubric . . . 'thus saith the Lord'.

Then again, in any sickness or even major operation, they never complain; they have such trust in the future. If you make enquiries as to how so-and-so is—although he or she may be suffering very acutely—the answer you invariably get is 'Oh! she's fine; she's not complaining'. Am afraid I am far from being so courageous; if I have any little ache or pain, I let everyone know of it! But there it is; we are not all made in the same mould. Some of us are mouldier than others!

* * *

I have given some indication of the crofter's life in his inner home; and his inner outlook.

As to his seasonal, practical occupation—well, he is hard at it all seasons of the year. After the winter and slight falls of snow there comes the spring.

'If winter comes, can spring be far behind?' In March the days have lengthened; the larch and the birch begin to herald spring; and towards the end of May nature has begun its revival. The cuckoo pays us its annual visit from across the ocean; and we get bored with its constant song; the bluebells of Scotland burst into bloom. The earth, surely, seems to receive instructions from Heaven to reclothe all Nature. In the springtime, a young man's fancy turns to love, 'tis said. But as to a crofter, he has work on his hands; he is far too busy to be thinking of love. At the beginning of March he starts to turn over his land with the foot-plough—the *cas-chrom*—quite a tricky, Old Testament type of primitive implement to handle. By the middle of April most of his spring work is done and then 'the peats' have to be cut—here again with a special primitive cutting tool (a turfing spade CABAR LAR—stripping the sods from the heather thus exposing the peat proper—and the peat knife, a tool to cut the sods into shape and to throw them on to the bank to dry. When partially dried they are put on end in small stacks, thereby letting the wind and sun thoroughly dry them out. They are then ready to be carted home for the winter's fire. *Peat*, the very name gives one the real smell o' the mystic isles and the north-west Highlands. It is the real crofter's main fuel. A very large part of Wester Ross is covered by peat bogs, and to the casual visitor these bog-lands with their characteristic vegetable life seem uninteresting except for just a passing glance, to say to their friends 'back home' they had seen 'peat growing'! to say what a lovely smell pervades a room with a peat fire burning. To a visitor there is no more evocative smell than that of burning peat; its smell brings to one's thoughts the hard work involved in cutting it on the moors, the loneliness of the many croft houses where it is used, and the friendly warmth of its fire; the kettle for ever singing on the hob, a harbinger of what is most indispensable—a cup of tea. Peat is evidently a post-glacial deposit, and in the long ages past with the weather cool and wet, the growth of 'sphagnum' moss would be encouraged, and this is the main formation of peat. So it grew and accumulated over the long, long years. Peat deserves to be classed among the most interesting natural phenomena of the Highlands; not only the peat itself but the many objects preserved in it. At some depth at the bottom of bogs, hazel, birch, alder and willow have been found in perfect state—after centuries of time.

In some bogs hazel-nuts have been unearthed deep below the ground, as perfect as the day they dropped off the trees; some peat fields are full of the rose-beetle wings, still glittering in metallic lustre which must have lain there embedded in these black airtight 'silos' long ago; and from the masses discovered in many districts these beetles must have swarmed like the locusts in the old Egyptian days. It is very evident that in those far-off ages a different vegetation covered the earth when peat began to form and that the land was full of plants and insect life now extinct.

The usual impression of peat is that it is a very modern growth and quickly formed. Nothing could be further from the truth. Forest upon forest; peat upon peat.

Peat is also found at the bottom of some lochs—submarine peat bogs; and these too must be thousands of years old.

The Scottish Peat Committee has been investigating this peat problem for the last thirteen years, and in their early 1962 final report, state that a peat industry providing jobs for 4000 workers and reclaiming tracts of land for farming, could be developed in Scotland.

More than 1,600,000 acres in Scotland are covered with deep peat, and workable deposits are put at 600 million tons of peat solids, equivalent to some 500 million tons of coal. One of the attractions of large-scale peat utilisation is the prospect of agricultural reclamation of the basal soil after clearance of the peat. It is to be hoped—for the sake of the Highlands—this considered opinion will not lie dormant.

Adverting to this preservation aspect, an interesting matter came to light in the Orkney island of Hoy during the last war. One day some children found a coffin in the middle of a lonely moor, whilst digging 'the peats' there. The corpse was as if it had only been recently buried. This was found to be the grave of one Mary Corricle, a young woman who hanged herself last century after being jilted by a sailor. The body was so preserved, for it had been years beneath six feet of peat. Her body now rests under a slab of concrete in the peaty ground; and some time ago an American missionary arranged to have the grave marked with a cross, and surrounded by a chestnut fence.

Early on in the year, say February to March or April, the heather needs burning in order to produce more and better 'crop' for sheep, grouse and such-like. After four years, heather gets coarse, and needs pruning as we would a bush or tree; and pruning in this case means 'burning'. Vivid fires are to be seen on the hillsides during this period, and much care is needed to keep the 'burning bush' under control. It appears to be a real scorched-earth policy, but new growth quickly comes along, and all is well with man and beast.

At this time there will be fences to be seen to, crops reaped, potatoes lifted, out-houses repaired, drains 'sorted'; and so it goes on.

The sheep, of course, have to be cared for, and continually rounded up by the crofter and his faithful collie. Some of these dogs seem to have a veritable hypnotic influence on sheep, getting them to do exactly what their master requires of them; and a crofter with only a few sheep is really helpless without his sheep dog. Lovely animals they are, sensing one's mood like a loving, dutiful wife. It may be said sheep do not sit about the hillside at random. Experts tell us they have a social behaviour of their own. Each sheep has its own patches of vegetation— known as 'rakes'—over which it moves in regular daily fashion. So they are not as dumb as we would make them out to be; except when they're on the roadway, and particularly so with their lambs, when you and your car need to exercise every caution to avoid running over them. Many, poor things, are killed each year by careless motorists. The 1964 hit-tune 'There'll never be another you (ewe)', is often occurring up north.

One hears many strange questions put by visitors, namely, 'What's the point of dipping the sheep; are they dipped in the lochs, natural springs or in the sea; how often are they dipped and shorn; are they brought from the moorland in winter, to sleep with their crofters in their cottages?'

So you will realise, there is never any rest at all for a crofter; never a dull moment, and a woman marrying a crofter should appreciate this, before it is too late! They work far into the long summer evenings, turning their modest land into as rich and as productive a unit as is possible. Yes, they have a hard

F2

life winter and summer, so much so that one crofter told a visitor
they became eligible for their old age pension when they were
forty-five years of age here! The crofter will tell you the cure
for anything is salt water—sweat, tears or the sea.

*   *   *

I have already mentioned Faith. Believe it or not, the
Highlander has full faith in his country, for he cannot compromise
with its mountains, its lochs, and its glens; and the shaggy
Highland cattle that roam about, and which plod through the
bogs 'neath the misty landscape. Yet how many, as I have hinted,
have to leave this great country of Wester Ross, Caithness and
Sutherland by reason of shortage of work and pay, the self-same
bog and the self-same barren fields. The Forestry Commission
and the North of Scotland Hydro-electric Board ('*Noshels*' as
it is termed—not as many might imagine, the name of some
obscure Old Testament prophet!) have worked wonders showing
what honest-to-goodness Highland endeavour can do. Despite
all this (and I'd have you know *trees grow slowly*) the crying need
is for light industry in order to halt the drift southwards. This
is not a theory; it is an acknowledgement of fact. Without all
this, in another fifty years, the land will see yet another revival
—a revival of the clearances; a disappearance of everything
characteristically HIGHLAND. Again, this is true—not just
literary fantasy. Deep down, no Highlander ever wishes to
leave his native homeland. But what can he do? He *has* (the
young Highlander), to live, just the same as you and me.

Further on, I refer to the Mod and AN COMUNN GAIDHEALACH
(the Gaelic Society). In essence it is not functioning deep enough
to my mind; it should attempt more in regard to Highland
rehabilitation. Whilst it pin-points *culture*, one cannot survive
by that alone. Only can one live by *economics*. With the exception of say Perth, Aberdeen, Inverness and Oban, there is no town
big enough to accommodate a Mod gathering—a gathering of
interests far and wide; and so such conferences of Gaelic importance have to seek venues further afield than the REAL Gaelic
homeland, namely in the cities further south, which—whether
you like it or not—have no real *personal* interest in the far, far
north.

Yes, the whole story today hinges on Faith; faith in the

younger generation born and bred in the Highlands, not only to move mountains, but to bring them into use. I have termed this country, 'God's own country'—a second Garden of Eden. This may well be, but it requires an Adam to keep it going as such. After all, there is plenty of space here to move around in; oceans of room to think, and acres upon acres of land in which to employ great vision—a countryside of unlimited power still untapped in this year of grace 1965; a *vast* land, in truth. What is needed, in my view, is a Scottish-minded government; one that *acts*, not one that merely 'thinks'. It's action now in 1965 that is wanted; not in 1995, for most of us will be dead by then! If this were so, the Highlands would then be the dog that wags the tail. As it says in the Gospel, 'Whether the twain?'

*　　*　　*

The crofter; his religion and his work.

What about his recreation; his spare hours!

And here I bring you to Gaeldom, to the Mod, to the céilidh's and such-like. To the crofter and the Highlander, the Gaelic language is song, poetry and story all in one; and it is true to say it has enhanced the arts of the world. Many distinguished Gaelic scholars have said, that if Gaelic ever dies, it would be a sad loss to civilisation.

In general terms, the Gaelic-speaking communities (one of the oldest remaining cultures in Europe, possessing the same roots as the Irish Gaels) are almost entirely confined to the islands and the districts along the north-west coast. Whilst Gaelic is definitely giving ground, it is still as full of life up in the *real* Highlands, as a flowering hawthorn tree—and at the various Mods, well, Gaeldom runs riot! Before I became fully acquainted with Scotland and the Highlands, I used to imagine MOD was something you ate, or the name of a Cornish wine! Such was my ignorance.

Each year, however, the number of Gaelic-speaking persons diminishes owing to constant depopulation of the Highlands. There is little opportunity for those growing up to find lucrative employment at home; and so they leave for the south. In one of the islands in the Outer Hebrides, some twenty-five per cent of its population have left during the past ten to twelve years.

In 1800, one Scotsman in five spoke Gaelic.

In 1860, the ratio was one in ten.

In 1962, it was about one in seventy; or in other words only about 70,000 people out of the whole of Scotland's millions, know 'the Gaelic'. I trust I may be excused in quoting once again *Ça Donne Beaucoup à Reflechir* ('it makes one furiously to think'). It is so very apt in this connection.

It may therefore be asked, why does anybody bother to learn a language that is dying? No one learns Gaelic for any monetary value. For some generations now, Highlanders have been brought up in the comfortable belief that they can preserve their character, customs and traditions, and yet allow their language to perish. Gaelic now seems to be the fading language of the home, of the fishermen and of the croft; certainly not the language of the enlarging commercial and industrial world in which we are being so rapidly engulfed. One cannot revive a language by literary efforts or arguments alone. It can only be revived when its appeal reaches down to the deepest sentiments of a people; or of a race; when their faith and passions become aroused to the full. The only people who can save Gaeldom are the Gaels themselves. *Am Bheil Gaidhlig Agad?* 'Do you speak Gaelic?'

Up in the north-west where I live and have my being, the Gaelic tongue is spoken in its soft, native sibilancy. It is a great bulwark in the preservation of the traditional loyalties and the simplicity of life. Progress, such as we know it today, tends to obliterate the old forms of warmth, grace, charm and the very poetry of life itself. Albeit up here in these humble homes of the people, there is still to be found the greatest hospitality combined with an inborn courtesy and grace which can fittingly receive a prince without a qualm, or a queen without embarrassment.

Early in 1964 the executive committee of AN COMUNN GAIDHEALACH (the Gaelic Association) recommended the appointment of a £2000-a-year Director-General as chief official to the organisation in an effort to further develop its work. The post would be given to a fluent Gaelic speaker having a thorough knowledge of the language and Highland affairs. He would have a roving commission all over Scotland, visiting areas and organising activities to stimulate interest in Gaelic.

Many eminent Gaelic scholars have spoken out strongly as to there being not enough done to encourage the use and teaching of Gaelic; or to cultivate Gaelic literature, history and music; or to encourage the wearing of Highland dress. For myself, I think the main organisation should be based in the Highlands proper, and not in Glasgow; for, as such, it carries little weight in Gaelic-speaking areas. The Mod may well be a happy convivial affair, and a happy meeting place for friends out-of-touch. But to my mind, it does not seem to have any *serious* merit. There appears to be a certain amount of inertia, which is apt to lose sight of the purpose of strenuously embracing its own youth movement. Much more needs to be done—much more. Compared to the resurgent Welsh Gaelic movement, AN COMUNN is a flickering in the twilight. There are only two Chairs of Celtic in Scotland; at Glasgow and at Edinburgh. Language is the vehicle and medium of expression. 'The Gaelic' needs a shot in the arm, so that the Highlander, his children and his children's children may not lose their identity *as a race*. It is now close on seventy-five years since AN COMUNN was founded. There has recently been inaugurated in Inverness a Gaelic amateur dramatic club; and they envisage a festival in the near future. Good for them.

Even in the churches, the Gaelic is dying out, where less than a century ago, most ministers held weekly services in the old tongue. Now there are so few Gaelic preachers that the number of Gaelic charges is being cut down. Previously there were two classifications; one where it was necessary for the minister to speak Gaelic, and one where it was desirable. Now, the first grade has been dropped entirely.

* * *

Now for the MOD . . .

The Mod is a yearly festival of Gaelic music, song, dance, oral competition and the like; and it is held for a week at different centres each year and to which all Gaelic-lovers (gentle Gaels with true speech on their lips) wend their way, young—even the very young—and old; for music is a universal language; a language which all the world understands, be it Gaelic or otherwise.

The vocabulary of Gaelic is much greater, and less defiled, than most; it is not a 'mongrel' language like English. Gaelic is a clear-cut, pedigree language, with a subtle gradation of meaning in the words it employs. It is a living, and therefore a spoken language. The longing for things gone beyond recall is probably the most moving note in Gaelic poetry; not so much Celtic gloom, but rather the hard facts of a people forced by poverty and by other men's greed years ago, to cross the seas to new homes, as I have stated already. Gaelic is more a language of description. Every year these great Mods are held, Gaeldom abandons itself to a week of glorious music and the renewing of auld acquaintances. There is the thrill of the tartans, the pipers, the joy of meeting old friends and 'feeling' the soft touch of the Gaelic accent, their lingering on the 'r's'; the softened consonants. The Mod is a unique gathering; colourful, impressive and electrifying. As someone once said, 'A gran' language the Gaelic; profanity in it just sounds like poetry in any other tongue!'

The word 'mod' comes from a word 'mot', so Gaelic scholars say, which is common to Norse and to Anglo-Saxon, but whether it came to us from the Vikings is uncertain.

The Mod is not an entirely musical festival such as some would suppose; for at the last Mod held, over 40 per cent of the entries in the junior section were for the oral competitions, which is indicative of the desire of Highland youth to become proficient in the Gaelic language.

Invariably on the Sunday before 'the week' commences there is a traditional Gaelic service held in the town's main church, and is attended by the Provost, Magistrates and members of the Town Council.

At such gatherings, people come who want to meet others similarly imbued; people who want to sing and dance in the old traditional manner, for to such folk these songs draw strength from their wild hills and misty moors; warm and fragrant from the heather; and amongst the whole assembly of such kindly folk, kith and kin are woven and knitted together like the strands of wool in the Fair Isle jerseys still being made by old knitters in out-of-the-way places.

These songs of the isles delight all ears—even English ears— as do the gaily-coloured kilts (with hues like the tint of heather, the greens resembling moss) swinging and swirling; that and the women wearing the brooches of their respective clans.

Tartan uppermost and everywhere; the shops making

beautiful displays in their windows; and the Council 'goes to
town' also, in stretching a banner across the main thoroughfare
emblazoned with the words CEUD MÌLE FÀILTE (100,000 welcomes); a cheering thought even on a cold day. I suspect many
English folk would enquire of the first Highlander in kilt they
met on the street, as to what 'those foreign words mean?' And
if the six-foot tall, hairy-kneed kiltie was the usual Highland
wag, he would tell them in all seriousness that it literally meant
'I can't give you anything but love!'

Most of the elderly women who steadfastly attend these Mods,
and who come from all quarters of the Highlands and Islands,
are of a shy, retiring disposition; but the memories of song and
laughter still abound in their bosoms. And as these women and
wives (some mayhap bereft of their menfolk) listen to the young
performers ('the young in heart'), they smile happily to the
speech and to the tradition which, to them, is a sure, and living
force; for there are things which can be expressed only in
Gaelic; truths in life that can only be put to Gaelic verse. For
life in the Highlands is hard, as hard and as dreary as the barren
rocks that surround them and their crofts; yet, all the same, the
love of life lies lightly on their chiselled faces.

Young farmers have left their crofts for the week, and whilst
they are away their cattle will be roaming the hillside at leisure,
crushing back the old invader—the bracken. Some of the
youngsters only have enough money saved to come for the one
day they are 'performing'; and then back they must go to their
homes which may be in one of the far-away islands of the Outer
Hebrides. A hard existence; a stocky people indeed.

Young and old; junior choirs, assiduously coached by their
Gaelic teacher, come to re-live, to revitalise one part—and to
them *the* part—of Scottish home life which, to these young boys
and girls, spells contentment of their own wee Highland homes.
Until they grow up—and there's the rub. For youth in the
Highlands, there is small chance for a career, for self-expression,
for incentive.

Yes, everyone of any note or having any Highland connections try to attend these Mods. No one ever seems to go to
bed on such occasions; and meals are not the only things that
'stagger' during Mod week! Those behind cocktail bars work
and sweat at high pressure—breakneck speed, for we are not

west of Garve now! They seem to work into the small hours
of the morning, for there must be a 24-hour licence. After the
mad Mod days, am certain the many cash registers will need a
general overhaul; especially the bells, for they'd be either worn
out or jammed!

So, after a week of tireless energy, tireless talking and tireless
Slàinte Mhaths, the annual Mod closes down and everyone goes
back to the Islands and Highlands—to the croft, the sheep and
the heather. To extend this Mod idea, and promote even greater
interest (and finance too) I think, if these Festivals embraced
Gaelic, Welsh, and Irish songs, music and dancing, they would
produce an immense impact on society generally.

The Mod-ites return to their homeland; to the crofts and
cottages where the burn babbles round the back door, and is
heard from the bedroom, lulling one to sleep; and then in the
morning fretting like an infant to waken you up. Many have
no water laid in to their wee houses; so they just go outside
to wash under the tap in cold peaty-brown-coloured water.
Then come in for breakfast, glowing, and ready for the new-laid
eggs picked out of the henhouse they've just opened up; warm
oatcakes and oatmeal porridge, thick as can be; home-made
marmalade—and the burn continues to babble. No luxury;
just Highland life; no wealth—just a wealth of happiness and
freedom. The mountains and lochs by day; the stars by night.
IONNDRAINN—the longing for things gone beyond recall; the
most moving note in Gaelic poetry. The 'Clearances' cannot
be forgotten; those days when the cream sailed overseas leaving
the skimmed milk behind. But since those years, the skimmed
milk has turned full circle; it is cream again. During those
fateful days, man's greatest pleasure was when he was subduing
rebels, defeating enemies, wiping out all their kith and kin,
seizing all their property; causing wives to weep with tears
streaming down their cheeks; burning their houses, raping the
women and using them as pillows to sleep on.

Now, all that is over; though forgotten, never. The Highlander has a long memory, and a long life.

As a rule, the men are virile to a ripe old age. They die
when their bodies wear out, and their hearts stop beating. They
get more relaxed as they grow older—whereas townspeople
grow more tense.

All in all, this is a blesséd land in every way. To quote Edna St. Vincent Millay:

> ... How can I tell, unless I go
> To Cairo and Cathay
> Whether or not
> This blesséd spot
> Is blessed in every way? ...

I can only add, it is indeed a blesséd country.

Then, of course, in the old days there were the *céilidhs* (cayleys)—meetings for gossip, stories and song held in the various houses, told round the fire during the winter months. At such gatherings one would listen to stories of ghosts, goblins and water-horses; all of which thoroughly thrilled the children. And then on the way home, these youngsters would feel that some terror or other might be lurking round every tree or every corner. A great deal of knowledge was acquired at these old-time céilidhs. There is not so much of all this nowadays; the village halls have, to a great extent, replaced the homely meetings, and in these halls are held dances, concerts, badminton, whist-drives and film shows provided by the Highlands and Islands Film Guild. Their cinema van generally makes weekly or fortnightly visits. There is, in a way, still *céilidhing* in a sense of meeting and talking and so on, but the age groups now seem to keep more to themselves.

Not only does the Mod provide a certain relaxation to the Highlander, but it should be remembered this is the land of Games, (with a capital G—and at such games, 'the Tartan'), and of 'the pipes'. To hear the bagpipes playing on the moorland at sunset is a very moving sound. The Scots, and particularly Scottish regiments, took bagpipe-playing all over the Empire; down to New Zealand and across to Africa and India. Only Scotland has produced bagpipe music of such sophistication as the Macrimmon (of Skye) pibrochs. That much-sung ballad 'A Scottish Soldier', is based on a bagpipe tune called 'The Green Hills of Tyrol'.

The Highland Games held nearest to Gairloch is in Skye, at Portree, and take place the last week in August in a hollow—a natural amphitheatre—only five minutes' walk from the square. The brae to the hollow is generally lined on both sides with tents put up by gypsies professing to tell you your fortune and selling also many odds and ends. You sit around the hillside looking down on the hollow where platforms have been built for the Highland dancing contests. Near by, in the specially reserved seats, sit the 'gentry'—the judges—all bedecked in their full Highland regalia, sashes and kilts, the whole setting a veritable colourama; an afternoon that will remain long in your memory.

I have seen some athletes of wonderful 'frame' at these games; some who can lift and throw a 28-lb weight as far as 70 feet or so, as though it were but a small stone; nae bother at a'. I think some of the porridge-makers must have photographed these giants for their carton covers; Tarzans of the Tartans we could rightly call them.

Thousands attend these games and the contestants come from far and near.

Of course, Braemar on Royal Deeside, miles away from here, is the 'hub' of the Highland games, and with Royalty present, it dominates the world in such sports. 'Cabers and capers', a wonderful day of events, personalities and splendour, the like of which you will never see in any other realm of sport. August and September are the most colourful months in Scotland when all the various clans foregather and wage war in the tossing of the caber, putting the weight, throwing the hammer, dancing the Highland flings; the tug-of-war, playing the pipes, and in so far as Portree is concerned the 20-odd mile marathon race up the mountains and down the glens.

A great deal of these Highland games date back to the days of Queen Victoria, who used to spend many happy months at Balmoral and who so loved the Scottish country.

I have read of one great barrel-chested Highlander—a veritable Hercules—who turned professional and during his long career all over the world amassed 11,000 prizes and some £30,000 in cash. Brawn combined with Brain? Truly up in the north, magnificently built men match their magnificent mountains.

Whilst of old, the Highland games were essentially Scottish, recently a few 'outsiders' have crossed the border and crashed in, not only to casually engage in the friendly sport, but to carry off prizes and prize money. There was one Yorkshireman, a blacksmith from Barnsley, who for the last two years has literally run away with nearly all the prizes; throwing, putting and tossing the caber—and all in a borrowed kilt! Am thinking

he was not entirely welcomed. Be this as it may, you will still
find hundreds and hundreds of people turning up to witness
these games of skill and brawn. The piping, dancing, and the
variety of all the coloured tartans continue to be a magic draw;
and when all set, you feel there is a true sense of occasion permeating the atmosphere.

Games and the Tartan. It seems these days tartan is much to
the fore; in fact in some districts it is becoming the rage; tartan
kilts, scarves, ties, rugs, knickers, shirts, waistcoats, slacks,
pyjamas. On some of these labelled 'Scottish Tartan', should
you look closely, you may see on another smallish tag 'made in
Switzerland'. But let it be here stressed; the kilt is the dress
of the Highlander; it is not the national dress of the Scots. 'The
Kilt is for Hielan' men!'

In chapter 12, one will read as to the wearing of Highland
dress being forbidden by law after the Jacobite rebellion defeat
at Culloden. It is interesting to learn how the kilt came into
use. Originally the Highlander wore a very simple, utilitarian
garment, and the kilt as we know it today, all arose from a
certain Thomas Rawlinson, an Englishman (a Sasunnach) who
became a legendary figure in the 18th century, about 1726,
eleven years after the first Jacobite rising of 1715.

Thomas Rawlinson, a Quaker, who had iron foundries
('bloomsmithies' as they were then called) in Furness, was born
in 1689, and was a man of unusual vision and energy. In 1726
he launched a project for the smelting of iron in the Highlands;
in Glengarry in the Great Glen. His selection of this spot was
on account of the great wealth of timber there. Unfortunately
this venture was a failure, due to high freightage costs and poor
quality ore; and it only lasted ten years. He had an agreement
with John Macdonell, 12th of Glengarry, to restore Invergarry
Castle (which had been burnt down by Government troops, as
the Macdonells had supported the Stuart cause) for his own
occupation during his lease. The idea of a Sasunnach living in
the Chief's castle was bitterly resented by Glengarry's followers,
and many attempts were made on his life.

In 1729, Highland dress consisted of the belted-plaid (breachan-
feile), a single garment gathered in and belted at the waist,
covering the upper and lower parts of the body. It consisted of
a single piece of cloth, 12 ells in length. Although Rawlinson

thought this dress was attractive and maybe just the thing for their moorland life, it was extremely awkward whilst working in his foundry. That they should wear trousers, like an Englishman, would be unthinkable to these dour Scottish workers. One night, some soldiers sought shelter from a storm in Invergarry Castle; and there was one, a Private Parkinson, who was a Regimental tailor from England, who was very taken with seeing this Highland dress. A Highlander came in, wet through, took off his belted-plaid to dry it at the fire; and then Parkinson saw it was but *one* single garment. Rawlinson mentioned to this tailor how awkward the dress was for foundry work, and wondered if it could not be made into two garments; a garment pleated as before, attached to the belt, and an upper garment to be used as a cloak or blanket? Parkinson took the necessary measurements, and thereafter the *feile-beag* (the little kilt) came into being. This 'crime' of altering the national, Highland dress, proved at once popular and became the official dress of Highland regiments. And this is the kilt as we know it today.

Rawlinson returned to England in 1736, and he died the following year, only forty-eight years of age; yet it was he, an Englishman, who designed the kilt.

In Edinburgh you can often go into a tartan store shop in Princes Street and hear an American woman asking for a certain clan tartan, explaining that her grandmother, or great-grandmother, had some Scottish blood in her and therefore she herself must also surely have Scotch blood surging through her veins, and thus can legitimately wear 'the tartan'; and as all this is good for trade—whether it be Festival trade or not—Mrs. Hap J. Hazard gets her tartan skirt, and maybe a suitable kilt for 'junior'—a wee brainless looking boy with heavy-lensed glasses.

Concluding the Highlander's relaxation, one must not forget the immense joy and activity attached to a Highland wedding—and in the islands especially, such festivities carry on for at least a week; long after the happy couple have left; for one cannot allow the imported crates of liquor to be dumped outside, so long as there are uncorked bottles. Oh! no indeed. Even on the mainland, such a wedding is meant to be an occasion outdoing all other occasions! Yes, sir!

Prior to 'the day' it is the custom to waylay the intended bride (we will call her Mairi) and her young man Donald; and this is done in a manner far excelling any English custom. The lassie is kidnapped, smeared all over with black boot polish, hair saturated with wet flour and sticking up like an O-Cedar mop, and carefully guarded by her 'friends' whilst being driven on a fish lorry up and down the village several times to the tooting and blasting of the horn so that all but the bed-ridden could not fail to see the fun of the fair. Her Donald is also waylaid, held down and rolled in the mud along the street, or square, his face and legs being similarly given a sun-tanning. In some cases, he is gradually bereft of his clothes, and when it comes to his underpants being torn off, the womenfolk rush indoors and draw the blinds! And if either or both events were deemed not to be 100 per cent successful, then the ritual is repeated.

Comes the day; one not readily forgotten. Cars of every vintage appear, taking young and old to the church; generally the church to which the bride belongs. After the service, guests are whisked away to the local hotel for drinks and the cake-cutting ceremony; and then the 'feed', washed down with whisky galore; telegrams read and speeches with stories that sometimes are tinged blue—the colour of the bridesmaids' dresses—but what does that matter, west of Garve! A local band is engaged to provide Scottish music from accordions ('boxes') and piano, with a piper thrown in if possible to lead the bride and groom to the floor, whereupon everyone follows suit and trips the light fantastic. Sets are arranged for eightsome reels, and as the evening wears on, the whole 'ensemble' becomes wilder and wilder, the drams being knocked back in routine fashion, for 'reeling' is thirsty work, and thereon 'reeling' becomes the operative word. Young and middle-aged, and even the not-so-middle-aged are almost lifted off the floor by the energy displayed by the manly men in kilts. The band is kept oiled by a special brew and their feet are tapping in unison with those on the slippery floor; and the 'Road to Stornoway by Oronsay' gets rougher and rougher!

Some of those in the inner circle repair to the corridor outside the rooms where the bride and groom are changing, and when ready both are lifted shoulder high and borne downstairs preceded by the piper into the hall, where an avalanche of confetti and

even kippers await them. Finally both are 'plonked' into the
waiting going-away car. Sometimes they are brought back
again, just in case somebody has missed seeing them off!

With the principals away, more music, more drams, and for
those who get peckish, tea and helpings from the mountains of
cake and sandwiches laid by; a means of steadying one up
temporarily for further sessions of drams and singing and dancing.
Towards 4.0 a.m. a thinning-out is noticeable as signs of weari-
ness and unreliability gain ground (or lose ground might be
more apt!). Then it is that a real problem presents itself; the
journey home? Fortunately the local P.C. is kept engaged in
conference, so he cannot hear or notice the cars being plunged
into gear as they make the attempt at a special 'reel' over the
hills and into the darkness of the glens. Perhaps he too, next
morning, was feeling the strain and responsibility weighing
heavily on his shoulders, for a wedding is not to be taken lightly
by Her Majesty's guardian of the Law. 'Tis a serious affair if
taken in the right spirit. 'Chust that. Better to wait till you
see five roads ahead of you before saying goodnight, for if you
then take the middle road you're sure of having two others on
either side of you to help keep you straight!

Yes, I came away from my last Wester Ross Highland
wedding hearing 'myself' saying to 'myself'; if it's 'myself'
that's getting married 'tis a Highland wedding for 'myself';
for there is every chance of the groom driving off with the
prettiest bridesmaid instead of the pretty bride! and no one would
know much about it, till next morning! Och aye!

*   *   *

The crofter, his life, his religion, and his relaxation.

And now to touch upon the Gaelic itself, which as I have
said, is seemingly dying out. There are many Gaelic speakers
who do not use Gaelic when talking to their children. No
language can survive such treatment for long.

In the Gaelic alphabet there are only 18 characters: 5 vowels;
12 consonants; and 1 'h'—the sign of a breathing or aspiration
only.

There is no indefinite article (nor is there in Greek or Latin
for that matter) and there are only two accents, grave and acute.
Some words are spelt the same, but the accent and pronunciation

gives them a different meaning; *i.e.* BÀTA (a boat), BATA (a staff or rod). These accent marks are easier in Gaelic than in, say, the French language. Thus:

A, U, and I when given a long sound are written as À, Ù, Ì; sounding as in the English words dam, doom, and deem.
Ó is like O in the English word tone
Ò ,, O   ,,   job
É ,, A   ,,   say
È ,, E   ,,   get
s before E or I is pronounced as SH in the English word show.

This letter 'h' is rather intriguing. It is simply a breathing which modifies the letter into a *softer* sound, sometimes smoothing it away altogether. *B* when aspirated becomes a *V*, and *S* when so aspirated, vanishes altogether. In short, the aspirate is to silence or euphonise the consonants when their initial sound would injure the easiness of flow; and so this aspirate power and correct use is most important. This 'h' is not included as a letter in the alphabet and there is not a single word in the Gaelic language that commences with the letter 'h'.

It is an aid to inflexion and is also used to denote gender, number, case and tense. Thus in BEAN MHATH (a good wife) where MATH appears as MHATH the aspiration shows that BEAN (wife) is feminine; and this aspiration may take place at the middle or end of a word.

The Latin word for *Mother*, MATER is MÀTHAIR in Gaelic and pronounced MA'UR, the original hard 'T' completely softened by aspiration. Gaelic is therefore a soft language; harsh, hard sounds seldom occurring. The music of the Gaelic speech is due in large measure to the use of this 'aspiration', thus causing sounds to glide into one another.

The Gaelic *vowels* sound very similar to the continental vowels. Thus A (ah), E (ay), I (ee), O (oh), U (oo).

There is no silent final vowel, like the English *e*, as in *home*, *house* or *give*.

The *consonants* are sounded each in their own way, and it would take too long—and be very uninteresting here—to give them all. Just to quote a few examples:

B is like B in boat, but tending towards a P sound
BH is like a V; BHA (VA)
C is always hard like C in cat; never like an s

FH is always silent; FHEAR (ER'R), meaning MAN
MH like a v with a nasal touch; MHATH (VA)
PH like F, as in English
TH like H in 'him'; the aspirate washing out the *t*.

The Gaelic *verb* always precedes the noun or pronoun and is *not* declined; it is the same for all persons and numbers, being very different from the English verb in form and structure.

All verbs (except 10) in the Gaelic language are regular and have only past and future time tenses.

As a matter of interest, I give the verb 'to be', and not being declined as I have said, is the same throughout:

THÀ MI (ha mee) I am   THÀ SINN (ha sheen) we are
THÀ THU (ha oo) thou art   THÀ SIBH (ha sheev) you are
THÀ E (ha ay) he is   THÀ IAD (ha eent) they are.

As THÀ ('is', 'are', or 'am') always precedes its nominative, we get the impression of a constant asking of questions. Example, 'it's a cold day' in Gaelic would literally be 'is the day cold?'

There is no affirmative word corresponding to the English 'yes'; nor a negative 'no'. A question is put by the interrogative form of the verbs, and the answer must be made by the affirmative or negative form of the verb; its tense corresponding to the form used in putting the question. And certain idioms seem to 'rotate'. To translate 'I hate him', the literal Gaelic wording would be 'hate is at me to him'. Again, 'I remember' forms itself as 'it is memory with me'. And 'I love you', in Gaelic becomes, 'Love is at me on you'. (Far too long a sentence, I'm thinking, in English for an ardent lover!)

In English, posing the question 'Did you go to town?', you would answer, 'I did'—not 'I did go', for the verb 'go' is understood. But in Gaelic, however, no such suppression as this can occur, and you must enunciate the whole verb; thus 'I did go'.

Nouns such as the names of males, young of all animals regardless of sex, trees, vegetables, liquors, colours, metals, elements, seasons, days of the week, are *all* masculine.

Usually feminine are names of females (including animals), countries, musical instruments, diseases.

The Gaelic *adjective* is immediately after the noun it qualifies. Thus CU (a dog), and DONN (brown)—and 'a brown dog' becomes CU DONN (a dog brown).

Regarding the points of the *Compass*, the observer—like the Druids and sun-worshippers of old—is supposed to face the rising sun. Thus, *East* is EAR (in front of); *South* is at the right hand, DEAS; *North*, the left hand, TUATH; and *West, i.e.* where you are standing, is IAR (the land at the back of you).

Gaelic therefore is a very different make-up to other foreign tongues we hear. Each word seems to weave a story of its own composition to both the casual labourer and the learned don. As I have said earlier, those speaking Gaelic are getting fewer and fewer, although it forms a language subject in the Higher leaving exams.

The following words, phrases and meanings, taken at random, may be useful to visitors coming to these parts:

THÀ E BRÈAGH (ha breeah): its fine
THÀ E FLIUCH (ha fluke): it's wet
THÀ E FUAR (ha fooar): it's cold
THÀ E GAOTHACH (ha guur): it's windy
BLÀTH (bplah): warm
MO GHAUL (moh voil): my love
CÉILIDII (cayley): a meeting for gossip and song
CIA MARA THA-THU (Kamera-ha): how are you?
THÀ GU MATH (ha goo va): I'm well
STRUPAG (strupack): cup of tea and a bite to eat
FÀILTE (faltchy): welcome
GLÉ MHATH (gley va): very good
ACHNASHEEN: field of storm
ÀIRD, or ÀRD: a height, promontory or headland
STRATH: a broad valley
GAIRLOCH: short loch. GEARR (short), spelt GHEÀRRLOCH in Gaelic
BADACHRO: BAD (clump), A (of), CHRÒ (trees, or nuts), might therefore mean a 'clump of trees'
GLEN DOCHERTY: properly GLEANN DOCHARTIE, is believed to have been the name of a man; in essence it means 'the glen of excessive scouring'—indicating that its sides and base are scoured by spates
BEINN DAMH (or DAMPH): mountain of the stag
CARN DEARG: red cairn
GRUINARD: in Gaelic GRUINAIRD; origin vague, may be Norse. GRIAN, the sun; AIRD, height

MELVAIG (or MOLVIG): in Norse it would mean a shingly bay;
   in Gaelic MEALL BHEAG, a little hill
MELLON UDRIGIL: Hill of Udrigil. Norse
OPINAN: little bays
SAINT MAELRUBHA: Maree, is a corruption from this saint's name.
SLIOCH, or SLEAGHACH: resembling a spear. From certain angles
   this 3217-feet mountain on Loch Maree appears as a broad
   spear-head
ULLAPOOL: an old name probably from UILE (all) and POLL (pool);
   or a pool large enough for all.

DUBH: black
FIONN: white
BUIDHE: yellow
GORM: blue
DONN: brown
GLAS: grey (or green)
DEARG: red
BREAC: trout
BRADAN: salmon
FRAOCH: heather
EILEAN: island
INVER: mouth of river:
   (Gaelic, INBHIR)

UISGE: rain
GRIAN: sun
CAORA: sheep
UAN: lamb
CIOBAIR: shepherd
FANG: sheep pen
BÓ (BA): cow
EACH: horse
BAINNE: milk
HAAR: Scotch mist (not Gaelic
   merely broad Scotch)
KINLOCH: head of Loch (Gaelic
   CEANNLOCH)
TIGH: house
KYLE: strait (CAOL, in Gaelic).

It is certainly very sweet and restful to listen to Gaelic being
spoken; especially wondering what it is all about—if *you* are
being talked of in terms good, bad, or indifferent.

Going back over the years, the Education Act of 1872 ignored
Gaelic, but in 1874 a concession was made whereby an inspector
might allow pupils to express themselves in Gaelic if they had
difficulty in doing so in English! Gaelic is now to be offered as a
language in Civil Service examinations. I would go further and
say that some Civil Service posts in the Highlands and Islands
should only be filled by those who have Gaelic.

It may be recorded with pride, I think, that Ross-shire has
the highest percentage of Gaelic speakers of all the counties.

Can Gaelic survive?

It is up to youth to decide. If the trumpet give an uncertain
sound, who shall prepare himself to the battle ? Disraeli said
almost everything that is great has been done by youth.

The Queen's 1964 Christmas broadcast was characterised by

her great and stirring challenge to all young people.

The Gaelic language has deeper roots in the soil of Scotland than any other institution; much more than the Saxon tongue. If it were to die on the lips of the remnant who still master it, the most that is distinctive of Scottish life would be meaningless. The Scots might then reconcile themselves to becoming substitute or 'ersatz' English. It is of special interest to record that Gaelic has recently been introduced into the liturgy of the Roman Catholic Church. Let it not be said Gaelic has withered and died on the vine. The Highlands never recovered from Culloden, nor did Scotland's quasi-independence of the English. After the '45 the whole country seethed with suspicion and bitterness. The clearing for sheep broke the old ties of affection between the people who owned, and who lived on the land; and so it left this enduring bitterness that is part of the mental heritage of the present-day people.

I might here explain how *Slàinte Mhath* (good health) came into existence. In the days after the 1745 rebellion, no Jacobite was allowed to mention the name of Charlie (Bonnie Prince Charlie) in any shape or form, under penalty of death, and whilst they always toasted his name in secret, in public it had to be otherwise. They had to toast the 'King of England'.

But the Jacobites got over this stigma.

In Gaelic, *mor* means 'big'; and it can also mean 'Marion'; and 'Marion' was the underground password for Charlie— Bonnie Prince Charlie—and they composed many songs to 'Marion', unsuspectingly.

At all Hanoverian dinners, banquets and like occasions, they would get up and say *Slàinte Mhor*, and the authorities, Quislings and so forth thought it was Gaelic for 'Big Health'; whereas, of course, they were drinking to the good health of Marion, alias Prince Charlie.

And so it has come to pass, down the years in history, corrupted as *Slàinte Mhath*, pronounced the same (*vhor*) as in those days of 1745.

This then is my humble compliment to Highland life, to the crofter and all he stands for. God bless him! And, of course, it should not be forgotten, the Highlander has a sense of *quiet* humour. Motoring once along a desolate side-road I came across a lonely railway level-crossing. Nothing peculiar about that you'd say; but the odd thing about it was its gates. They were half across the roadway and half across the rails. I got out and asked the old Highland keeper what was the meaning of having the gates halfway? His quiet reply was 'Well, I'm *half-expecting* a train shortly!' Slàinte!

Almost as subtle as the Irish. Two Irishmen were detailed to shoot a traitor from the I.R.A. at an appointed bridge, where they were told the man would pass over at twelve o'clock. By one o'clock he still had not arrived; two o'clock and no sign of him, whereupon one assassin said to the other, 'I hope nothing's happened to him!'

*   *   *

Concluding Highland life then, even in this year of grace 1965, we still have to learn that what the Highlands *could* and *should* offer us, besides their unequalled beauty, is not money, but men living and women and children living in tune with their background—a race which has given great things to the world, but which nearly two centuries after the 'Clearances' began, is very nearly gone.

Their unbounded kindness, however, will last for ever; a kindness which sows the seeds that in due season burst into a living and sincere respect to all who may be fortunate enough to cross their paths. I have been one of those fortunate ones.

I know full well a lot of English folk look upon the Highlander as 'dour'. As a race they have perhaps a leaning towards dourness; but think of all the trials and tribulations they have gone through. I would rather place upon the word, the meaning 'bold' or 'determined', not as those south of the border are apt to do in terms of 'harsh', 'rigid' or 'glum'.

Many English folk also regard northern Scotland as a wild remote area, inhabited largely by people who are crafty and cunning. I think if you are searching for an adjective, a more suitable one would be 'deep'.

Highland life ... Highland hills ... Highland beauty.

> Blue hills that rise up to the skies
> Blue hills that are tipped with snow;
> At the close of day
> Guarding the bay
> While the evening sun sinks low.

Your beauty is hard to impart
Poor indeed are these words of mine;
But list to the song in my heart
As I humbly kneel at your shrine . . .

*   *   *

Adverting to comments earlier in this chapter, as to the
crofter needing to be encouraged, the Western Isles Crofters'
Union are pressing the Government to establish a *college* of
crofting, for—they say—education in crofting activities has never
had a proper deal. The college should be completely separated
from the existing colleges of agriculture in Edinburgh, Glasgow
and Aberdeen; for these are concerned mainly with farming,
to the neglect of crofting. True, the recent crusade for land
improvement in Lewis (on which I have touched) has been
given further impetus by the establishment of the Crofters'
Commission with new grants for crofting. This development
has reached a plateau, and the crusade has lost its fire; and the
major reason for this is that there are insufficient colleges of
agriculture advisers of the calibre of the originators, to lead on
the revolution at the new level. The work of advisers could
well be extended into the Junior Secondary Schools, when the
leaving age is to be raised in 1970. However, that is five years
off!

In short, and as I have hinted before, crofters are alive to
all possibilities, but lack the technical knowledge and *capital* to
gear themselves to any real and new developments.

Location fashions behaviour and character, be it city, town or
village; even more so in the closer knit units of the Highlands.
The sea breezes blowing off the bay, combined with the winds
from the Torridons, make men rugged here.

CHAPTER 11

SPORT IN THE HIGHLANDS

THE main sport in the Highlands, disregarding climbing mountains and ski-ing, is fishing and shooting; fishing for salmon and trout; shooting grouse and deer. Maybe I should add two other 'sports', whisky and the haggis?

For the fisherman, Scotland provides first-class sport amid unrivalled surroundings on the many lochs and rivers. We all know the impulse at certain seasons of the year for the Englishman to come to Scotland to try and 'kill' a salmon or land a trout; shoot a stag and taste real haggis washed down with *real* Scotch whisky which he will tell you always seems to taste so much better than in England. And why? because you are sipping it neat in its natural surroundings; and as soon as the double is poured out you place the palm of your hand over the top of the glass to keep the flavour in! 'Hush! be quiet!' (a Gairloch expression this).

Fishing. Taking up any new sport can often be a frustrating business, until one gets the hang of it. Fishing is a sport that not only requires the hand and the eye, but patience. There is the story told of an Englishman fishing from a boat just close to the loch's side. On the shore a local watched and watched. The Englishman fished for four or five hours, catching nothing. All the while the local sat and watched and watched. Coming ashore the angler said to the local, 'Why don't *you* try fishing?' 'Och', said the local, 'me? I wudna' hae the patience for yon kind o' thing!' It's no use casting a fly and expecting a bite at once; you can maybe expect it a few days later, unless you may have had what is termed 'beginner's luck'. A trout or a salmon is a very wary fish. In a slow-moving stream it has plenty of time to inspect the stream-borne food that it lives upon, such as fly larvae and other submarine aquatic mites, a decimal of an inch long. He looks leisurely at it, deciding whether it is fit for him to gobble up or not. In a faster stream, he has to move and decide quickly what is or what is not, palatable to his needs. It means a split-second decision. For myself then, not being an adept at the game, I would plump for a fast stream, so that our friend below water wouldn't see that I was an amateur in casting the fly; or casting the right type of fly that he was fancying! Believe me it is quite an art to be able to make the knots to fix the particular pattern fly to the line. There seems to be so much tackle in the way! Fishing bag, the gaff, the catching net for the big fellows, boxes of flies, two or more rods, and so forth. Then there is the casting; another art, for more often than not you'll find the fly-hook tugging in the long grass behind you, or else it has attached itself to your trousers, and here again you need patience to unhook the 'Bloody Butcher' from penetrating further into your bottom! (Oh! yes, these flies have some funny names).

Salmon fishing begins 11th February; trout fishing 1st March. Normally you can't expect good firm fish till April. Of course everything is in the lap of the gods; so it's no use predicting things for certain. If it has been a mild, dry winter, then the burns and pools will not be so full of good fresh, peaty brown water as they should be. One needs therefore to pray for wet weather! You may or you may not get it; in short the whole essence, charm and delight of fishing, I'm thinking, lies in unpredictability—a good word for a good sport.

The atmosphere of a small fishing hotel has an air of its own. You are met at the front hall by masses of rods, lines, fishing bags and nets, Wellington boots, waterproof trousers and macs, generally coloured yellow, all thrown about; and further on see the kitchen tin-plates with their glistening, speckled fish lying side by side—sardine fashion—the product of one of the visitors' proud catch that evening or early dawn; and you gaze on them to the sound of a babbling burn running round the hotel side, weaving up various stories of them; how that one is a real beauty, the other would have taken some landing, some patience, some skill, and you say to yourself, 'I hope I'll have such luck tomorrow. I must think out my technique when I'm in bed tonight!' Should you meet with no such success, it will all boil down to the weather; too wet, or too dry; too windy, or too calm. There's always plenty of excuses. Not enough ripple on the loch, or too much; that, or a Southern Belle touring motor coach passed just as you were about to land the 'biggest ever', and the thirty-five or forty Lancashire loud-throated visitors (trippers) suddenly let out one mad cry of 'cheerio'—and away went my fish!

Yes, the behaviour of the salmon is fascinating. Breeding under similar conditions as trout, his early sojourn is in the rivers, and what lochs are to brown trout, the sea is to the salmon. It is the region of rich feeding with growth and habit culminating in the urge to return to the parent rivers. So in its life, an adult salmon makes at least two long journeys; as a smolt in the second or third year of its life it journeys to the ocean from which some years later it returns as an adult. How far it wanders, no one knows. The up-stream migration as I have said is fraught with all the hazards of waterfalls and rapids. There is a hatchery board at Contin, shortly before one comes to Garve. The trail to the rivers in Wester Ross is blazed by young fish which are assisted at Contin by the introduction of numbers of unfed fry. They are placed in the upper Conon river and develop their growth into parr, and then after a year or so, into smolts which move down-stream to the sea. After growth they return and make use of the newly available spawning grounds. The annual production of the upper Conon river is about 20,000 smolts. Pike, trout and gulls take a heavy toll of these young fish.

Some of these small hotels don't rise to a reception desk; just an oak table in the hall with a vellum-bound book, which a peremptory notice merely says, 'Please register'. In the tiny lounge there is generally a small bookshelf with a queer assort-ment of old thumb-marked books ranging from fishing tomes to Percy's Reliques of Ancient Poetry; with somebody's racing almanack (the local butcher's, perhaps) stuck on the wall with a drawing pin that could tumble down any moment—the calendar not the wall of course!—and when you plonk yourself down on the one and only settee, the worn springs meet up with you with uncomfortable closeness, bringing forth squeaks and twangs like Big Ben about to strike the hour! You think of fish; you reek of fish; you dream of fish—but who cares. You're here on your own; you've forgotten all about catching the 8 o'clock morning train to the office, your wife and your typist (at least we presume you have forgotten the latter!). You've *got away from it all*, and you don't care a hoot whether you locked the office safe or not, before you set sail for the Highlands.

You think back on all the joy it was of carrying all your outfit—Wellington's and all—along the station platform as you embarked northwards from the south, and letting people see you are a fisher, outward bound. 'My!' folks say in the other compartments, 'What a lucky chap that is, going fishing to Scotland; doesn't he look happy (and funny) with all those flies stuck in his fore-and-aft. He's probably some laird!' A young child tugs at its mother saying 'Look, Mummy, at that man with all those nappy safety-pins in his bonnet!' If they only but knew you lived a humdrum life at No. 15 Accacia Avenue!

Yes, you are now away from it all, in Ruritania; though not in one of those small whimsical, music-sounding foreign states of Andorra, Luxemburg or Liechtenstein. You're no longer a Prisoner of Zenda; you are Rupert of Hentzau, and who's to question how or why? You are up in the Wild West of Scotland, at Altnadamph, looking on to the loch at Altnadamph, miles away by 'Wells-Fargo' stage-coach from Beeching's railways. You are sitting drinking far more Scotch than you're used to (for the drink is flowing to match the conversation), but then you have a number of Scottish pound notes to spend, which you had left over from your last holiday, and which you had not cashed for fear your genial (?) English bank manager might have charged you 6d. commission on each note. And you've become 'canny' in your old age! There is from time to time a certain amount of argument as to Scottish notes presented in England. Scottish notes were, and are, issued by Scottish banks for their own convenience and were meant for issue within Scotland. Of course if Scotland had a government of its own, its issue of notes would be recognised abroad—even in Ruritania, to say nothing of our friend Liechtenstein! Actually there are no 'English' notes. The Bank of England issues the notes for the British Government, and they are really in lieu of sovereigns; so in effect they are British Treasury notes. Some of these Scottish £5 notes are quite big and look very impressive, so much

G

so, that when in an English supermarket shop and tendering one of these notes, I was told they didn't accept cheques!

At this moment, therefore, I leave you sitting, drinking and thinking. Thinking 'midst the tang of the blue peat smoke fire which the hotel owner's wife has just made up and spoken to you in so sweet and so soft a Highland accent (bless her!) that you've now captured the 'wave in the heart' and the 'dream in the eye' (*her* eye, mayhap ?), that you've heard so much about in the Gaels; thinking how wonderful it would be if you hadn't to work and toil in a dull uninteresting town; cursing in a way that you had not been left all your Uncle's money, so you *could* live and enjoy this life at the back of beyond (forgetting, of course, that your Uncle in the 1890's worked much harder than you do, or ever will do); whereas you should thank your lucky stars you *have* a good steady job at home, denied so many these days, and which should bring to your mind that Chinese saying, 'I cursed when I had no shoes, 'til I saw a man who had no feet'. And then as the hour is getting late, you feel you should go to bed to get ready for the morn's morn; and as you go upstairs, having marked the slate to be called at 6.30 a.m. with morning tea (should Highlander's ever get up at that time), you say to yourself, 'Yes, I *am* Rupert of Hentzau; I am no longer George B. Smith of Suburbia; *I am away from it all!* The red fire will soon be out of the peat, and if all's well, the sun in a matter of hours will be ready to start on its orbit once again. You look out of the window from the half-way landing on the stairs and see a pageantry of clouds through the mist, and you think you can discern the rim of the mountains as the mist and cloud drift along; and then you see the gem-like surface of the near-by loch reflecting for a brief instant the cloud lights and shadows moving across the sky. In one fleeting second there is a billowy pearl and alabaster outline—resembling the Taj Mahal mausoleum at Agra in India—and then ... nothing but dense mist, like foaming crests rolling down from Ben Pibroch. Yes! I'm going to empty Altnadamph Loch of all its fish, before I leave here! Goodnight!

It should not be forgotten, fishermen are very superstitious. Should any relative of the Captain's die, the boat is painted black the next time it goes in for overhaul. There is never any whistling, or singing at sea. Wind or disaster were sure to overtake the boat if that occurred. A man would get luck if he cut his hand and the blood dripped on the bait. To meet a cat whilst making for the boat was bad. No one cared to meet a cripple or a weakling on their way to the pier; it could only foretell a bad omen. They speak very little whilst going ashore, and not much whilst afloat. Shetland fishermen are perhaps more superstitious than around Gairloch. The crew would not care to go to sea if a minister should happen to come down the pier, and attempt to put a foot on board. When setting sail, the boat is invariably turned 'by the right'—for that is a lucky turning. You seldom, if ever, see a fisherman unless he is wearing some sort of a hat, cap or bonnet. You'll never catch fish, unless your head is covered!

Many north of Scotland fishermen wear *one* gold ear-ring in their ear; for it was said if they chanced to be drowned and their bodies washed up on a part of the coast where they were unknown, then the value of the one ear-ring would ensure sufficient money for a proper burial.

Such is superstition, and legend has a melodramatic appeal. In the old days people up in the Highlands firmly held on to the adage of 'coming events cast their shadows before them' in the fullest supernatural ways.

There is an old Gaelic saying which translated means 'close the north window, close the south, close the west window, evil never came from the east'.

An east wind in May is supposed to augur a bountiful fruit crop.

In some old churchyards the eastern and southern aspects were reserved for the good and affluent; the western area for the poor. Criminals and suicides were allocated the north side. Funerals in some isolated districts still approach the grave 'by the right'. Housewives stir food in the pots 'by the right'. Omens can be pictured by flocks of birds wheeling right or left.

At baptism it was thought lucky if the child cried when water was sprinkled on it—originating from the fact that, according to the scriptures, unclean spirits cried out aloud when driven out by our Saviour.

As to marriage, a Highland girl should adopt the Latin motto 'SI VIS AMARI, AMA'—if you wish to be loved, love!—and at the same time try to find out all she could of her young man by

various old-time means, such as counting the cuckoo notes when
first she hears them in spring, to learn the number of years she
would be single. Dreams, too, were respected. If after eating
salt herring the lassie dreams of her lover offering her a drink,
then her wedding day would be soon.

I am not sure though if the Highlander is superstitious of the
number *thirteen*; particularly Friday the thirteenth; as are quite
a few folk in England. 'TRISKAIDEKAPHOBIA'—the fear of Friday
the 13th! This day can not, however, occur more than three
times in a year. Some say it was the day that Adam ate the
apple, though research shows that no apples grew in Mesopo-
tamia; followers of Islam believe the seductive fruit was either
fig or banana. Because thirteen people sat down to the Last
Supper, some say thirteen must be unlucky; and Friday was the
day of the Crucifixion.

In England many people will not have their houses numbered
'*thirteen*'; they would prefer it to be 12A, 12B, or not at all. Up
here it doesn't seem to matter, and houses are numbered 13 as
occasion arises. Whether agenda items in the local Council
proceedings appear as No. 13, or as No. 12A, B, or C, I cannot
say! In the East, the number thirteen is not regarded with any
awe, for one comes across many effigies or symbols on mosques
or pagodas which, if you counted them, would total 'thirteen'.
No more, no less. There were thirteen states originally in America. George Washington received a salute of thirteen guns
when the Republican standard was unfurled; and the American
eagle has thirteen feathers in each wing.

As to death, the howling of a dog was ominous; and a
cockerel crowing more than naturally at night was an indication
of death. Horses when driven along a road and shying for no
known reason, were supposed to see the phantom of a funeral.
Laughter of an owl, another omen. Highland carpenters long
ago used to say that when there was an unseemly rattle of wood
in their workshop it was a sure sign that a coffin would soon be
needed.

For toothache it was said that carrying a cheek-bone of a
sheep in the pocket would charm away the pain. In Yorkshire
it was said if you carried a potato in your pocket it would cure
rheumatism and gout! 'Aweel.' A degree of sanctity clings
to many of the old standing stones, especially those referred to

in Gaelic as 'stones of worship'. In many old byres (cowsheds), a hallowed stone used to be kept and milk was spilt on it to ensure that cream would rise and the churn would yield a goodly quantity of butter. And so the old stories and legends can go on and on. Fairies and yet more fairies. Someone once asked me, during a night's talk on superstition, 'What goes over the road and never touches it?' I said, 'A fairy? Elf? Leprechaun? Hobgoblin?' 'No', said my old Hielan' friend, as he moved his glass along the bar counter for another dram. 'Well, what does?' I said in all seriousness. 'The County Council!' said he. 'Same again please, Alec.'

* * *

Shooting

We all know of the crowded trains going northwards on the eve of the 'glorious twelfth'—grouse, 12th August—and of the fantastic efforts of the poacher to rush the first grouse of the season down to London on the 11th, so as to be on display at opening time on the morning of the 12th and at an outrageous price, too.

Yes, there is much paraphernalia involved in the entourage connected with this 'glorious twelfth' business. There's the gamekeeper, the beaters, the loaders, the guns, the cartridges, the shooting-sticks, the dogs, the food, the drinks, the ice for champagne, the glasses, the flasks (not only of coffee but of brandy), the shooting-brake, the Mercedes-Benz and the party itself—particularly the womenfolk all dressed up for the part in tightly knitted sweaters—proclaiming in no doubts that they *are* women—and, of course, their slacks! even down to the padre's wife's pyjama-looking jeans!

We're off, and by jove what a shoot! Everything laid on; nothing left to chance, and you return to the 'big hoose' so proud at bringing down so many brace with so few shots. A glorious day, and someone is paying a glorious price for it too. But who cares? So long as it's not you who has to foot the bill!

And at night, during the house-dance supper interval, and you're sitting on the stairs with your host's attractive daughter, apologising for your poor dancing, saying, 'I'm a little stiff from Badminton, you know', to which she looks up at you with her blued eyelids and mascara lashes, her eyes full of 'you', saying

'I don't care if you're a big stiff from Badachro!' And you carry on telling her of the days you were out in Ceylon and ask 'where have you been all my life', then raise your unsteady hand and drink to her health in Pimms No. 1; and you spin the old yarn, sitting closer as you spin it; then putting on more airs to impress, say, 'for years I've had a month amongst the Cairngorms in June, and a month in Wester Ross in September when the heather is at its best; but this next year I'm having a change'. 'Yes,' says Sheila (for that's her sweet name of course), 'there's nothing like a change; where are you going next year then?' 'To Wester Ross in June and the Cairngorms in September', you reply! *Slàinte!* and you both '*Slàinte*'; and then with the dance ended and the lights switched off, the sheep commencing to herald in the dawn, you mount the wide staircase, holding on to the balustrade, and turning the handle of your bedroom, hold her in your arms and kiss her goodnight in the one and only 'glorious twelfth' fashion. Ah! me! you say, if only this glorious twelfth was every day—and every night! It would then be worth fighting for, let alone shooting for! And most certainly worth all Sheila's kisses.

Grouse exists naturally in certain parts of the Midlands and north of England, but its true home is Scotland. All attempts to rear and keep this little game-bird on the Continent have failed. The grouse pines away and dies outside of Scotland.

The golden eagle, that has its home in many parts of the Highlands, is a killer of grouse—the killer that the law protects in fact; and recently some hard words have been given vent to in the Highlands as to the law concerning the protection of wild birds.

The golden eagle is a beautiful bird—but a beautiful bird of prey. It is thought there are close on 300 pairs of eagles in Scotland—protected—and it is calculated that each eagle accounts for one grouse a day; and that in the nesting season, far more. One case can be cited, and which was confirmed by camera, of nine grouse in an eagle's eyrie one day, and two days later, thirteen.

The grouse is esteemed as the best game for its superior flavour of its flesh; there is more of a 'tang' in it than partridge (1st September) or pheasant (1st October).

As I have said, these small out-of-the-way fishing and shooting hotels have an air of their own. You don't look for anything 'posh' in such isolated spots as Lochfaroff. The manager and his wife seem to be on duty all 24 hours. I have known one place that would give you a full-course meal at nearing midnight. Nae bother! And as mine host and hostess had a pretty daughter, I asked them to join me over coffee and liqueurs in the sma' hours, and wished them all BEANNAICH S'O (Bless this house).

* * *

Deer

The *Deer* is an animal that cannot be left out in writing of the Scottish Highlands, for the red deer is indigenous to these northern parts. There are so few obstructions it is possible for these wild beasts to roam from the north of Caithness to the south of Argyll. The antiquity of the red deer in Gairloch itself is substantiated by their cast-off horns having been found deep in peat bogs, where they must have lain many centuries.

Deer stalking holds all the elements of eternity. Fishing is a brisk sport compared with this crawling, whispering vigil. Deer stalking is the crowning glory of the shooting season. I am told it is an arduous and absorbing sport.

There are a number of deer forests within easy radius of Gairloch: one across Loch Maree at Letterewe and another fine forest a friend of mine has between Garve and Ullapool, near Aultguish Inn—Strathvaich, in extent 25,000 acres.

From a recent survey it was estimated that Scotland has a deer population of about 150,000, occupying about six million acres. The marking of new-born calves with ear-tags is being tried out, and the coding of some can be read from about 100 yards, and at even greater distances, for their colour alone can give useful information in establishing the rate of growth of these animals, when they start to breed, and when they die of natural causes; for up to now there is not sufficient known as to the life of a deer, herd movements, and how long they live.

To be a successful deer-stalker you must be a keen sportsman of athletic frame and hardy habits, with perfect eyesight, and be capable of covering 20 or more miles a day over the roughest of rough ground. Suitable clothes are important; clothes that match up to the nature of the ground over which you are shooting. And of course you must sport a deer-stalker hat! now much in evidence at the various Highland weaving shops you come across in the Highlands; known as a 'fore and aft'.

The greatest possible caution is required; any false move in your approach may wreck your 'stalk'. Notwithstanding all your carefulness it may sometimes happen that the suspicious stag gets an alarm from a previously unseen sheep that has strayed into the forest, or from a crowing grouse, or a frightened mountain hare, or even from an eagle. You have to approach your quarry by such a route as not to be visible and that no breeze may convey your scent to the wary animal.

In fine weather the biggest stags are to be found on the highest hills; in wet weather they are on the lower slopes. They move up wind when they feed. Your keeper must take due credit for any successful shoot. A good keeper has an unlimited and intimate knowledge of the habits and habitats of game. He has to be successful with dogs, and humane, too, preventing any unnecessary suffering to the beasts that might arise in the course of the chase.

An interesting—and maybe in time, a serious—matter came to my notice in talking with the head keeper of Letterewe Estate, Loch Maree. They are subject there to a very heavy rainfall, between 80 and 100 inches a year, and, with strong winds coming across the Atlantic from the west, a certain amount of radioactive fall-out had been discovered in the livestock, in the thyroid glands of both sheep and deer. A very small lump, the size of a pea, seemed to form. A careful watch is being kept on this matter and investigations are now being carried out as to this 'activity' occurring, it is thought, from the number of nuclear experiments being made by the Americans in the South Pacific.

In this Land of Venison, where, in some of the 'Deer' hotels innocent stags heads gaze down on you in the hall with such imploring eyes, you, who are not a stalker, feel acutely 'out of it'; afraid to talk of such a sport for fear of using the wrong technical phrases (I do know you 'kill' a salmon, not 'catch' it; as for a deer I think the term is that you are a 'slayer'!). You have venison for lunch, venison for dinner and venison sandwiches for your packed teas. Personally I am not partial to it, even with red-currant or rowan jelly; it seems too lean a meat with little taste.

I am now picturing myself in a 'Deer' hotel; at the dining-table with venison as the main dish, and served me by a waitress as though she was offering me her entire dowry. Poor girl, if she did but know! Then at the next table, I listen to the one-time Lieutenant-Colonel saying to his wife (both looking yellowish, denoting they had spent the best years of their lives in Poona!) 'That was a beautiful beast, my dear, a 12-pointer, a "Royal" you know'. (I didn't know, of course, but I later learnt that a stag having twelve points to its antlers is called a 'royal'. At the same time a 'royal' may not necessarily be a first-rate stag; oh! no; the best heads are distinguished by their wide spans, thickness and long points of the antlers and the length of horn.) But who am I to say all this. I should leave it to the officer-commanding at the next table to recall all that happened in the chase. He is wearing a monocle in his left eye for dinner, and for 'effect'; if he had only donned his Crimea and Mafeking medals—and one for the relief of Lucknow—he would have looked the part of one who had upheld the Flag in days of yore. He looks askance at me, a mere individual having no sense of duty or reason; muttering to himself and doubtless to his wrinkled wife, whose 'sex' had left her many moons ago, that I was a nobody—just a drag on the nation; then loudly proclaiming, 'Yes, a beauty, and we'll have his head stuffed when we get home, and hang him up in the porch at the Manor, m'dear, for all to see and hang their hats on! Stalked him for five hours, you know, my sweetie (oh! dear me!); then, blow me down, the wind changed; he smelt us (he must have smelt his whisky breath, or seen his beer-stained moustache!) and we had to alter our line of approach. Another cherry-brandy, my love?' In the end, yes, there he is, hanging on the Manor porch; poor old Charlie-boy, he's called. Truly, the stag at eve had drunk its fill. And then later on in the lounge-cum-bar he would condescendingly say good evening to me, hoping I'd stand him a 'double', for, with all his swank, loud talk, and medals, he would have little to come and go upon in standing *others* a drink. But for 'myself, myself' having met these types before, I don't bite. I merely say something cryptic, putting them both in their place—and where they belong—saying I know more of the East than most folk. 'Oh, indeed'—'Yes, indeed'; and goodnight!—and good riddance!

A good stag is generally 8 to 10 years old at least; and they are usually in condition for killing between mid-August and mid-October. Roaring begins towards the end of September, and a week or so later most of the older stags are out of condition. There is no close time fixed by law for killing stags.

Three mild winters increase the deer population; but one bad winter after three mild ones may result in a 25 per cent loss in population. It is not generally recognised what a big factor a mild or a severe winter can be on the deer population.

A stag casts its horns every spring and it is said the hinds eat the old horns. They—the hinds—have only one calf a year, about June. In the case of a stag with a very fine head, the sportsman may not wish to shoot it until its horns are quite free from velvet.

* * *

Whisky

Although by no means a 'sport', Scotland being so famous for its whisky, it may be of some interest to say a little of this beverage. The subject needs no introduction; as the secretary at a Board Meeting generally starts off, *inter alia*, as 'we will take it as read', in this case we will take it as drunk! Scotland has sold and exported this product all over the world; and over the years sales have risen astronomically. *Exports* have more than trebled since the end of the war and now stand at something like 23 million proof gallons. In 1960 the whisky industry sent 3 million proof gallons to the Commonwealth alone. Since 1945 whisky has earned a mammoth £500 million in foreign currency. America drinks 'Scotch' to the tune of £36,000,000 a year. At home this rise is not so pronounced on account of the prohibitive tax. In 1849 the duty per proof gallon was 3s. 8d.; by 1914 it had risen to £1: 10s.; in 1920 it was £3: 12: 6. Then during the war years it advanced by stages to £10: 10: 10. In 1961 the Chancellor of the Exchequer raised it to £11: 11: 11 per proof gallon; and in 1964 it advanced once again. The Chancellor of the Exchequer now takes about 30s. in duty on every bottle.

There are just over 100 distilleries in Scotland producing some 32 million gallons a year, of which nearly half are owned by one giant company, the D.C.L. As late as 1820 more than half of Scotland's whisky came from unlicensed stills! In Glenlivet alone there were over 200, for in the valley of the Spey the burn-water there has some magic, indefinable quality, making its malt whisky so famous. Glenlivet is the heart and soul of Speyside whiskies.

There are well over 2000 brands of whisky on the market, practically all 'blended', and being so, they really have no geographical identity.

Malt whisky is made in pot-stills from malted barley; that is, barley that has been allowed to germinate for several days. There are about 90 pot-still distilleries in Scotland, each producing their own characteristic brew, and this malt whisky goes off to the blenders.

It is this malt whisky that gives to blended whisky its flavour; for grain whisky—made from a mixture of barley and unmalted cereals in patent-still distilleries—has far less flavour and character.

Invariably wherever you travel, people prefer the blended whiskies; malts are more heavily flavoured and of course more expensive.

As you drive through the whisky country, Speyside in particular, there seem miracles at work and 'afloat' in the brown burns tumbling through the glens, and in the peat-reek. But a distillery is run on exact scientific lines just as you meet with in a laboratory. The whole quality of whisky revolves around the quality of its water. There is spring water, limestone water, peaty water, soft and hard waters and chlorinated water. Almost as many differing kinds of water as blends of whisky; they may be small, insignificant, minute differences, but differences all the same, and that is what 'does it', a distiller told me.

To have a lovely whisky and add some indifferent water to it—if you really *want* to add water—is pure sacrilege. To the whisky of the place you *must* add the water of the place. I have said the differences in water may be minute, but are not the whiskies? Try for yourself; two glasses of the same whisky, adding to the one the water used by the distillery, and to the other, say, some of your own local water. You will be astonished at the difference in taste of each glass. In America today there is being offered for sale 'genuine Scottish water' to go with the brand of whisky you may buy. An export firm is planning to send 'cans' of Scotch water to suit all the blends exported all over the world; a great effort, to be sure. So any hostess, at home or abroad, who wants to be 'up' with her neighbour should have cans of such water 'on tap'.

Recently I learnt that five gallons of water from the river Tay had been flown 12,000 miles to Brisbane, to be drunk with Scotch whisky at a banquet organised by the combined Scottish Association of Queensland.

When tourists come to Scotland (to drink the whisky!) I think they should be asked which kind they prefer, not just given anything out of the bottle that chances to be opened at the time. Barmen (in cocktail bars especially) should be able to *explain* what the different whiskies are, *where* they come from and *what* makes, or does not make, for one whisky being better than another. It is a real art, and this art should be cultivated as a salesman would in his particular line of business. You would then get the tourist enthusiastic over a certain brand and he would go around praising it up; our friends need guiding with the local knowledge of these whiskies; their origin and the why and the wherefore, etc.

It is said the only thing that will keep a Scot from drinking is illness! and then someone is sure to prescribe a gargle of 'Scotchotis'—a special proprietary brand! The line of the song, 'When I get a couple of drinks on a Saturday, Glasgow belongs to me' needs revising, for in 1960 it is reported that for the first time there were more drunks arrested in Glasgow on *Fridays* than on Saturdays!

To be in at the making of illicit whisky must have its moments; its thrills. And I believe there are yet to be found such stills, and not so far distant from where I live! Hush! be quiet! Thrills in procuring and making the apparatus; and thrills in keeping a watchful eye on 'Mr.' Duncan the Excise man, travelling around at all times of the day and night on his specially 'silenced' silencer of his motor-bike.

The main difficulty was in getting copper for the worm (a long length of copper pipe wound spirally, through which the whisky is distilled). A local ironmonger appeared to be getting a far greater number of copper hot-water cylinder tanks, for far more houses than were built, or ever likely to be built, in a certain village, and those cylinders contained the very thing, copper piping wound round and round. 'Chust the chob'; much of which found its way into other 'water' channels until such time as 'Mr.' Duncan's nose took on a more than reddish hue with inglowing suspicion and anger—'the whiles'.

Then it was Willie and Hector had to turn to other quarters to get piping, but get it they did. Next, how were they to bend it, for Angus, their 'ironmongering' partner, was now too nervous to oblige them in this direction.

After a few drinks from the old illicit brew, kept handy in a small cask in cases of dire emergency (and if ever there was one, there was one right now), they went out into the darkness and wound the piping round the garden post at the back of Sandra's house that Willie had just thought of; this was done perfectly as though Percy himself had plumbed the job from start to finish. Next, and the simplest job of all, to push the worm up off the post and then all would be ready, and away to the hide-out. But it seemed a long, a very long, way to the top of that post, far higher than their own 5 feet 9 inches height of manly growth. So they thought it would be better and quicker to saw off the post at the ground and carry the lot to their workshop. But then again, it seemed thicker and tougher than they had bargained for, and their saw was not of the kind a lumberjack would use. Exhausted, another wee drink and another try, with no success at all. It was stuck good and hearty all ways and such a beautiful job, 'chust sublime'. Drunk with fatigue, excitement and 100% proof, they laid down their handiwork, to take up the cudgels the 'morn's morn'.

But being roused at sunrise with the rain beating down on them, they found themselves looking up at the pipe coiled round an electric standard and a hydro-electric chappie on the spot looking angrily at his high-voltage pole being so ultra-violated. And what was more, he 'himself it was', a friend of 'Mr.' Duncan, and knowing his telephone number also! Poor Willie; poor Hector; for 'Mr.' Duncan's motor-bike—this time without its special silencer so he could gather more speed—came purring round the bend; yes, both Excise man and his machine were indeed purring. And the sequel could be read in that week's local journal under the caption, 'Sheriff Court, Dingwall, High Noon. Illicit whisky; fine paid;' and then in smaller print underneath, 'Gairloch men back at work again!' Yes, Willie and Hector will be at it again, have no fear o' that; for they have not only courage, but a great 'spirit' to urge them on, as

well as many ardent followers wishing them *Slàinte Mhath*.
Besides, 'Mr.' Duncan retired shortly after this affair, and the
new man . . . well, bless him! he's still new to the job. And as
whisky needs time to mature, so will—they hope—'Mr.' Donnie
Mackenzie need time to mature; his nose in particular!

*   *   *

Haggis

Another sport? well not exactly, but a sure necessity now
you are in Scotland, 'absorbing' as well as imbibing all that
goes to make up a Highland holiday. Although haggis, 'the
haggis' as it is invariably called up north, is an all-the-year-
round morsel, it generally comes more into prominence on
25th January (Burns' night) or on 30th November (St. Andrew's
night), when literally tons of it are eaten at home and abroad.
When this 'Chieftain o' the Puddin-race' makes its appearance
then upon ladened tables, it is usually given full honours in being
hailed in with much pomp and ceremony, to the skirl of the
pipes by some well-known piper. And all on account of Rabbie
Burns (1759–1796), whose favourite food it was. In his poor
days it would be cheap to prepare, and so, more or less, a regular
dish. (It may not perhaps be a coincidence, but Burns' date,
25th January, is known in the English calendar as the Conversion
of St. Paul on the Damascus road.)

If you look at your cookery book, it's 10-to-1 you will never
see the recipe for haggis unless you turn to the index for the
chapter 'Cooking for the courageous'—the dish that someone
said contributed to the decline and fall of the Roman Empire!
Earlier, I hinted that a number of people had no idea what a
haggis is at all. Some think of it as a kind of rugged Highland
dog, and if you got two of different sex, you could start breeding
haggis! Some imagine it to be a boy's name, Haggis, Hamish or
what-not. Some believe it is hand-reared and home-fed. I've
even heard it thought to be some kind of manure! or an animal
whose outside legs are longer than its inside, so that it can run
around the hills easily. Och aye! To put the ignoramus wise,
I would say it consists of sheep's heart, liver, suet, oatmeal,
onions, soup-stock and seasoning; and when sold in shops, it
is sewn up into a sheep's stomach in the manner of sausage skins.

Of late there has become at Cannes, South of France, a special

Scottish Festival to coincide as near as possible with Burns' birthday, at which many Scottish dignitaries attend, from Ministers of State down to Lord Provosts and Bailies; and the haggis is then generally of giant size. Yes, on such occasions the haggis graces tables the world o'er. Although the word 'haggis' (from HAG: to chop) is thought to be exclusively Scottish, it seems the Scandinavians were making a similar concoction long, long ago. Who knows, but the Chinese first thought of it? but with the Lion rampant stamped on its casing—like our familiar shop eggs—when it travels abroad and reaches India, Malaya, Australia, Peru and Ghana (and all the other places where it has gone 'away from it all') it passes purely and solely as 'all Scotch'.

As to its making: you wash and boil the heart and liver for a while; then mince it finely, put everything into a large bowl —the chopped suet, oatmeal, chopped onions, soup stock, salt and pepper—covered over with grease-proof paper. Put into a large enough pan of water and steam for two or three hours until the mixture is dryish and crumbly. Serve hot, steaming hot, with swedes and mashed potatoes. It is eaten, not with a spoon and fork as though it were curry, but with the usual knife and fork; not, may I say, by brandishing a claymore or a skean-dhu at it, for a haggis is a temperamental exclusive morsel and quick to sense if you are acquaint with 'himself, himself'; just as a horse can judge if it has a novice astride its saddle. With a tot of whisky poured over it, you then feel you can call the Duke of Lonemore your uncle! Take courage in your hands and make a hearty meal of it, for a haggis respects courage. Haggis, the haggis, ranks as a V.I.P.—Very Important Pudding. As I have said, Rabbie Burns termed it 'Great Chieftain o' the puddin' race'; that turned its head and it became famous overnight.

There is on record a true case of a haggis being ordered from Scotland by an Ontario Burns' Club, and being interned by the Canadian Agricultural Department; the official reason given being that the haggis arrived without the Government seal, which every parcel of imported meat must have.

And yet another case, this time from Australia; a present sent from Edinburgh to a Scotch lassie there never reached its destination. A letter from the Adelaide Customs said it was not allowed into Australia, and consequently it was in quarantine, would be confiscated and destroyed. A similarly worded letter was sent her from the Health Department for Animals, 'Seized, and to be destroyed!' They must have a great fear of foot-and-mouth disease 'down-under'?

So English folk who thought, and think, a haggis is an animal, are not alone, are they?

The Medical Research Council, in all seriousness, have had 'the haggis' under test recently and pronounced judgement on it, that it was 'no obscene bag of rubbish'. Just that. Except they add a corollary to the effect that it is 'only slightly inferior in food value to fish and chips'. What cheek! What consternation *this* will cause up in Wester Ross, to be sure. Of course, they are silent about its taste; and after all does not taste—in life's mild enjoyment—sometimes overrule 'vitaministic' values? If it's 'a meal you want, then it's haggis you want' is a bright and snappy slogan, despite its vitamin content or its basic formula.

Should you be a laird and own a few thousand acres of moorland, then you would kill a stag and eat deer haggis.

To the native Scot, the haggis is akin to porridge. He has been happily brought into this world and subsequently reared in this land on these two fundamental dishes, which many term as succulent. Those who look askance on the dish, scorn the dish, ridicule the dish may—for all we know—do so in envy? Whatever is said for or against it (Medical Council included), nothing will shake the real Scotsman—or me, for that matter— in being a staunch addict of this grand onion-flavoured oatmeal, with all its chopped-up what-you-may-call-it ingredients, steamingh ot, with its modicum of 100% proof Highland Malt Scotch Whisky from Glenlivet distillery (8 years old, no less) poured over it, with reverence, precision and great precaution against spilling even one precious drop on this one precious dish. I would almost go so far as to say, 'A haggis a day, keeps the doctor away!'

Och, aye; the snow is on the bens, the haggis is on the boil, and the hunter home from the hills. At times it rains; but who cares, for a rainbow curves all over the village and over the bay, its colours reflected in the sky and on the snow-capped peaks— a wonderful background to the mountains of Torridon 'that sweep down to the sea'; far more majestic than 'the mountains of Mourne that sweep down to the sea'; for they are grandeur personified looking outward from Gairloch.

Yes, the haggis is in Dan the butcher's shop; the venison is dressed looking tempting to buy; and a nice juicy trout looks up at you from its cold, cold slab—with cod-like eyes.

All told, you murmur *Slàinte Mhath*! For indeed there is really nothing more appropriate you *can* murmur!

In considering the making of the haggis, and indeed of most of the Scottish meals, soups, stews, puddings, shortbread, pancakes, scones and so forth, there is a great amount of time and preparation involved; and with but few hands the kitchen is a busy place. There is always something boiling or bubbling on the fire or cooker, even though it be only the kettle; for ever spouting steam. Take the case of soup—Scotch broth; most of these Highland housewives are monarchs of the stock-pot. Soup is *really* soup in Scotland; none of your watery consommé concoction. I have seen a whole side of brisket, or a chicken, in the stock-pot, lying snug and bubbling amongst a score of different vegetables, nicely cut up and diced 'intil 't'; and my! the wholesome smell of it all. And an old dodge of putting a dessertspoonful of sugar in, to bring out the flavour more. Yes, here, in the Wild West, you get soup made, watched over and nursed, like a young mother gloats over her first-born child; soup unknown anywhere else in this country—perhaps in the world. Soup, the whole(some) soup, and nothing but the soup! Scotch broth indeed, stiff with vegetables, so stiff that the spoon almost stands upright in it without any means of visible support! Tell me of any other place you find this, but up in the Highlands?

As I have said, you need patience and leisure in a Scottish kitchen in the preparing of these true Highland dishes. And when you've tasted them, and had second helpings as is more than likely, will you *still* want to 'get away from it all' to Tokyo or Patagonia? Just send me a postcard to let me know! Remember, though, newly-baked pancakes and warm flowery scones, you feel you want to cuddle, are *always* ready waiting for you in the Scottish Highlands.

*   *   *

It may serve of use to our visiting friends to list a few special sporting dates, so they may be acquainted as to what they can

look forward to, at various times of the year. There is good
fishing of some kind available every month of the year in Scotland; and game fishing—for salmon, sea trout or brown trout
—can be enjoyed at some place or other for more than ten months
of the year.

January	1	Haggis season opens!
December	31	„　„　closes; an all-the-year round love!
February	11	Salmon fishing begins
November	1	„　„　ends
March	15	Trout fishing begins
October	6	„　„　ends
August	12	Grouse shooting starts
December	10	„　„　ends
September	1	Partridge shooting begins
February	1	„　„　ends
October	1	Pheasant shooting begins
February	1	„　„　ends
September	1	Deer stalking (for stags) starts
October	12	„　„　„　ends
November	10	Deer stalking (for hinds) begins
March	31	„　„　„　ends

May (the last week): Skye Week.
June: Skye Provincial Gaelic Mod.
July (3rd Thursday): Highland Games, Tobermory, Mull.
August: Gairloch Sheep Dog Trials.
August (1st week): Oban Regatta Week.
August (last week): Skye Highland Games, Portree.
September (2nd week): Oban Highland Games.
December 31 'Hogmanay', when all true Scots bring in the
　　New Year with customary high 'spirits'; and visit friends
　　('first-footing').

*　　*　　*

　　Sport in the Highlands! and who's not to say the Highlander
is not a 'sport' in trying to keep up-to-date? Brassieres for cows
is the newest thing down on the croft; and these come from a
Dutch factory, and are made of nylon and stretch cotton. Its
purpose is to support the swollen udders of cows in calf. So
now you know!

CHAPTER 12

ROSS-SHIRE NIGHTINGALES

'A NIGHTINGALE sang in Berkeley Square ...'
This was a touching love-song of World War II period; of the loves brought together during the bombing raids on London, and during lulls in the summer nights, there would suddenly be heard a nightingale singing sweetly in the shade, when everything else was seemingly at rest. There were a great many American air-force boys stationed around Grosvenor and Berkeley Squares.

This chapter, however, has nothing to do with the song, or the small bird that sings at night, but of people ... nightingales of sweetness and devotion; of the Florence Nightingale character, to wit.

Florence Nightingale (1820–1910), an English nurse who did yeoman service in the Crimean War—a heroine in fact—and whose system, in principle, has since been universally adopted, and who received the Order of Merit in 1907, is surely a name that conjures up the best of our ideals.

In 1853, when England, France and Turkey fought Russia, and British troops landed in the Crimea and won the battle of the Alma river, the cry went out from the sick and wounded 'why have we no sisters of mercy?' In short, Florence Nightingale assembled nurses and equipment and went out there into a veritable Hell of chaos; this soft-voiced women with only the love of humanity as her reason and purpose. Not only was she an organiser, purveyor and schoolmistress, she was a nurse dressing wounds and comforting soldiers, and assisting at operations, hours at a stretch, with an utter disregard of contagion.

She was known as the soldiers' angel, and when the war was over, and she returned to England a weakened woman, a fund was started for a school for nursing, and in one year a sum of £50,000 was raised; and it was then, in 1859, Florence Nightingale began, at St. Thomas's Hospital in London, the very first training school for nurses.

That school reformed the so-called hospitals of England, and, indeed, of the whole world. Her life of 90 years was full of action, despite the fact that for some fifty years she was a sick person.

Now, in Gairloch, I record with all honour and respect, there lived—until her death on 2nd October, 1962, aged 77 years—a similar soft-voiced dedicated woman born and bred in Gairloch, and, after a life-time of nursing service, lived in a small cottage that veritably touched the edge of the sea, devoting the closing years of her super-active life to looking after and caring for her two invalid sisters, one of whom had been bed-ridden for many years.

I call her 'My Lady Alice'.

She was born, as I have said, in Strath, Gairloch, in her aunt's house, a small cottage, *Beul-na-Mara*, Gaelic for 'mouth of the sea'. When in her teens, her mind turned to nursing; in fact even to this day, many or most of the young girls in Wester Ross take up nursing as a career—far more, I believe, than in any other part of Scotland. Nursing and the sea appear to be the call of the women and menfolk. In due course, towards the close of the 19th century she left home and went to train at St. Marylebone and St. Thomas's Hospitals in London, closely following in the steps of Florence herself. Whilst there, she was not long in showing her outstanding capabilities, not only as a nurse but as an organiser. A 'Florence Nightingale' indeed.

Time marched on, and soon the First World War loomed ahead and, in 1914, having come into personal contact with many Harley Street doctors, she headed a team of workers and was drafted out abroad; Italy—who was then our ally (in which country Dr. Castellani's name comes to my mind, as he was many years previously in Colombo and the doctor to my Company there, and who became world-famous in respect of his discoveries of new serum to combat diseases caused by the ravages of war)—Salonica, Greece and up to the Austrian border; and in many instances she and her team actually were in some of the districts in advance of our troops, preparing, ordering; for ever watchful.

When the war finished in 1918, she returned to England and was fittingly honoured and decorated by King George V himself (and Queen Mary) with the Royal Red Cross medal, the military counterpart of the British Red Cross—a beautifully designed medallion and ribbon. She also prized a scroll, personally signed by Queen Alexandra.

But this was only the beginning of 'my fair lady', as her attention began to focus on the Far East, and for over fifteen years, from 1923, she was in Colombo, Ceylon, where I first came to know her. We were close friends, relaxing in our odd hours by golfing, dancing, dining and so forth. Of course, we were both much younger then. However, though young, we had a modicum of reason and a sense of proportion; she in her sphere and myself in mine. During those years she was the propelling figure of the Kandy hospital—Kandy, the old capital of Ceylon, 2000 feet above sea level, a real jewel, set amidst a semi-tropical background, and which in the Second World War was to become Louis Mountbatten's Eastern headquarters—then on to the hospital at Nuwara Eliya (pronounced *new-railia*), a fascinating health resort 6000 feet up, with mountainous scenery and a climate very like Scotland. Later she was sought after to become the matron of the extensive General Hospital in Colombo itself, and finally the supreme head of the De Soysa hospital, also in Colombo; a hospital devoted to sick native children and women—Ceylonese, Tamils and Indians. Here she worked wonders and was looked upon as the 'Great White Chieftainess', literally transforming the whole institution. Strange to relate, one of the leading doctors who formed her team in Italy eventually found his way to, and set up practice in Colombo, and we three became very drawn to each other.

Eventually she retired early in 1939 (two years after I had shaken the tropical dust off my feet) to live in peace and enjoyment at the old wee cottage at Gairloch again, and where the sea still lapped the front-door steps; and the mountains of Torridon, in a sense, swept down to the sea, like the mountains of Mourne.

Did I say retired? Only a few months later, the Second World War broke loose, and again, at her advanced age, she volunteered for active war work and was drafted to Devonport Military Hospital. But not for long there, for the Scottish Department of Health, St. Andrew's House, Edinburgh, which was virtually in charge of all nursing arrangements in Scotland, soon claimed her, and she was to be a dominating figure once more in Scottish nursing history.

She was appointed head of the hospital that was made available by the Ministry of Works in the huge mansion of 'Mellerstain' in Berwickshire—situated 6 miles north of Kelso and 10 miles south of Lauder—the stately home of the Earl and Countess of Haddington, where she was the king-pin for six years, 1943–1949. Whilst at Mellerstain she was sent off at times to deputise at various other war hospitals, where the matron might happen to be away ill and so forth. Such places included Stirling and Killin, where near by at the Duke of Breadalbane's large and sumptious Taymouth Castle which had been converted into a special hospital, patients came under her charge.

Then in 1949 she really *did* retire, four years after the war had ended, mark you, although the authorities were loth for her to do so; and despite her countless activities, as well as fifteen years in the sweltering heat of the tropics—for Colombo is only 7 degrees off the equator, and with the constant humidity of a green-house, it certainly does take toll of one's stamina and particularly so of a woman's—she still remained active, though living on 'borrowed time', and daily cared for her two dear and near ones.

When she left Ceylon she visualised and planned quiet travels to Scandinavia, America, Canada, Australia and so on and so forth, as she wished to see even more of the world as well as enjoy her well-earned leisure years. But though we may plan, we cannot foretell.

In September 1962 her sister, who had been ill for so many years, died. The week-end following the funeral 'My Lady Alice' suddenly took a stroke, was rushed to hospital in Inverness, but never recovered. She was laid to rest on Friday, 5th October 1962. The hundreds who attended her funeral, that cold October day at the Gairloch Free Kirk, testified to her virtues and to the great love the village had for her. I, too, was there, being privileged to take a cord of the coffin as it was borne from the Kirk to the cemetery a quarter of a mile away. Poor 'Lady Alice'. I shed tears in remembering those Ceylon days when all was so well with us both. But such is Life, and we have no option but to accept what lies before us.

Hers was a life of devotion. Knowing her so well, it is no small wonder that I especially—and with continued sorrow—write these lines in remembrance. I question if many reading this can even touch the fringe of such a dedicated life; a life of self-denial.

Today a figure of Florence Nightingale stands on a lofty pedestal in London. Surely it would not be out of place that alongside such an illustrious woman should be recorded the name of 'My Lady Alice of Strath'?

Her truest monument, however, is not one modelled and set up by hand.

It is to be found in the realms of unrelentless energy and aid to the suffering which, in times of nation-wide trouble, the world opens its arms for, and not in vain; namely the noble profession of Nursing—and written with a capital N.

* * *

This brings me to yet more of the 'Nightingale' spirit, namely the care and attention given the old folk at the many homes for the aged dotted around the country; but only sparsely dotted, I am afraid. We could do with many, many more.

In Strath, Gairloch, there happens to be one such home, named 'Strathburn'. This home was opened by Sir John Stirling, County Council convener, who is related to the Mackenzies—the Lairds and owners of Gairloch—on 12th May 1960.

The opening was quite a signal occasion for Gairloch, and colour was added to it by a notable piper—Alex MacRae, a member of the Duke of Atholl's Highland Army, who was Gairloch born and bred—who came up from Blair Atholl, where he has a business, specially to 'play his pipes' at the luncheon and at the opening ceremony. The luncheon was given at the hotel to quite a large gathering of those who were closely connected with this new institution, and who had come a distance. When the luncheon was ready Alex piped the guests from the lounge into the dining-room playing 'The Mackenzie Highlanders', and whilst the main course was being served, marched round the tables playing a selection of marches; and before finishing stood in a recess and played a Strathspey Reel.

At the Home, 2 miles away in Strath, after Sir John had declared its opening, Alex played an appropriate slow march— a Gaelic melody called 'Mo Dhachaidh' (my home), the translation into English of the commencing Gaelic words of the song being 'Sing cheerily, couthily, canty and free; Oh this is the hour of sweet solace to me . . .'

A word, in passing, of the Atholl Highlanders—the only private army in Britain—may not be out of place. The Duke of Atholl lives at Blair Castle, Blair Atholl, situated 7 miles from Pitlochry and before you start the climb to Dalnaspidal (1500 feet), to Dalwhinnie, Newtonmore, Kingussie and on to Inverness.

The Atholl Highlanders were first raised in 1839 as the personal bodyguard of the Duke. The army remained an illegal force until 1844 when Queen Victoria and Prince Albert visited Blair Castle. For three weeks a detachment of Highlanders kept guard over the Royal couple, and the Queen was so impressed with their efficiency that she presented them with a set of Colours the following year. The regiment does not appear in the Army List; it has no barracks, nobody gets paid and its last proper parade was in 1913. The army has never fired a single defensive shot in the line of duty. Its only purpose is as ceremonial guard to the Duke of Atholl at Blair Castle, which has been the fortress home of the earls and dukes of Atholl for 700 years.

Membership is strictly by personal invitation of the 30-year-old Duke. Officer rank is an honorary commission bestowed on family friends of the Murray clan; lower ranks are usually drawn from employees on the Blair Atholl Estate. The private army boasts one V.C., a D.S.C. and a D.F.C. Our Alex named, in particular, was, during the last war, H.Q. Coy. piper in the 1st Battalion of the Black Watch. He has been a piper in the Atholl Highlanders since 1938, and is a corporal. He and the others play round the Duke's table, usually at Christmas and New Year or at other times when His Grace's friends are staying with him. Altogether, at the moment, there are seven pipers and a pipe-major and they play as His Grace's pipers on special occasions throughout the county of Perthshire. The pipe-major, the Duke's ex-head-gamekeeper, is 75, and has been a member of the Highlanders for forty years. Another has been in the regiment since 1911.

The 'Strathburn' Home has thirteen bedrooms and can accommodate twenty-one people in all, and is exceptionally well planned; everything being thought of to ensure the maximum efficiency and the maximum of comfort with the minimum of trouble. The staff consists of a matron (a fully qualified trained nurse who left a Glasgow hospital as ward sister to come here), a nurse auxiliary, cook (and a very good baker too, for I can testify to her scones and pancakes the day I had tea at Strath-burn), kitchen and bedroom (ward) maids and of course Duncan, the 'man about the house'.

The staff quarters with their own dining- and lounge-rooms are beautifully fitted out, just as the Matron's private suite is so fitted. The general building comprising the big lounge (and radio), smoke-room for the men, dining-room, luggage-room—this latter particularly systematically arranged—and other minor rooms, are 'polished to the nines', and I felt I should have brought my slippers with me to change into as I stepped from the wet muddy pavement into the delightful warmth of this 'haven'. I talked with many of the residents, all of whom had a smile of contentment, and who went out of their way to say how happy they—and everyone—were. In the ironing-room, I spoke to an old lady who must have been nearer 90 than 80 years of age, who daily gives a hand operating the electric pressing/ironing machine and she said she 'loved being here and giving a hand'; in all this I felt I might have been Prince Philip himself paying an official visit. It was most touching.

The architects have certainly 'gone to town' on this job at 'Strathburn', and the one who designed the kitchen comes in for my loudest praise. The Home caters for those living in Wester Ross, and entry—when there happens to be a vacancy—is per agreement of the House Committee-members who meet at intervals under the chairmanship of Gairloch's Church of Scotland's minister.

There is, unfortunately, no sick bay attached to this Home, or allowed for in any way; the matron has certainly made use of a little chiropody room, turning it into a glorified first-aid room, but this is far from sufficient and I think when such Homes are built they should be designed to include a proper clinical bay and staff it accordingly; for it should be remembered we are 80 miles away from Inverness, the nearest hospital. I am sure our Welfare State could afford this essential, for it certainly cannot be classified as a 'luxury' addition.

As I remarked earlier, the country can do with hundreds more of these Old Folk's Homes. Modern medicine continues to increase the number of years old people can expect to live; but when will we strike the solution of making those extra years happy ones? Our population is getting older. Fifty years ago, elderly people represented only 7 per cent of the population; today they represent 15 per cent—more than double. I am afraid we have little reason to be proud of our treatment of the elderly, seeing to it they are happy in the spending of their remaining days in peace and quiet comfort, but rather we should hang our heads in shame! In other countries the elderly are venerated. Here the fate of many is to be shoved around from one son or daughter to the next, like a pawn in a game of chess. Those who, whether they be individuals or Councils, are engaged in this work and programme of looking after, and catering for, the old folk, are always spoken of in a glib manner as doing a 'great work'. Well, how about joining in the greatness?

We must accept the fact that it is impossible to stay young in years. Time will not stand still and we all grow old. We are not as active at 60 as we were at 30 or even 40 years of age; and there is nothing to be gained in seeking to hide the fact. We must needs go slower as the years advance. There is much wisdom in the words of Old Father Thames who 'never seems to hurry, but gets there just the same'. Youth is not mainly a matter of age, but of the spirit. Many older folk with a youthful spirit will gladden anybody. To be youthful in spirit in one's old age, is to have faith in something, an enthusiasm in something that makes life worth living; not to get stale by being lost in one's own littleness. Time will then not drag, for it will pass all too rapidly; and I write from experience, and as Coleridge said 'experience can be likened to the light on the stern of a ship at sea, for it only sheds light on the track that has been passed over'. To have the joy of helping where help is needed is one of life's greatest satisfactions. We must not get bogged down in narrow ideas; if we do, life will be stunted. Our horizons need to be kept wide. Friendship and love know no selfish barriers. We might well ponder over what St. Paul means when he wrote, 'though our outward nature is wasting away, our inner nature is being renewed each day'.

The French have many apt sayings; but, of course, the French language is sheer music. As to old age there is the beautifully worded saying, and I make no excuse in giving it here: *si la vieillesse pour les gens ordinaires, c'est la décadence; pour les hommes d'esprit, c'est l'apothéose* ('if for ordinary people, old age is decadence, for men of genius it is apotheosis (deification)'); the word *esprit* in this sense meaning brains, cleverness or brilliance.

In the Old Testament days, the Jewish race placed old age into three categories. They said from 60 to 70 years was only the beginning of old age; the next ten years, 70 to 80 was regarded with 'white-hair' reverence; whilst from 80 years onwards till one's death, THE BOOK has it as saying 'well-stricken in years'. Old age to them was looked upon as grandeur. Both Aaron and Moses at the time of their deaths went *up* the hill, not *down*.

* * *

It is not an over-statement, then, to say I look upon the Matron and her staff of the Old Folk's Home in Gairloch as being 'Nightingales' ... neither should we overlook the district nurses in all these Highland parishes—further 'nightingales'— and their little black bags, constantly out and about looking after, and administering to, the sick and needy in their homes, working with, and under, the resident doctor of the particular parish area. All these local doctors and nurses have much to do, and are on call throughout the twenty-four hours of the day; as is the ambulance driver taking any serious cases to hospital in Inverness, 80 miles away.

So up in this so-called Wild-West country, far from up-to-date hospitals, clinics and the like, there are to be found many 'Florences'. All such, with the 'vet' as well, constitute a praiseworthy team—a team the inhabitants in all these scattered villages rely upon in times of sickness and distress.

And they do not rely in vain.

Yes, one of the most distressing things about old age to many is its loneliness. Would we could summon into effect the words of Joel 2: 25, 'I will restore to you the years that the locust hath eaten'. We need companionship, and above all *love* during the days of our years upon this earth. Old age has its perils; we should not think dangers are over for us. Moses the meekest man in all the earth, spoke unadvisedly near the close of his life. In consequence, he *saw*, but was not *allowed* to enter the promised land.

CHAPTER 13

SKYE AND FLORA

SKYE and Flora; Flora Macdonald of the 1745 Jacobite rebellion and Bonnie Prince Charlie; Flora, the most illustrious woman the Highlands and islands have produced.

Why, it may be asked, should a special chapter be devoted to Skye, when this book is mostly concerning the Gairloch district of Wester Ross, and 'sunset' on the Gair Loch?

It is a question that can be simply answered, for I look out on to Skye as I write; to the Cuillins and the 'Old Man of Storr'—a conspicuous obelisk of black trap-rock rising sheer 160 feet high; the Storr rock itself rising to a height of 2400 feet above sea-level. It seems only a stone's throw away; and appropriately enough my house is called 'Skye View'. Besides this, many visitors as a rule coming or going from here, 'take in' Skye in their itinerary; and a very pleasing three or four days may be spent in touring that island. Another island that I like is MULL, which is the third largest island of the Isles (Lewis and Harris, with Stornoway as its chief town, being the largest —the Long Isle; it is in the county of Ross-shire); Mull is in Argyll; Skye in Inverness-shire. Maybe Mull is becoming more into prominence now, since there is more nobility associated with it than in any other part of Britain. From a 'Who's Who' of Mull, one can say there are almost forty notables having houses or landed interests in that small island, ranging from the Duke of Argyll, to Brig.-Generals, Lieut.-Colonels, Majors, Viscounts, Captains, Sirs and so forth. Mull (and Iona) is easily accessible on one's way up north, from Oban; merely a 2½-hour journey by MacBrayne's fine steamer, the *Claymore*, to Tobermory, a beautiful little spot. Only 28 miles by sea, and as a rule the trip is a sheltered one, for the sea passage is almost land-locked. Perhaps I like Mull, because I found Fiona there!

But we must get back to Skye; for there is seldom a day in looking out and seeing Skye from my house, but my mind turns to Flora Macdonald, the preserver of Prince Charles Edward Stuart, who was 'not only a Hero, but a Great Prince'. This eulogy is recorded by a Mr. John Cameron, Presbyterian Preacher and Chaplain at Fort William, in his writings of 1746; who went on to add that the Prince submitted with patience to his adverse fortune, was cheerful, and frequently desired those that were with him to be so. He was cautious when in the greatest danger, never at a loss in resolving what to do, with uncommon fortitude. He regretted more the distress of those who suffered for adhering to his cause than the hardships and dangers to which he was hourly exposed. It was said of Prince Charlie that all Europe was astonished at the greatness of his enterprise, for though Alexander and other heroes had conquered kingdoms with inferior armies, he was the only one who ever engaged in such an attempt without any.

*   *   *

'*Eilean A'cheo fo Sgail Nam Beann Mor*'—or 'The Isle of Mist under the shadow of great mountains'—that is the Isle of Skye described in the native Gaelic language of its people. The late King George VI called Skye 'the isle of kind and loyal hearts'.

Almost the whole of the north-west of Scotland (and the many islands) is charged with history; but with Skye, not only history, but highly romantic history too; that and the Cuillins with their practically world-known jagged knife-like peaks climbing upwards to the clouds, never dropping below 2500 feet. There are some 15-odd peaks in the Skye Cuillins over 3000 feet in height; and surrounded by a bodyguard of lesser peaks they form a unique panorama unparalleled anywhere in the British Isles. Corries and wild mountain passes abound. The highest is Sgurr Alasdair (3250 feet), ascended from the wild but beautiful Glen Brittle. Not far distant, at the head of Loch Scavaig, is the most weird and awesome loch that any country can boast of— Loch Coruisk. Sir Walter Scott immortalised it in *The Lord of the Isles*; and on a rock near by, chiselled out his initials. Loch Coruisk has been extolled by artists and poets alike. Its waters are dark and deep. All around are the grim Cuillin mountains; and here desolation reigns supreme; desolation upon desolation.

You cannot reach Skye by either rail or air. You *must* travel 'over the sea' to Skye; a beautiful island about 50 miles long and about half that across.

It was first mentioned by Ptolemy in the 2nd century. St. Columba arrived in Skye in A.D. 565. Danes and Norsemen ravaged most of the Western Isles in their time. In 1098 the

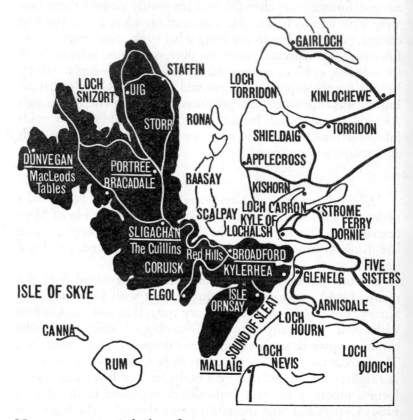

Norsemen occupied Skye for a considerable period; but in the 12th century the son of Gillebride, Celtic Lord of Argyll, turned them out and became First Lord of the Isles. His grandson, Donald, was the first of the Clan Donald, and thereafter the MacDonalds, MacLeods and MacKinnons ruled Skye, being independent of the Scottish Crown. After King James V's visit to Skye in 1536, the Skye chiefs gave their support to the House of Stuart. They fought for King Charles II in 1651, and for King James VIII in 1715. When Prince Charlie raised his standard

at Glenfinnan on 19th August 1745, he counted on the support
of the Skye chiefs. But only the aged chief of MacKinnon was
loyal. Later on he paid the penalty, for his lands were forfeited
and his Clan scattered to the ends of the earth.

Except in the south of the island, Skye is really treeless. It
enjoys, like Mull, very mild winters; the islanders are mostly
crofters, some engaged in weaving beautiful cloth, sweaters and
the like, at Portnalong on the west side, even to this day.

The usual gateway to Skye is across the ferry from Kyle of
Lochalsh—the railway terminus completed in 1898—to Kyleakin,
a matter of minutes only. From London one travels from Euston
via Perth and Inverness to Kyle; from King's Cross, via Edinburgh (or Glasgow), Fort William to Mallaig.

This latter town, a fishing and curing port mainly, is on the
mainland, and one can now take a Government-chartered vehicle
ferry (which carries 52 cars and about 600 passengers) across to
Armadale, Southern Skye, where at this point of disembarkation
there is a fine, large pier. The cost of taking your car across is
30/– single fare (according to size) and passengers 4/–.

Other new car-ferries opened in 1964 are from Oban–
Craignure on Mull (50/– and 5/– passengers); and from Uig,
North Skye to Tarbert (Harris) and Lochmaddy (North Uist)
65/– and 12/6 passengers. The journey Mallaig/Armadale takes
20 minutes; Oban/Craignure, 40 minutes; and over the Minch
from Uig, roughly 2 hours.

Mallaig is approached by a lovely run of some 50 miles,
shortly after leaving Fort William. The road follows the railway
closely all the way, and is almost unmatched for its combination
of mountains, moor, loch, glen and coast scenery. You also pass
Glenfinnan (aforementioned), and the monument—now vested
in the National Trust—was erected in 1815, where Prince Charles
raised his father's (James VIII's) standard that fateful day of
19th August 1745, at a rally of the Cameron and MacDonald
Clans, under Lochiel and Tullibardine. He had come to remove
George II from the throne and place his father there—as had
his father tried thirty years before.

Armadale, just named, has a fine castle, the modern Gothic
seat of Lord MacDonald, open to the public during the summer
season. Armadale is called 'the Garden of Skye'; its southern
exposure and protection by the near mainland, and the lofty isles

of Eigg, Rum and Canna save it somewhat from the ravages of the winter gales; and there is a 'Riviera' feeling in the air on a soft summer's day.

The little village itself is clothed in tall trees, interspersed with the ubiquitous birch, giving it a very English look along the narrow roadway.

Journeying inland, up to Broadford, and making for Portree—'the King's Port', the name being a corruption of 'Port-an-Righ', a title given when King James V with his fleet anchored there in 1540—capital and only town really of Skye, you pass Knock, where the remains of the old castle of the Lords of the Isles refuse to surrender to time or tempest. This whole area is known as Sleat; 'brindled Sleat of the beautiful women'.

The quickest route of course is by Kyle of Lochalsh ferry; in 1964 these spacious ferry-boats took 200,000 passengers and 73,000 motor vehicles. Altogether, from all quarters, 220,000 people crossed 'over the sea to Skye'.

Coming up from the south by the Caledonian Canal, one invariably takes the 'Road to the Isles', turning off at Invermoriston on the canal; and to Lochalsh it is 56 miles. This road was originally constructed by General Wade. For myself, I consider a prettier way is to turn off the Canal lower down, 7 miles before Fort Augustus, at Invergarry, taking that road, meeting the one from Invermoriston at Clunie Inn, and carrying on to Shiel Bridge at the head of Loch Duich—surrounded by the 'Five Sisters of Kintail', which form part of the Kintail estate, a National Trust Property, of 15,000 acres.

Near Shiel Bridge was fought the battle of Glenshiel on 11th June 1719 in which General Wightman's government troops defeated 2000 Highlanders—mostly MacRae's and Mackenzie's. The Highlanders were led by the Earl of Seaforth and assisted by a few hundred Spaniards who had landed from Loch Alsh from two frigates; the remains of a storm-tossed fleet of thirty vessels sent from Cadiz by Cardinal Alberoni, to help the cause of the Old Pretender. The Spaniards surrendered, but the Scots escaped to the hills.

Travelling on to Dornie, a magnificent run, you then look down on the ancient Eilean Donan Castle—the Earls of Seaforth—which in 1932 was restored by the MacRae's. The Castle, on an island connected with the mainland by a stone bridge (but it can be reached by the shore at low tide) is a striking picture, set in magnificent surroundings. Once a stronghold of the Mackenzies, it was held by Spanish forces when British warships destroyed it in 1719.

Thence onwards passing Balmacara, where you can see the Cuillins rising grey in the distance—over the waters of Loch Alsh, you see the Sound of Sleat weaving a sea-quilt of green and purple, and you speed up and over the hill to Kyle of Lochalsh, where, if you stretch out your arm, you feel you can almost touch Skye.

As we are at Lochalsh and before taking the crossing over the ferry to Skye it is fitting to refer to this busy port as well as making mention of a very short, but pleasant, detour to Plockton.

The great Ptolemy, geographer of Alexandria, Egypt, appears to have recorded the existence of Lochalsh as far back as the 2nd century.

Lochalsh originally formed part of Argyll (not Ross-shire as today) along with the neighbouring parish of Kintail; and early in the 18th century one half of that parish was split into the parish of Glenshiel and the 'Five Sisters'—those notable mountains above Loch Duich—were transferred by Parliament from Kintail to Glenshiel. Be that as it may, they are still known and spoken of as the 'Five Sisters of Kintail'.

In the 1200's Lochalsh was held by the Clan Matheson, whilst Kintail was inhabited by the Mackenzies. For many centuries, rivalry and intrigue existed, and in the early 1600's, Lochalsh was dominated by the Mackenzies of Kintail. Eventually Lochalsh came into the hands of Sir Alex. Matheson, Baronet of Lochalsh.

Early in the first quarter of 1800, Matheson went out as a young man to India, joining the firm of Jardine, Matheson & Co. —a firm which expanded and still functions as such, but more particularly so in Hong Kong.

In 1801, the last Lord Seaforth sold Lochalsh to Sir Hugh Innes, whose descendant, Mrs. Lillingstone, became owner. She in turn sold out to Mr. Alex. Matheson.

Elsewhere I refer to the extraordinary prophecies of the Brahan Seer (born early in 1600, be it noted) and in connection with Lochalsh, I give the following prediction he made some 200 years before the event; viz.: 'The day will come when the Mackenzies will lose all their possessions in Lochalsh, after which

H

it will fall into the hands of an Englishman, who shall be distinguished by great liberality to his people, and lavish expenditure of money. He will have one son and two daughters; and after his death, the property will revert to the Mathesons, its former possessors, who will build a Castle on Druim-a-Dubh, at Balmacarra.'

So much for the prediction.

Well, the late Mr. Lillingstone was an Englishman. He was truly distinguished for his kindness and liberality; and he had a son and two daughters. After the death of his wife, the whole of Lochalsh came, as noted above, into the hands of Alex. Matheson, so fulfilling the prediction. A castle was built, but at Duncraig, not so very far, really, from Balmacarra.

I give yet another and astounding prediction by the Seer concerning Lochalsh, viz.: 'A Lochalsh woman shall weep over the grave of a Frenchman in the burying-place of Lochalsh'. Here again a native woman of Lochalsh did marry a French footman, who died and was interred in the burying-ground of Lochalsh, thus leaving the widow to mourn over his grave. Truly extraordinary. In those far-off days it should be remembered that a Frenchman in Lochalsh, and a Frenchman whom a Highland woman would marry and mourn over in the Brahan Seer's day, was a totally different set-up from the present day.

Reverting to Matheson and his voyage to India, he returned after about fifteen years to his native Highlands. He spent money in improvements of Lochalsh and other lands in Ross-shire, building Duncraig Castle, near Plockton. Since his death in 1886, the estate naturally changed ownership on several occasions. The present baronet is General Sir Torquhil Matheson who formerly resided at Duirinish Lodge, but now lives in Camberley Surrey. The proprietors of Lochalsh are the National Trust.

The population of Lochalsh, given at the last census in 1961 is 1800. Just over 150 years ago it was 1300. The population of the three parishes of Lochalsh, Glenshiel and Kintail in 1961 was 2264.

The railway was firstly laid only as far as Strome ferry—on the south bank; boats sailing up Loch Carron connected with the railway, taking and bringing passengers to and from Skye and Stornoway.

It was only in 1898 that the old Highland railway was extended to Kyle itself. Here again I record another remarkable prediction of the Brahan Seer's, viz.: 'The day will come when long strings of carriages without horses shall run between Dingwall and Inverness, and more wonderful still, between Dingwall and the Isle of Skye'. Over two centuries later, that prophecy was fulfilled. Truth is stranger than fiction, to be sure.

This train journey is as picturesque as motoring, for always there appear many, and varied, scenic vistas as the Iron Horse rounds the several bends. One moment one may be looking at the majestic Cuillins; another, back at Loch Carron and the mountains of Applecross; and again at one moment looking out to sea at the Isle of Raasay with its flat-topped, volcano-type, Dun Caan.

There is one main street in Lochalsh, as in a number of these Scottish towns and villages; and it is a narrow street as visitors will doubtless soon realise; and walk with caution in these days of such endless streams of motor-cars, lorries and buses.

As we pass out of the town (inland) approaching the next small scattered crofting village of Badicaul, we look out to sea to that imposing island, Crowlin. Then onwards following the main roadway we come to the village of Erbusaig (a 7th-century hamlet), another beauty spot of the west, where one can still see peat stacked near each cottage and sense the smell from peat-reeking chimneys. Shortly afterwards we take the minor road off to Plockton, passing another old-world village, Drumbuie, and then to Duirinish: situated on the river bank and overlooking this village is Duirinish Lodge, mentioned before. In the 1400's a serious dispute arose over Duirinish between the Chief of the Clan Matheson and Lord Sutherland; and in the resultant battle the latter was killed. Matheson was arrested, taken to Edinburgh, found guilty, and was beheaded.

Leaving Duirinish we soon reach Plockton, which long ago was engaged in boat-building. It is a charming, picture-postcard village, nestling on the sheltered inlet of Loch Carron. From the War Memorial on a hill above the village, one obtains a wonderful panoramic view of lochs and hills and of Duncraig Castle on the far horizon.

Plockton has a fine old school, and above the Gothic doorway the Arms of the Matheson's are carved.

We must needs return from Plockton the same road back to

Duirinish; then forking left we soon rejoin the main road to Lochalsh and/or Balmacara and beyond.

This little 'circular tour', Kyle–Plockton–Kyle, is but 12 miles and should certainly not be missed; for it is a 'must' for visitors to Kyle and Skye. Lochs, moors, heather and hills unaltered in their pristine glory.

The strait at Kyle is only half a mile wide. We cross at last to Skye and land at Kyleakin on the old stone pier that has withstood the storms of centuries.

As we land at Kyleakin, we see, on the left, the ruins of Castle Moyle, said to have been built by a Norse princess who married a Mackinnon. Mary was her name, and it was built to exact tolls from passing ships. The princess constantly pined for her Norwegian home, and when she died she was laid to rest on the mountain top, so that the winds from her homeland might waft gently over her grave. The name of the hill has been given Beinn na Caillich—The Old Woman's Mountain.

Now having reached Skye, with a population of 7765 according to the 1961 census, what briefly are we to put down in our diary that we must see, within a matter of a few days?

We go to Portree, the capital of the island, with a population of a little over 1000; its ancient name I have already given. It has a fishing fleet, woollen factory, large hospital and the mail steamer is domiciled there. It sails daily at 8 a.m., except Sundays, for Raasay, Kyle and Mallaig, returning each evening to the little port on which the village looks down from the surrounding heights; and this proves to be a most interesting day's outing.

Portree occupies a good position in Skye, as coach services radiate from there to all parts of the island. It was at Portree in one of the rooms of the Royal Hotel, facing the harbour, that Prince Charlie said goodbye to his preserver, Flora Macdonald, on 30th June 1746. In St. Columba's Episcopal Church there is a beautiful stained-glass window, dedicated to the memory of Flora Macdonald.

Taking at first a small tour north of Portree one goes by the Old Man of Storr, Staffin—where there is a youth hostel, bathing beach and cliff scenery. Overlooking here is the famous Quirang with the sharp needle-rock as well as other fantastic chaotic pinnacles. The Table of the Quirang is a grass-covered platform several hundred yards long.

Then on, passing Flodigary (where Flora Macdonald had her first home after her marriage) to the northerly township of Kilmaluag and the fragmentary ruins of Duntulm Castle, the ancient seat of the Macdonalds of the Isles. This has a wonderful site on a cliff overlooking the sea and must certainly have been impregnable as a fort from all attacks by sea. It is a fortress proclaiming its proud history, the joy and sorrow of the great chiefs and clan activity, the brilliant scene of war and peace. Near by is the ancient burial ground of Kilmuir, the 'Relig Mor' of the Macdonalds, where Flora Macdonald, that owner of a proud name in Clan and Highland history, is buried. A fierce wind generally blows over this old churchyard. Flora Macdonald's son erected a marble tombstone over her honoured grave. The slab of marble, conveyed by boat to Skye, was cracked in its journey but it was placed in position on 9th November 1871, but only after a few months was the stone base remaining. Pilgrims to the grave had taken away fragments of the stone—sacred relics from a dearly loved shrine. A large granite Celtic cross was then erected, but the Atlantic gales blew it down and shattered it in December 1873. But the head of the broken Cross still lies on her grave; and a restored Cross, erected in 1880, now exists as a landmark far out to sea.

The Cross bears the inscription:

Flora Macdonald,
Preserver of Prince Charles Edward Stuart.
Her name will be mentioned in history; and if courage and
fidelity be virtues, mentioned with Honour.

Across the grave is a granite slab bearing the following words:

Flora Macdonald
Born at Milton, South Uist, 1722
Died at Kingsburgh, Skye, March 1790.

Flora died after a lingering illness, aged 68 years, *not* at Kingsburgh as noted on the granite slab, but at Peinduin, which was a small village, now in ruins, about 1½ miles north of Kingsburgh House just over the river Hinnisdal, which flows into Loch Snizort Beag, where it joins Loch Snizort, and is about 5 miles south of Uig.

Her husband, Allan Macdonald (whom she married at Armadale, Sleat, Skye, on 6th November 1750), died two years later, 20th September 1792; and he too is buried with Flora in the Kingsburgh burial place at Kilmuir.

Near by is Port Kilbride, where Flora landed from Benbecula with the Prince, disguised as her maid, 'Betty Burke', on 29th June 1746; further on, coming southwards on this peninsula known as Trotternish, back to Portree, there is Kingsburgh House, where Prince Charlie had refuge and where in later years Boswell and Johnson were entertained by Flora and her husband on 12th September 1773. It is said Dr. Johnson occupied the very bed in which Prince Charles had slept.

From Kingsburgh we return on our tour to Portree; a run of some 40 miles.

The next tour (about 50 miles) would be from Portree to Dunvegan and back by Bracadale and Sligachan. Though these mileages sound insignificant compared with distances on the main motorways of Britain, yet owing to the narrowness of the roads, to say nothing of the hundreds of blind corners and bends, it takes one many hours to travel it all in comfort; besides there are so many stops to make; so much scenery to drink in and admire.

In this northern area of Skye there are great stretches of purple moorland, queer mountains and rocky cliffs; of hardy, kindly, quiet crofter folk and historical places of Clan and Scottish interest.

From Portree then, for Skeabost Bridge, and inner Loch Snizort; onwards skirting Loch Greshornish, another loch flowing into the bay of Loch Snizort. Further on, one comes to the Fairy Bridge, where one road going north serves the peninsula of Vaternish, via the village of Stein. This is a Norse name. Such characteristics are to be found in plenty in Skye (Skeabost and Carbost, to mention but two). King Haco and his fleet must have visited here as well as Kyleakin.

Carrying on northwards (it is well to see this Vaternish or Waternish area and then return to Fairy Bridge) the land grows fierce and wild. At Trumpan can be seen the ruins of the church that saw the massacre of the MacLeods by the Macdonalds of Uist, who in their turn suffered heavily when their boats could not escape because of the ebb-tide. It was in this parish that the MacLeods, sorely pressed in clan-battle, waved their fairy flag and saved the day. And as I soon record, the flag is to be seen this very day in Dunvegan Castle. It was originally captured from the Saracens and supposed to be possessed of special virtues.

Retracing the 10 miles back to the junction, the Fairy Bridge, we continue for a few miles when we reach Dunvegan, and its world-renowned castle lying at the top of the loch bearing its name. All roads lead to Dunvegan; the castle standing on a rock, where it stood a thousand years ago, is the lure.

This castle and Glamis Castle in Angus are the two oldest inhabited Scottish castles. Dunvegan is the home of MacLeod of MacLeod; and Dame Flora MacLeod of MacLeod, D.B.E., is the present chief of the Clan MacLeod. She has travelled the world over in the interests of her clan, never sparing herself, constantly speaking for and upholding her great big 'family'—strengthening the bonds of kinship which unite MacLeods everywhere. No Scottish clan has a more romantic or exciting history than Clan MacLeod; and today no clan is more active—as a clan—than the MacLeods.

The story is told hundreds of years ago of one of the first ever MacLeods who had a hump and a long beard, as though he had swallowed a horse and stuck on the tail! This ugly MacLeod in his endeavour to perpetuate his race, tried to woo the three daughters of Lochiel; the eldest flatly refused him, so did her next sister; but the youngest and prettiest said, 'there never was a mound or a hump but had a sheltered side to it'; and she married him and so the MacLeods today are as plentiful as midges!

Dunvegan Castle is so pre-eminent, that in Gaelic it is spoken of always as 'An Dun'—the fortress; similarly the loch is always referred to as Loch an Duin. It is supposed to have been built in the 9th century by a Viking named Began. During the latter part of that century Norse colonies were founded in different parts of the Hebrides, and like many other Highland families the MacLeods are of Norse descent; the founder of the clan being Leod, son of a Norse ruler. Of all the heroic figures of the Clan MacLeod, perhaps none remain so persistent in memory as the 25th chief, Norman, who ruined himself financially in saving his people during the potato famine of 1846–48.

The keep—the 11th-century sea-gate—and the lower part of the tower are all that are left of the original castle. The fairy tower dates from 1490.

It is a venerable building of various periods, looking, as Dr.

Johnson commented when he spent a week there, 'as if it had been let down from Heaven by the four corners, to be the residence of a Chief'.

Although today the Castle has been greatly reconditioned and is in first-class modern order inside, it still presents a proud defensive front to the beautiful bay. It has come to be regarded as the Buckingham Palace of Skye.

Originally it was a traditionally Highland keep, surrounded by ramparts; water on three sides; ghosts on all four sides! The great chief Rory Mor is still associated with its character, and his two-handed sword is there, a mighty weapon on the corridor wall. The fairy flag (already alluded to) is safely and religiously preserved in its glass case. It is a small square piece of very rich creamy coloured silk—one time of course much larger—and on it are crosses wrought in gold thread, and several elf spots stitched with utmost care. This flag is supposed to have the power, on being waved, of saving the clan from three great dangers. It has already been waved twice; at the battles of Glendale and the Stony Dyke.

The past of Dunvegan dominates the west of Skye; it is the Iliad of Skye—a saga in stone.

There are many treasures to be seen in Dunvegan Castle; Jacobite and St. Kilda relics. There is a very rare 'Amen' toasting-glass bearing the inscription, 'Donald MacLeod of Gualtergil in the Isle of Skye. The faithful Palinurus. Anno 1747.'

Palinurus was Aeneas' steersman in that Latin epic and the inference must be to Donald's aid in ferrying Prince Charlie from place to place in the islands and in assisting Flora Macdonald's passage.

There is also a lock of Prince Charlie's hair. I may say I have come across so many alleged locks of Prince Charlie in so many different parts of Scotland, even down to the Border country, that I should imagine the time the lovable Prince left these shores he must have been on the bald side!

There are many beautiful large-sized family portraits by Ramsay and Raeburn hanging carefully on the walls, and in these days of destruction of big family houses, Dunvegan stands unique in its hopeful, helpful future, as a real home for the Clan Chief. For nearly seven centuries now, the MacLeod family have held unbroken occupation of this Castle. The appointed successor to the Chieftainship is Dame Flora's twin grandson, John MacLeod, who, in the summer of 1961, had been filling a principal role in a film of the Misty Isle. He portrayed a romantic young hiker who is keen to learn all there is to know about 'timeless' Skye— the isle that is a mixture of the modern and the old. The local 'lass' who paints a picture for him of Skye, is Fiona, the pretty young wife of the proprietor of one of Skye's hotels. The film is a documentary, in colour, and is mainly for showing abroad to boost still further the attractions of the Isle. Crofters, weavers and fishers all play a part in the film.

Trust Dame Flora, that indomitable charming 86-year-old Scotswoman, Skye's greatest emissary, to always be 'upsides' in the advertising of Skye!

> Dame Flora with so many world-wide relations
> Would do well as a member of United Nations! . . .

Looking down from the towers, one sees a panoramic stretch of moors and mountains. The green MacLeod's Tables are the Norse-named hills of Healival Mhor and Healival Bheag and high from the ramparts can be seen the hills of Harris. Further on, the famous township of Glendale, the home of owner-occupier crofters—the scene in the past of Land League revolt with crofters' security of tenure as the prize. In this area is Boreraig near the northern tip of the peninsula known as Duirinish, the home of the famous MacCrimmon pipers, hereditary pipers of the MacLeods, where there is a memorial cairn erected in 1933 to this famous school of piping maintained here in the 16th, 17th and 18th centuries. They held their land of MacLeod by tenure of their piping. The course lasted seven years and the student had to learn by heart nearly 300 tunes.

Returning now from Dunvegan (visitors are admitted to the castle every afternoon except Saturdays and Sundays from 1st May to end of October, and one may wander round the lush, verdant gardens at will), one makes for Sligachan via Loch Bracadale and its two arms, Loch Harport and Loch Beag, embracing another peninsula, named Ullinish. Passing along the north shore of the loch one sees the little crofting township of Struan. Then the majestic Talisker Head stands out on the coastline. The far western isles of Barra and South Uist again seen

H2

from the head of the moor road joining in from Portree to Struan. The main road continues inland until it reaches the head of Loch Harport, a branch road leads down to Carbost (another Carbost is near Skeabost aforementioned) on the south side to the famous Talisker distillery. This name Talisker surely hangs 'peaty' on the tongue and lingers on the ear. The distillery is set in a lovely part of the country, miles away, it would seem, from anywhere; everything there is so perfectly quiet, peaceful and restful. I paid a visit a few years ago and looked with great enjoyment to being shown round by the manager and sampling a little of the distillery's product, and when he met me getting out of my car, I felt sure I was in for a pleasant and 'absorbing' morning. All was going well, when suddenly, looking out of his office window, he espied a car drawing up with his directors in it and already disembarking! He exclaimed to me that 'we'd had it' or words to that effect; and that he would not be able to show me round or even offer me the hospitality of a 'Talisker'. Shaking hands, however, I said, with a knowing wink, 'I'll be back'—and back I will go one day! Before coming into Carbost is a road leading to Glen Brittle, the road that winds through rolling machair till it reaches the foot of the Cuillins, giving another view of these famous hills. This area is now being gradually afforested, and the traveller has new relief to the eye in the stretches of plantation surrounding Eynort, where new hope in the reopened school has been given to an area that was previously a depopulated hinterland.

Arriving at Sligachan we turn northwards the 9 miles to Portree; the same road we came along when we first put foot in Skye at Kyleakin ferry.

Sligachan is, to all intents and purposes, the hub of Skye. Roads and paths branch from it in all directions. On the south of the river a path leads up Glen Sligachan. Here Prince Charlie came one day in July over 200 years ago, his companion being Malcolm MacLeod. He tramped along this desolate glen on his way to Elgol and the sea. From Sligachan one has a wonderful view of Glamaig (2537 feet high)—a Vesuvian-type of conical mountain; and with the sun rising behind this monumental mass of nature, the effect is terrific.

These quick journeys just enumerated have—in essence— 'done' Skye. Skye remains an unspoiled island to be sure, and

as I have said—and it bears repeating—its people are quiet and
kind, and the Cuillins majestically awesome, with their long
jagged ridges, are undoubtedly the most challenging mountains
in Britain; and with the Golden Eagles soaring in, and about,
and above them—well one is really lost for words.

Aye, the Cuillins bring back memories . . .

> The Cuillins stand silent; and so
> As one wanders alone on the shore
> One thinks of the old MacLeod motto
> 'Hold Fast'; but the Cuillins say more.
>
> Entranced, you behold and recall
> They were formed in the timeless past;
> A message so simple for all
> Endure, Fight on, and Hold Fast.

When day wears to the gloamin', one likes to relax and be
cushioned in comfort and care, no matter how romantic or beautiful the surroundings. I feel sure Skye has these attributes—
comfort and care—and more.

Yet let it not be forgotten Skye has had its full share of poverty
and famine just as the mainland had. The potato famine of
1846–48 was more severe on the islands than on the mainland.
When the Laird of Gairloch planned the road-makings around
Gairloch, Loch Maree, etc., hundreds of Skye men came over
to Wester Ross to find work; for the MacLeod's fortune then
was at a low ebb.

Skye has in the past given much to the British army. It is
said during the early years of Queen Victoria, 666 officers, 10,000
private soldiers and 120 pipers enlisted during a space of forty
years. There are hardly that number living in Skye today; but
if and when the call comes, the active men of Skye will be
there.

The crofters—the backbone of Skye—are now receiving direct
help and encouragement from the Crofters Commission, as well
as from Skye's own social council. The subsidies that agriculture
in general is obtaining, have done great good to the small-holders,
and now special loans and housing improvements, of a capital
nature, are being administered by the Department of Agriculture.
These, together with the wonderful work of the North of
Scotland Hydro-Electric Board in bringing light to the majority
of the crofting townships in Skye, have enabled the crofters to

have and enjoy every modern convenience; and it is only right they should, not only in Skye but all over the Highlands; for the advent of electricity helps the housewife in her labours and it is well known for years and years she has had a hard, a very hard, struggle and existence in having neither light nor water 'on tap' —that and living in primitive low dwellings, the rough thatch of which is weighted with stones, just to help keep the roof on!

*   *   *

Nor must we forget that Skye is *the* land of the pipers in Scotland, the MacCrimmons—the greatest pipers of all. This family is supposed to have been descended from the Druids, and to have been of Royal Irish line. One of the Irish Kings was Crimithan; and there are some today who believe the Mac-Crimmons were descended from that King. There is popular tradition that the first of the MacCrimmons was brought from Italy to Skye by the Macleod of the day on his return from a crusade in the reign of King Alexander of Scotland; and that the name MacCrimmon is derived from Cremona in Italy, the piper's birthplace.

The piping college of the MacCrimmons was known as the *Oil-Thigh*, and it was at Boreraig, about 6 miles north-west of Dunvegan in the Duirinish peninsula, this college was situated. In the 18th century they gave diplomas to their successful students. On such diplomas were drawn a picture of Dunvegan Castle, the galley of the Macleod and various musical instruments.

When in 1745 the Chief of MacLeod decided to support the Hanoverian King, many of the clansmen refused to follow him, but Piper MacCrimmon put duty to his chief before anything else. He went into battle with a heavy heart knowing he was to be on the side of the butchers of Glencoe. He was to fight against kinsmen who were supporting Prince Charlie; and he could never return to Skye with their blood on his hands. He knew he would never return; his 'second sight' told him that. He plays farewell to Dunvegan for ever; and his words to his piping go down in history as follows:

Farewell to each cliff on which breakers are foaming ;
Farewell, each dark glen, in which red deer are roaming ;
Farewell, lonely Skye, to loch, mountain and river ;
Macleod may return—but MacCrimmon shall never!

The MacCrimmons, hereditary pipers to the Macleods, have gone; their pipes remain; but of their ancient school at Boreraig nothing remains but a memorial cairn, erected nearly 40 years ago, when *Salute to the Cairn at Boreraig* was specially composed and played by one of Scotland's leading pipe majors. In the old days it was said that no Highland chief would be content until his own piper had taken lessons at Boreraig.

Of course it is not everyone that cares for bagpipe music. Not so long ago, the Glasgow College of Piping had its summer headquarters in Tobermory, Mull, and were told they were no longer welcome there, as visitors apparently had objected to the noise. So they moved their 'retreat' to Skye. It is true that whilst mastering the art, many discordant notes can arise; in fact the MacCrimmons used to teach their pupils in many of the seashore caves, where maybe only gulls would be likely to complain! Yet the bagpipes played on a hillside, at a graveside, or at a wedding can have a poetry and an eloquence all of their own.

At Dunvegan Castle is preserved the renowned *piob ballbhreac* —or Speckled Pipe—said to have belonged to Padruig Mór MacCrimmon.

* * *

I would now like to dwell more fully on the '45 rebellion, Bonnie Prince Charlie and Flora, and first of all to record the principal dates and journeyings relative to the Great Prince. Good judgement or bad, the '45 will always stir the heart of man though many other well-planned and successful campaigns are long forgotten. The 'cause' is now a thing of the far-off past; the 'ifs' and the 'buts' are buried long ago.

The inspiration of that romantic adventure, from the raising of Prince Charlie's standard at Glenfinnan until after Culloden, is found in poems, songs and ballads over the past 200 years. The adventure will *never* die.

Prince Charles Edward Stewart or Stuart (Bonnie Prince Charlie) first set foot on British (Scottish) soil on the Island of Eriskay, south of South Uist, in the Outer Hebrides on the 23rd July 1745, spending the night with his seven companions (known as the 'seven men of Moidart') in a cottage. Before he came to Britain he had consulted a soothsayer who had told him he would win the English crown if he killed the first living creature he met in Scotland. When he landed that fateful day on Eriskay there chanced to be a beautiful, shapely, young maiden milking her cow, and she came along with milk to the Prince. He took it, thanked her, and went on his way. One of his followers at once said to him, 'That was the first living creature you met and you didn't kill her as commanded by the prophet'. 'No,' said Prince Charlie, 'I did not. Not if I lost the crown and my head with it, would I have killed her.' Hence, according to the seers, that was why he never became King; and thus it came to pass. He was only 25 years old.

On 25th July 1745 he landed at Borrodale on the north shore of the loch (south of Morar) from a French frigate, the *Du Teillay*. (He was later, on 20th September 1746, after spending five months since Culloden as a fugitive in the Highlands and the Hebrides, with a price of £30,000 on his head, to be taken off again at the same spot by another French vessel, the *L'Heureux*, fourteen months later in fact.)

He thus passed through Borrodale twice, sailing thence for Benbecula (26th April 1746) and landing there from Skye on 10th July 1746.

From 25th July 1745 he gradually travelled the road to Glenfinnan where he raised his standard, 19th August 1745.

The monument there today—a wonderful monument in a wonderful setting—has inscriptions repeated on the walls surrounding the pillar in Gaelic, English, Latin and French, to commemorate the generous zeal, the undaunted bravery and the inviolable fidelity of the men who lived and died for Charlie.

> Let them tear our bleeding bosoms,
> Let them drain our latest veins,
> In our hearts is Charlie, Charlie,
> While a spark of life remains.

The fiery cross had summoned the clansmen to Glenfinnan. With the Macdonalds of Clanranald, the seven men of Moidart, Prince Charlie rowed up Loch Shiel to Glenfinnan to await the Camerons and others who joined to see the Marquess of Tullibardine raise the white, blue and red silk standard proclaiming James III of England and VIII of Scotland. And so it all commenced. Can you visualise a more inspiring, romantic setting?

For my part I cannot; and once you see Glenfinnan for yourself, I am certain you will agree and more than agree. It is 'splendiferous', to coin a word.

From Glenfinnan he wended his way south towards Fort William on 28th August 1745. He carried onwards achieving a notable victory at Prestonpans over General Cope, 21st September. When he occupied Edinburgh the Prince made Holyrood his headquarters from 17th September to 31st October 1745. He reached Jedburgh, on the Borders, on his way into England on 6th November 1745.

We all know his invasion was checked, and on his retreat from Derby, early December 1745, it is recorded he lodged at the County Hotel in Dumfries on 21st December 1745. Continuing his retreat he vainly besieged Stirling Castle early 1746. At Falkirk, 17th January 1746, he obtained a victory over General Hawley on his northward journey.

Then came Culloden; Culloden Moor, 16th April 1746, where the fate of the House of Stuart was sealed. At 1 p.m. Prince Charles's 5000/7000 Highlanders, tired and hungry, were engaged by 9000 Government troops under the Duke of Cumberland, the third son of George II. The battle lasted less than half an hour, in which the Highlanders lost 1000 dead, and another 1000 or so in the subsequent flight. The English killed amounted to less than 100. Prince Charlie spent the day after Culloden at Invergarry Castle, later that year burnt down by the Duke of Cumberland.

Thence came, as I have said, five whole months of wandering trying to evade capture—which, of course, he did.

From Culloden the Prince wore the clothes of his guide and travelling companion, Edmund Burke, and on 18th April this band of four, Burke, O'Sullivan, O'Neal and the Prince himself, set out going southwards towards Loch Morar and reached Meoble the following day, rested awhile and then made for Lochailort, south of Morar and Arisaig, where, as always, Prince Charlie was expecting news of his followers; and particularly from his friends in France. His party remained here four days, receiving sad reports from his scattered followers, news of further losses and little hope of any possible strong rally. There was no alternative but to leave Scotland, saddened and dejected, and as soon as it could be managed despite reports of continued patrols of the western coast by King George's ships and soldiers.

Charles thought of Skye as a safe haven until a French ship could pick him up and carry him back to France.

On the night of 24th April 1746, the Prince and party put off in an 8-oared boat from Loch nan Uamph, a sea-loch below Arisaig, and safely landed in Benbecula, at Rossinch on the south-east end of the island on 27th April. Owing to a heavy storm, they were unable to leave Benbecula till 29th April for Storno-way. They were blown far out off course, eventually landing on the shores of Loch Seaforth, some 20 miles south of Storno-way, which distance they had to walk.

They were not to be long in Stornoway, for the townsfolk were greatly alarmed and so, on 10th May 1746, the Prince, who needed no publicity—far from it—set sail again; once again for Benbecula, still escaping the pursuers. (Scalpay, an island at the mouth of East Loch Tarbert—off Harris—was also a frequent refuge for Prince Charlie during his wanderings between 27th April, when he arrived at Benbecula from Borrodale, and 28th June, when he left with Flora Macdonald for Skye.)

From there to South Uist, Glencoridale, 15th May–5th June. This hide-out at a forester's cottage was most acceptable, and although scores of the islanders knew of the Prince being in their midst, none would sell the secret, even for £30,000. (In those days this amount of money—in English gold—was truly 'worth a million'.) In South Uist, 2 miles north of Askernish on the west side of the island, and 5 miles west of Lochboisdale, the island's steamer port, is the village of Milton where are the ruins of Flora Macdonald's birthplace; and it was in a hut near Ormaclett, 3 miles further north, that she first met Prince Charlie and agreed to take him over to Skye.

The Prince's party left Glencoridale on 14th June and made for the island of Wiay, off the south-east coast of Benbecula. Here they stayed four days, then back to Rossinch, Benbecula, again for two days, only to be pursued by English men-of-war, but with luck they managed to get to Lochboisdale (South Uist) two days later. However, they were still living every hour in great danger, so decided to return to Benbecula once more. But with one companion only, O'Neal; and this was on 24th June 1746; and it was here, in South Uist this time, that he first met his new preserver and companion (if only for a brief while) in

his travels, Flora Macdonald, who was then visiting her brother
and was due to return to Skye.

Should he now leave the Hebrides—where he was known to
be—and risk adventure on the Isle of Skye?

With government forces all around, Flora, who was an artful
woman, landed herself in a guardroom until released by an officer
known to her family, not before she had obtained a pass for
herself, her maidservant, and an Irish woman helper by the name
of 'Betty Burke' whom she said she was taking to her mother in
Skye. The plan succeeded, and Prince Charlie became 'Betty
Burke' disguised in clothes obtained for the purpose.

The party then left Benbecula and set course for Skye.

> Speed, bonnie boat, like a bird on the wing,
> Onward! the sailors cry.
> Carry the lad that's born to be king
> Over the sea to Skye.

As fate would have it, a French ship called in the South Uist
area to pick up the Prince; but he had just left.

That night, 28th June 1746, was, as usual, a stormy one when
they set sail at 8 p.m. making towards Vaternish Point the
north-west tip of Skye. They arrived safely on the shores of
Loch Snizort near Kilbride. 'Betty Burke' was left on the shore
sitting on her baggage whilst faithful, artful Flora went to
Monkstadt House to see her friend Lady Margaret Macdonald,
through whose goodness she obtained a safe conduct for her
Prince to Kingsburgh House, some 14 miles south close to the
shores of Loch Snizort Beag (the inner loch of Loch Snizort
proper).

At Kingsburgh House he rested and was nursed by Flora, and
was soon on his way again, disguised still, until they reached
Portree. Here he discarded the 'Betty Burke' rig-out for the
clothes of a Highland gentleman; and it was on 30th June 1746,
in a room at an Inn (now the Royal Hotel, the landlord's name
was Charles MacNab), that he bade a fond farewell to Flora
MacDonald, with hopes of meeting again. He gave her his
miniature and repaid a small sum of money he had borrowed
from her, then cautiously left. But that reunion never took
place. He set off with a small party in a small boat from Portree,
crossing the waters of the Sound of Raasay to friendly, young

MacLeod of Raasay, arriving there on 1st July 1746. Poor Flora, and I am sure all our hearts go out to her; as I quote from the *Lament of Flora Macdonald*:

> She looked at the boat, which the breezes had swung,
> Away on the wave, like a bird on the main,
> And aye as it lessened she sighed and she sung,
> Farewell to the lad I shall ne'er see again.

It has been said in later history that the Prince was not worthy of such devotion. He saved his own skin, but never remembered the woman who risked so much to aid his escape. Ah! well; such is life.

From Raasay, Prince Charlie roamed between Skye and the west mainland, always in hiding. August saw him at Glen Cannich, the furthermost point reached in these 'wanderings'.

In September news reached him of the arrival of the French ship *L'Heureux* at Loch nan Uamph, near Borrodale again, where he had landed just over a year before. That ship took him away to France, with a legend, on 20th September 1746.

He arrived in Scotland a man young in years, and young in outlook; 6 foot tall, brown of eyes and with rich brown hair. He left a bedraggled fugitive—with a price of £30,000 on his head; but as we have read, none would sell their souls for 30 pieces of silver, let alone of gold. Had there been a real Quisling among any of the Highlanders, he would have been an easy prey. But even though a number of them refused to help in the campaign—and some even fought against him—*none* would ever think of handing him over to the Redcoats. Such was the Highland race. And one island in particular, whose population is predominantly Catholic, cherishes his memory to this day —Benbecula; where the army now has established a rocket range.

Thus ended the abortive, inglorious episode of the Jacobite rebellion of 1745; and of Bonnie Prince Charlie.

Charles Edward Louis Philip Casimir, to give him his full name; 'Charles Edward, Prince of Wales, Regent of Scotland, England, Ireland, and the Dominions thereunto belonging'; the Young Pretender (son of the Old Pretender James Francis Edward Stuart, son of James II of England, who in turn was the 2nd son of Charles I, 1633–1701, deposed in favour of William of Orange

1688; the Jacobites, so-called, being adherents of James II after he abdicated the throne) was born in 1720 and was only 25 years of age when he hoisted his colours at Glenfinnan in 1745 (19th August); and subsequently died a dissolute wreck in Rome in 1788; and was buried in the Cathedral Church of St. Frescati.

He was a Catholic, and when he landed in Scotland, all the Catholic priests of the Catholic glens became his most enthusiastic recruiting agents. Bishop Hugh MacDonald, Vicar-Apostolic to the Highlands, blessed his standard at Glenfinnan for the battles to come.

I suppose when he landed, so young, with good fresh looks, beaming and bounding with energy and enthusiasm, everyone— chiefs and womenfolk alike—fell for his 6-foot debonairness; that, and the cause, cemented everything and everybody and one can well picture the shouting and uplifting of the claymores and swords, staffs and cromags, as his standard was unfurled that day of August 1745. But for fate, would British history have been differently written ?

The 30th June 1746—a fateful day to be sure—when he bade goodbye to his preserver, Flora Macdonald, at the Portree Inn.

> Royal Charlie's now awa,
> Safely ower the friendly main;
> Many a heart will break in twa,
> Should he ne'er come back again,
> Will ye no' come back again?
> Will ye no' come back again?
> Better lo'ed ye canna be,
> Will ye no' come back again?

There was no return; no reunion; not even a letter. She was forgotten. . . . Sad, very sad.

Of Prince Charlie's many battles and wanderings, Culloden comes uppermost to one's thoughts. Culloden put an end to the '45 organised rising—it put 'paid' to the hope that the Stuarts would ever again be Kings. It was not, however, the end of Highland bravery, loyalty or self-sacrifice; nor was it the end either of slaughter, suffering and humiliation.

Culloden is a name of tragedy for countless Scots, a day— 16th April 1746—of futile sorrows echoing down the centuries; the last battle fought on the soil of Britain. The battle and its significance can only be matched by Waterloo, Dunkirk and El Alamein. It is the story of Scotland's saddest defeat.

'*Bliadna Thearlaich*', the Highlanders called it—Prince Charlie's Year 1745. It was indeed! After Culloden the wearing of Highland dress was forbidden by law; the clan system in the old familiar sense—namely, a 'family', not a social hierarchy— was completely shattered by merciless measures.

Glens were emptied by deportation or emigration. By the rigidly repressive Acts of 1746 and 1748 the old ties of clan kinship were cruelly broken. Henceforward until 1782, except by stealth, the tartan was unseen in the hills and glens, where before it has been the people's pride and joy. It is fitting to record the chief of a Scottish clan is entitled to wear a crest badge surmounted by three feathers. It is the practice, however, for chiefs to allow their followers to wear the crest and motto in a silver strap-and-buckle badge. The plant badge of a clansman was a sprig fixed to his staff, spear or bonnet. It acted as a distinguishing emblem; but there is ground for believing that it was used as a charm, like an amulet or talisman.

In 1782 the Duke of Montrose fought nobly for the repeal of the hated Disarming Act and was successful, but there was no immediate enthusiastic return to the tartan and the kilt. The old attachment to the Highland dress had died in a generation. The old patterns were forgotten; so was the skill of making the dyes from the herbs on the hills. It was not until forty years later, towards the middle of the 1800's, that a romantic interest in Highland dress was reborn. During this melancholy period the oppressed Highlanders, dourly and silently, endured their wrongs, brooding upon the loss of their ancient heritage; but powerless. Gradually, and after the turn of the 19th century, Clan Societies grew up and multiplied in the New World and in Colonial Britain; then slowly wherever Scotsmen dwelt, the sympathetic feeling of kinship was kindled and the tartan became symbolic, not of the Highlands alone, but of Scotland as a whole. And that is as we know it today.

It was savage legislation indeed, for, to the government, a Highlander was looked upon as a savage from the remote regions of Scotland. There were plunder and killings long after Culloden. Cumberland (the bloody butcher as he became known) started a reign of terror to subdue the Highlands for ever; a veritable dictator, with one obsession, 'suppression'. All this made way for the 'Clearances', in which hundreds of thousands of clansmen were banished, 'that a degenerate lord might boast his sheep'. Then the sheep went too.

Such was the aftermath of 'Charlie's Year'. Misery for the Highlands; abject misery.

Today the site of the battle is marked by the cairn erected in 1881 by Mr. Duncan Forbes. The cairn is built of rough stones and stands 20 feet in height and 18 feet in diameter; and on it is the following inscription:

THE BATTLE OF CULLODEN
was fought on this moor, 16th April 1746
The graves of the gallant highlanders
who fought for
Scotland and Prince Charlie
are marked by the names of their Clans.

The burial places of the various clans are denoted by the stones upon which the name is engraved, whilst those High-landers who were interred irrespective of sept or clan, were buried in trenches, the inscribed stone stating whether the grave is that of any particular clan, or the resting place of members of several clans who fought under one standard.

There is a lot in a name, and Culloden carries a wealth of meaning. The legend of 'Bonnie Prince Charlie and a' that' can never really, in this age, hope to survive the misery and horror of this last battle in the north, still less the aftermath of sadistic infamy.

With the abortive night-march to surprise the Duke of Cumberland's camp, there was foot-slogging, misery and frustra-tion and bickering between the chiefs. Prince Charlie's army was distraught, rations non-existent, and they were out-numbered and out-gunned. The slaughter of the wounded, the mutilation of both dead and living had a bloody-minded perpetuation. Stench-laden prison ships, river hulks, distant gallows and scaffolds, pestilence, survivors slave-shipped to the Carolinas—all this testified to the completeness (and let it be said, degradation) of the Hanoverian victory.

Yet legend tells of Jacobite triumph in defeat!

Whatever else, certainly no situation, political or otherwise, has been preserved in poetry and song as that of the Jacobite rebellion. One of the most beautiful is 'MacLean's Welcome', from which I extract a few lines:

> Come o'er the stream, Charlie, dear Charlie, brave Charlie,
> Come o'er the stream Charlie and dine with MacLean;
> We'll bring down the track deer, and doe from the glen
>
> .   .   .
>
> And the loveliest Mari in all Glen McQuarry
> Shall lie in your bosom till break of the day.

Nearly 220 years ago the Clan MacLean offered everything to Prince Charlie; venison, drink and women. Such 'rewards' have been given the favoured ones in history since time began; and so it will continue.

I have mentioned the 'bloody-ness' of the Duke of Cumberland; and after the battle the butchery not only commenced but continued. More than half the Prince's army were slaughtered whilst lying wounded in the field.

There is the story told of a Highland officer who, wounded, still retained his proud bearing even in front of the victorious Duke. The Duke commanded a major of his—a Major Wolfe—to shoot the Highland scoundrel. The English officer, with all due respect to the Duke, refused to do so and said he would forfeit his commission rather. The Duke then got a common soldier to carry out his order and shoot the wounded Highland officer where he lay.

Thirteen years later, on 15th September 1759, that same Major Wolfe—then General Wolfe—stormed the Heights of Abraham and captured Quebec; an outstanding victory in the annals of British history as we all know. He was, however, mortally wounded in the victory; and strange though it may be —even stranger than fiction—Wolfe fell into the arms of the son of that self-same Highland officer whom the Duke caused to be 'murdered' in cold blood at Culloden.

Yes, the traditions of centuries lie buried at Culloden, but eventually this defeat *did* bring Highlands and Lowlands together to weld the Scottish nation as we know it once again.

Not far from where I used to live in Yorkshire, is Burnley in Lancashire; and this town is associated with the butchery of Cumberland in a remarkable way. In those days, Lancashire was referred to as 'Stuart Province', for that county was a great supporter of Prince Charlie's cause.

There was a Colonel Francis Towneley, who on behalf of the Prince was governor of Carlisle, being a staunch Jacobite supporter. Eventually in the defeat he was put to death on 30th December 1746. He was the first Englishman to be publicly executed for his support of the Stuart cause. Towneley Hall, originally built with its six-foot walls for defence in the 13th century, was the home of the Towneleys and is on the outskirts of Burnley. When beheaded, Towneley's head was stuck on a spike at Kennington, where the cricket ground, the Oval, now is. After some years, his head was obtained by some of the Towneley retainers, and they and their kin kept the skull until 1946—exactly 200 years after—when it was given back to what was left of the remote Towneley descendants, who authorised that the family vault of the Towneleys in Burnley's Parish Church be opened, and the skull of Col. Towneley was, with all reverence, interred there. There are no Towneleys remaining now; the last of the male line died in 1878 and one of the daughters in 1902 offered the Hall and all its parkland to the Corporation of Burnley. With her death in 1921, the long association of the 'Towneleys of Towneley Hall' came to an end.

It is said the Duke of Cumberland was visited by Col. Towneley's ghost and was grievously perturbed; so much so that he forthwith travelled south and told his father, King George II, of his vision. There is on record an old poem by some unknown writer, descriptive of what took place between father and son, namely:

> Cheer up, my boy, my darling son
> The bold usurper said,
> Never repent of what you've done
> Nor be at all dismayed.

> If we on Stuart's throne can dwell
> And reign securely here
> My uncle Satan's King of Hell
> And he'll protect us there.

*　　*　　*

Flora Macdonald was born in South Uist in the spring of 1722, and reared at Milton there, of which her father was tacksman (gentleman farmer). She was born into a family whose claim to high rank could be established both on the male and on the female side. Through her father she derived her descent from the Chiefs of Clanranald and from the House of Dunnyveg in Kintyre; whilst on her mother's side she had a pedigree stretching back to the Chiefs of Sleat. She was thus a genuine daughter of the lordly and aristocratic Macdonald House of the Isles, founded by the great and mighty Somerled, known to history as *Rex Insularum*. Flora was also descended from the House of Argyll, her great-grandmother—on her father's side—having been Agnes, daughter of Colin, Earl of Argyll. Through the Argyll family she could trace her descent to the Scottish Royal House of Robert II, as well as through her Macdonald line; her ancestor John, 1st Lord of the Isles, having married the Princess Margaret, daughter of Robert II.

Thus, Flora Macdonald was not a mere peasant girl, as is often alleged by many writers, but was one who had the best blood in Scotland—that of the Lords of the Isles, the Earls of Argyll and the Kings of Scotland—mingling in her veins.

Scandalous stories have been invented and circulated by many writers regarding the Prince's relations with his rescuer, Flora ; but these are not worthy of consideration. I have read through authentic data—particularly *The Truth about Flora Macdonald* (out of print now), by the Rev. Donald Mackinnon, D.Litt., of Portree, and later of the Free Church Manse, Kennoway, Fife (the greatest authority on Flora Macdonald)—and there is not the slightest foundation for thinking or assuming that any 'love' entered into their two lives. The whole episode in which they were together lasted less than two days—from a Friday to a Sunday afternoon; and the whole of their association was in the presence of several others. It was a perilous enterprise she was engaged in, solely and wholly; and for which she will always and truthfully be remembered. I am also indebted to Mr. Reginald H. Macdonald of Kingsburgh, O.B.E., of Pittsburg, Pennsylvania, U.S.A., who was a great-great-grandson of Flora Macdonald, for his great work on *The House of Macdonald of Kingsburgh and Castle Camus* (Skye), in his compilation of the genealogy of the Macdonalds dating back to Somerled Rex Insularum, who was well-nigh an independent King and Thane of Argyll, and who founded the Celtic Lordship of the Isles. Somerled married in 1140 Ragnhildis, daughter of Olave the

Red, Norwegian King of Man and the Isles, and from that marriage derives, broadly, the Clan Donald and directly the Kingsburgh family. Somerled was treacherously murdered in his tent in 1164 by an emissary of King Malcolm IV just before the Battle of Renfrew was joined, but his family suffered no particular diminution of its power after his death and remained in possession of the vast territories he had won.

It is said, when Flora lay dying, a smile came over her face as she breathed her last, on 4th March 1790, saying, '*Criosd's Ailean's Tearlach Og*'—Christ, Allan and young Charles.

There is another great book—a classic of three volumes—now out of print (and I believe only two or three copies exist in Britain today, one of which is available in the Advocate's Library in Edinburgh), dealing with the '45 rebellion and the affairs of Prince Charles 1746–1775, written by the Rev. Robert Forbes, A.M., Bishop of Ross and Caithness who died November 1775, entitled *The Lyon in Mourning*, originally published by the Scottish History Society. It is a collection of speeches, letters and journals all relative to this Jacobite up-rising. As to the title, it has been suggested it was in allusion to the woe of Scotland for her exiled race of chieftains; the *Lyon* being the heraldic representative of the nation. The writer, no doubt, identified the Scottish nation with the comparatively few Jacobites within the country. It is truly a masterpiece.

On the day of his execution, 18th August 1746, on Tower Hill, the Right Honourable Arthur, Lord Balmerino, said this of the Prince . . . 'the incomparable sweetness of his nature, his affability, his compassion, his justice, his temperance, his patience, and his courage, were all virtues seldom to be found in one person. In short, he wants no qualifications requisite to make a great man' . . .

Capt. O'Neill, who was the Prince's aide-de-camp and chief bodyguard after Culloden, had great difficulty in prevailing upon Flora Macdonald to undertake being guardian to the Prince in Skye. He said 'you need not fear your character, for by this, you will gain yourself an immortal character'. And so she did. He further told her, 'if you still entertain fears about your character, I shall (by oath) marry you directly, if you so please'. What a noble gesture. O'Neill fell down upon his knees imploring her; what a servant in all surety! (The Prince had told

Flora the sense he would always retain of so conspicuous a service.)

During their passage to Skye, a heavy rain fell upon them. To divert Flora's anxiety, the Prince sang several songs. She fell asleep, and to keep her so, he continued to sing. Happening to awake with some little bustle in the boat, she found the Prince leaning over her with his hands spread about her head, sheltering her body. When Flora was telling this particular part of the adventure to some ladies that were paying their respects to her, later on in life (on board the *Bridgewater* in Leith, when she was a prisoner), some of them with raptures cried out, 'Oh! Miss, what a happy creature are you who had that dear Prince to lull you asleep and to take such care of you with his hands spread about your head, when you were sleeping! You are surely the happiest woman in the world!' So, indeed; she was the envy of all. In fact one of the ladies whispered to her, saying, that she would with pleasure stay on board all night and sleep with her, so that in after years she could then say she had the honour of lying in the same bed with that person (Flora) who had been so happy as to be the guardian to her Prince. And it is recorded the two women *did* sleep together in the one bed that night. Several ladies made valuable presents to Flora in the manner of gowns, skirts, shoes and stockings.

As this is all authentic, I am not drawing on my imagination.

Originally the plan of escape to Skye, to be protected by Lady Margaret Macdonald, a true Jacobite, at Kingsburgh, was for Flora to really take the Prince to her mother's house, Armadale Castle, in the south of Skye. She declined, however, to implicate and risk ruin to her step-father, Sir Alex. Macdonald at Armadale, and so chose the better course—to go to Kingsburgh. The Prince's 'Betty Burke' outfit was made by some of Flora's women friends at Nunton on the west coast of Benbecula—flowered calico gown with purple sprigs, petticoat, and a mantle made after Irish fashion with a hood and cap, and apron. The Prince and a few members of the crew of the boat that had brought him to Benbecula went up to a small hill, Rueval, which commanded a view of the surrounding country, and not far from Nunton, and awaited word to set sail from Roshinish (or as it was then written Rushness) and on the evening of 28th June 1746 left for Skye. There were just three in the 'royal party'; the Prince (Betty Burke), Flora and Neil MacEachen, who acted as her man-servant. The Prince had strongly wished for Capt. O'Neill to accompany them, but as Flora only had a passport for three persons, that was impossible; also O'Neill did not know the language of the country, as did MacEachen.

The next morning they had reached Skye, south of Dunvegan Head, and eventually they landed in the small bay of Kilbride across Loch Snizort on the Trotternish peninsula. Flora, accompanied by Neil MacEachen, made for Monkstadt, to Lady Margaret's, leaving the Prince on the shore. After dinner at Monkstadt, much discussion took place as to the Prince's safety, and in the end all of them, including Macdonald of Kingsburgh, who happened to be visiting there, made for Kingsburgh House. It was here then, really, that Flora Macdonald's personal share in the Prince's escape ended. He had been under her care from 8 o'clock that Saturday morning of 28th June till about 2 p.m. on the Sunday, 29th June—some thirty hours altogether. From there on Monday, 30th June 1746, they left Kingsburgh for Portree; Flora and Neil leaving ahead of the Prince. Before leaving Kingsburgh House, the Prince parted with a lock of his hair, as a keepsake for Mrs. Macdonald and her daughter' Mrs. MacAlister. There are various accounts of this 'Rape of the Lock'. Mrs. Macdonald begged Flora to go to the Princes, bedroom and get it for her. Flora at first refused, but eventually with Mrs. Macdonald taking her to the door of the bedroom and telling the Prince what was their mission, Flora went in. The Prince asked her to sit down on a chair near the bed, then, laying his arms about her waist and his head on her lap, he asked her to cut off a lock with her own hands in token of future and more substantial favours. One half of the lock she gave to Mrs. Macdonald, and the other she kept to herself.

Another incident connected with the Prince's stay at Kingsburgh House regarding the sheets in which he slept, seem to be misrepresented in various quarters. It has been said Mrs. Macdonald and Flora went to the bedroom after the Prince had risen, folded up the sheets and pledged themselves to preserve them unwashed until they would be used as winding sheets when they themselves died. But as it seems from some biographers that Flora had left earlier for Portree, it could only have been Mrs. Macdonald and her daughter, Mrs. MacAlister, who took the sheets. Should Flora have had some of those precious sheets, one would have thought she would have mentioned the matter to Dr. Johnson and Boswell, when they visited Kingsburgh on 12th September 1773, and were entertained by her and her husband there, especially so as Dr. Johnson is said to have slept in the very bed Prince Charles had lain 27 years before. It would appear Mrs. Macdonald preserved all the sheets, folded them carefully, and charged her daughter that they should be kept as they were; and that when she died her body should be wrapped in them as a shroud. Her will was religiously observed. Some of the remaining sheets, however, came into Flora's possession thereafter.

Thence we come to the *finale* at Portree early on the Tuesday morning of 1st July 1746, when bidding goodbye to Flora (who had gone there ahead) the Prince left the Inn with Capt. Donald Roy Macdonald as guide, and walked slowly down to the shore at Portree Bay (spelt in those days as Purtry), where Capt. Malcolm MacLeod of Brae, Raasay, was waiting. From there, over the sea to the Isle of Raasay.

That was the end. Although the Prince lived for over forty years after that parting scene with Flora at Portree, he never communicated with her, or indeed with any of those friends in the Hebrides, to whom he owed so much—his very life and liberty.

Culloden, 16th April 1746; Prince Charlie's departure to France 20th September 1746—what five months of unparalleled danger and sufferings, of hunger, cold and thirst! not discounting the fact that he was surrounded by an army on land and on the sea, thirsting for his blood; for the £30,000 sterling on his head —the price of blood. Verily a suffering hero. In all truth it may be recorded down through history that the Prince could not have been so safe in any other place in Britain than in the Highlands of Scotland.

I think I cannot end on a better epitaph than that.

*   *   *

The Prince, before he said goodbye to Flora, also gave her the garters he wore with the woman's clothes (Betty Burk's) which were French, of blue velvet covered upon one side with white silk, and fastened with buckles that bore his royal crest.

At the Prince's farewell it is officially recorded in these words,

'I hope we shall meet in St. James's yet, and I will reward you there for what you have done'. It was not to be, though.

It would seem, apart from his defeat in the field of battle, that the greatest objections to the Prince in Great Britain were Popery and arbitrary government.

In regard to those journeying 'over the sea to Skye' with Flora, Neil MacEachen and the Prince, there were five of a crew, namely John Macdonald (cousin to Glenalladale) at the helm; Duncan Campbell; John MacMerry; Roderick Macdonald; and Alex. Macdonald. All five were people belonging to the Long Isle. John Macdonald was afterwards drowned whilst crossing the Minch a few years later. The boat and the rowers, as soon as their 'passengers' had stepped ashore at Kilbride, returned at once to South Uist; which was unfortunate, for they were instantly made prisoners and threatened with torture, if they did not declare everything they knew.

Previously, I have mentioned the 'butchery' enforced by the victor of Culloden, the Duke of Cumberland, and of his dictatorship obsession later on in Scotland. In November 1765, on the death of the Duke, a writer signing himself as 'No Flatterer', caused the following epitaph to be inserted in the *London Chronicle* in Latin . . .

HIC

MORTE VICTUS, JACET,

QUI

VICTOR OLIM

IN AGRO CULLODENSE.

QUALIS ERAT,

SCOTIA MOERENS INDICAT.

A few days later, he gave the editor a translation in English, to wit:

Here lies a victim to all-conquering death;
The man who conquered on Culloden's heath.
What else he was, or what his victims were,
The groans of weeping Scotland best declare.

How very true . . .

*   *   *

The above then, are, I think, most of the salient points and facts bearing upon the '45, the Prince, and Flora.

Concluding, I would quote the lines written by an unknown Aberdeen gentleman, which appeared in the Scots edition of the 'Journal' in August 1749, reading as follows:

> ... When rancour, malice, envy, all are dead,
> And future ages shall thy story read,
> Ten thousand pens shall celebrate thy fame,
> And latest ages shall thy worth proclaim.
> Nor shall the faithful Flora's memory die,
> Till the last trump rend the empyreal sky. ...

*   *   *

So I come to the end of Skye, 'Eilean a' Cheo', Prince Charlie, Culloden, and last but not least, of Flora Macdonald—Flora (or Funivella) of immortal memory. And of course the Cuillins; the black Cuillins with their peaks pitted against peaks; and in the early morning of shafts of light, grape-blue in colour, still, frightful, stupendously awesome; so much so that with the dawn and the rising sunlight one literally gasps at a sight which in certain aspects is 'out of this world'. The very names of some of the peaks—given them by the Vikings of old—speak of thunder and the God Thor—such as Sgurr-nan-Gillean, Sgurr Mhic Coinneach, Sgurr Ghreadaidh and Sgurr Alasdair. Truly Skye stands alone, for Nature made it so. The Cuillin peaks— sharp, dangerous, yet beckoning. Wildly beautiful to the beholder.

Yes, Skye is steeped in legends, romantic and otherwise. You feel the spell of Skye on you as soon as you cross over from Kyle. Most Skye names are a mixture of Norse and Gaelic, for in the olden days it was, as already indicated, a Viking land, Norsemen colonising it. In the wintry months when everything is at its loneliest, you can sense a Viking stepping out in front of you on the road or hillside with an uplifted sword, like the highwayman in far-off English days. The roads have tales of magic, of water Kelpies, of boys kidnapped by fairies, of boys killed by witches, of fairy bridges and of fairy cattle. You will see the small strongholds (or round duns) in which the inhabitants of those days took shelter from the Norse pirates, when they were seen coming in from the sea.

Legends and superstitions!

I have already mentioned the fairy flag at Dunvegan Castle;

the fuller story goes something like this. Long, long ago when the heir was born to MacLeod of MacLeod, the nurse left the room where the infant was sleeping to go down and join in the festivities. The Chieftain told her to go back and bring the baby down to be shown round to the clansmen. When she entered the room she found the child wrapped in the fairy flag; and as she carried it downstairs, fairy voices were heard singing out that the flag would save the clan in three great dangers. It was to be waved three times, and three times only, in case of great need; if waved for some trivial matter, a curse would fall on the clan.

So far, it is history that it has been waved twice; the first against the invading Macdonalds who were all killed though the MacLeods were hopelessly outnumbered; the second time the flag caused them to be saved from a cattle plague.

As to the curse, it was to involve the death of the heir, the rocks at Dunvegan would be sold to a Campbell, and when a fox had young in the castle, the MacLeods' glory would dwindle, and much of their estate be sold. In 1799 it is said, MacLeod's factor decided to test this curse and he took the flag out of an iron chest, waved it and put it back again. Shortly after that the heir was blown up in H.M.S. *Queen Charlotte*; the imposing rocks near Dunvegan (called 'MacLeods Maidens') were sold to Angus Campbell of Ensay; and they are still in possession of his grandson. A tame fox in possession of a Lieutenant MacLean *did* have its young in the west turret in the castle, and the MacLeods' riches declined. Strange indeed?

... There is an ancient belief that if earth and sea were swept away, there would be seen written on the basic rocks of Skye, the name of MacLeod ...

So we say, not farewell, but *au revoir* to the Isle of Skye— the Isle of Mist. For as likely as not we will return there again —and yet again.

Better lo'ed you canna be.

*   *   *

In a previous chapter I have said 'Skye Week' is the last week of May; and the Skye Highland Games, the last week of August. Begun in 1950 as an attempt to show people how hospitable the people of the Isles were, 'Skye Week' has developed in its fifteen years to being a great social occasion. It is the first, and one of the most romantic, of Scotland's many annual gatherings. Whilst pipers play on the battlements of the hoary Dunvegan Castle, and dancers perform, Dame Flora moves and chats amongst the throngs of people from all parts of the world; and a grand concert ends this notable week.

. . . Skye, Flora, Prince Charlie, Culloden, the Clearances and the Covenanters, the tragedy of the '45 is not only the tragedy of Prince Charlie; it is the tragedy of the Highland people. They were fighting not so much for the Stuarts, but for a way of life; and the '45 was really the beginning of that way of life. The Prince left the sinking ship and never thought very much about the Highlander again.

The century before Culloden saw the persecution of the Covenanters in full force. This body emerged as the direct result of the Stuart theory of the Divine Right of Kings in both common and religious laws. They had either to obey God or obey the King; it was as simple as that, and they chose God. They had no dividing line between toleration and submission. The King's dragoons pillaged and killed cattle and people at random. This era of persecution passed at the end of 1688, when the Stuart's were in exile.

CHAPTER 14

A GUID NEW YEAR!

A GUID New Year tac ane an' a'. And on Hogmanay (New Year's Eve) that is a saying broadcast all over Scotland—indeed all over the world. *Hogmanay*, the eve of Scotland's greatest feast; and the very name conjures up intrigue. Is it something you eat, or something you drink, or another form of haggis?

Hogmanay in essence is the eve of visiting and wishing one another a 'Guid New Year'.

The *very* old custom of 'first-footing' in the Highlands was that you gave the 'letter-in' a coin in exchange for something he or she brought in; and after a drink and a bite—both wishing each other well—you then let the 'first-footer(s)' out by the back door!

In a sense this bears comparison with the New Year resolutions many of us are apt to make. We readily make a list only to find them gone soon enough. We let them in, and then let them out!

Scots are born with the conviction that New Year's Eve was the invention of their own native genius; so it is well to bear that in mind when you go to a real Scots party in the Highlands, for you will doubtless be surrounded by strapping, six-foot, hairy-kneed Highlanders, and by buxom young lassies. Try to tell the party that other nations beside Scotland celebrate New Year and you will be asking for trouble, right, left and centre! Persist in your argument and you'll get properly 'clobbered' off and your head in your hands—shorn off, figuratively speaking, with a claymore as slick as Leask's bacon-slicer!

I

So face up to it and join in; that's your only salvation being an Englishman!

You need to learn up a few appropriate phrases in advance, in order to keep conviviality going your way, and if one of your party turns to you, raises his glass and says, 'Here's tae us', you say, 'Wha's like us?'—and at once you become the life and soul of the party; an Englishman acknowledging Scottish superiority!

There are, of course, many asides you can mutter as the evening wears on, as a help in trying to establish some faint claim that you have *some* Scottish blood in you; for instance, 'forbye'; 'Lang may your lum reek'; 'aweel' (this said deeply and solemnly is always a winner!); and since it *is* New Year's Eve you are celebrating—in case you had forgotten, and doubtless you will forget as dawn comes along—there's always 'A guid New Year tae ane an' a'', of course; and remember, it's always 'Rabbie Burns', never Bobby Burns!

Christmas and New Year: two great occasions, though up in the Highlands the majority 'keep' only the New Year; and in olden times, New Year's Day was celebrated on the 12th January. Some Highlanders today seem to keep it from the 1st to the 12th inclusive! There are no church bells ringing out the glad tidings as in England.

Up in these parts, the 25th December—a set calendar date—is not acknowledged as the birthday of Christ; for no such specific date is recorded in the Bible. 'Whilst shepherds watched their flocks by night' could not, they say, be the month of December; for then both shepherds and flocks would not be out in the open fields. What *is* observed is the ascendancy of Christ; Christ risen from the dead; and this is observed every Sabbath throughout the year; not as the Church of Scotland or Church of England do only at Eastertide. Therefore, Easter Day also is not observed as a *special* day.

On the morning of each New Year's Day, be it a Sunday or a week-day, the Free Church and the Free Presbyterian Church hold a service, which is more in the nature of a lecture than of an ordinary Sabbath-day worship service; a means of bracing and fortifying oneself for the coming twelve months' worldly affairs and pitfalls of life.

Be all this as it may, Christmas Day—so bound up with the childish belief in Santa Claus—is one, broadly speaking, set aside for celebration, decorations, little fir trees bedecked with fairy lights and presents for young and old; holly and mistletoe hung up around the house, and a general air of rejoicing; and looking back on life, I must confess it gave me great joy as a youngster. On this day, for the whole twenty-four hours, some special benediction descends on fallow hearts; for eyes that will see, for ears that will hear; in short, the floodgates of affection and generosity are opened wide. And why not?

Of all the gifts of that day, the gift of the very day itself— 1440 minutes—is the most precious, and is a gift bestowed on all. Everyone, no matter what their creed or race, could spare at least a few minutes of those 1440 to embrace its honest meaning; to give a soft answer; to turn the other cheek; to do unto others as you would be done by; to take the glibness out of 'Peace on Earth, goodwill towards men'; and to exchange with one another a right 'Merry Christmas'—and that coming cheerily from the heart. Ceylon, where I lived for a quarter of a century, is a Buddhist country at heart and as such does not believe in celebrating Christmas, as I have said before.

When I first went out to Ceylon, I lived in the company's bungalow bordering on the native quarter of Colombo—the Pettah—in which all races and castes lived and had their being; selling their various wares, and burning much incense, which conveniently drowned the otherwise stinking smells from the squalid humanity and open drains. There were four well-known beggars in the Pettah: Ahamed, Marikar, Podysingho and Mohideen, all professing different faiths. They were true rascals, doing nothing but sitting on the crowded pavement holding out their bowls to be filled with odds and ends that passers-by chose to give. It was Charity with a capital C that they were living on and nothing more, save perhaps their wits. They were sly creatures, although they were able enough to do an honest day's work.

At night they went back to their little hovel and squatted round the small charcoal fire that served as their only means of cooking. One day, one of them had nothing in his bowl save a few scraps of meat. The other, a few vegetables, the third spices, and the fourth a few handfuls of rice. They grumbled and quarrelled, feeling that they were living in a cruel, inhuman world. It was suggested on that particular night, when 'takings' had been so poor, they should hang the chetty-pot over the fire, fill it with water, and throw all they had into it and so make some broth which they could all have. Agreed it was, and the pot was filled with water.

It was dark in this small unlit hovel, and only the glow of the charcoal embers lighted their pitiable dwelling. Each was to put his contents into the bowl. But one who had the scraps of meat was cunning, and he said to himself, 'Let the others put their lot in the pot; I won't; I'll relish the hot soup and then later on eat all the meat myself. Good.' So he just pretended to empty his bowl into the chetty, and then sat contented and smug and waited. However, Marikar with the vegetables had the same sly mind, and he also pretended to empty his contents into the pot, keeping his vegetables for his own mean self later on. So did Podysingho with the spices; so did the beggar with his rice. Therefore, in effect, nothing was put in the pot, yet each one thought to himself all was fine.

When the pot was boiling and lifted off the fire, there was nothing but hot water in it—and, of course, that ended the night with upheaval and quarrel extending into the small hours of the morning, when they ventured out into the streets again to cry 'Alms for the love of Allah, Buddha' and so on.

The Christmas spirit of *giving* was not observed by these four beggars. How different would it have been if they *had* freely given?

But let us get back to the Hogmanay party and 'spirit' of *the* season; not forgetting to realise that the production of whisky is a fine art, and that all attempts to produce *uisge beatha* (water of life) by any scientific artificial approach has been found futile! And it may be worth recording, the very first man to discover the potent qualities of wine was Noah (Genesis ix; 20.21). At Hogmanay gatherings it is well known that this water-of-life laps the palate of nearly all Highlanders.

I have been at a few so-called Hogmanay parties in England, but they have nothing on those up in the Highlands.

You start at one house, the one that is to be—you think—the centre of the evening. Liberal supplies of sherry, port, gin and whisky are not only available, but overflowing. Then extra-specially made soup from extra-special stock; a choice of venison, chicken, or duck (mountains of it); dainty sweets like lemon

meringue pie, pear condés, Trinidad trifle and so forth emblazoned with mountains of *real* whipped cream, plum pudding,
cheese; 'whangs o' cheese', particularly 'crowdie'. Crowdie
is the traditional skim-milk cheese of the crofts and farms of the
North of Scotland. It is skim milk made into a curd. The whey
is drained off, a little salt is added; and there you have a white,
fat-free spreading cheese. Then there are oatcakes made with
fine (extra fine) oatmeal, that melt in your mouth, stacks of
newly baked pancakes and scones, that you feel you want to
cuddle. All in case you are still hungry. Not only the table,
but the sideboard is 'plastered' with food.

After all this, coffee, home-made cake and shortbread.
Surely a meal to end all meals. And we musn't forget the
liqueurs, Drambuie as a rule, for it has a whisky base! Then as
the hours slip by, other friends will phone up asking when are
we coming along to their place; and so to their places we go, along
dark, tortuous roads (for in the Wild West there are no street
lamps), and upon arriving, we are once more assailed with food
and drink. And you are glad of more food to stabilise you.
This can go on all night—well into the sma' hours—and so long
as you have a box of indigestion tablets with you, all may be
well! Gatherings that put the old year to shame with joy and
splendour, and at long last you come away, hoping you are car
conscious, saying *ceud mìle taing* (a hundred thousand thanks),
and my! what a nicht wi' Burns we've had! Or to mix and stagger
your metaphors more, you might say to your hosts, you expected
a *real* Hogmanay, but it was a much better Hogmanay than you
expected!

And so, at the close of a real good Hogmanay (with your
tongue the next day like the bark of a dead tree and you feel you
have been drifting in an open boat for days beneath the parching
pitiless sun of Capricorn) you come out into the cold of the night;
the cold air beating on your forehead which makes worse confusion of your befuddled mind; and as very often is the case
when you leave the house that has befriended you in its wealth
of enjoyment, people and warmth, you find it has been snowing
heavily during the hours you have been indulging, and the world
outside is nothing but a white blanket—and your spirits sink like
a wet blanket, and you think of what extra work this will
involve, up here in 'cut-off' Wester Ross: sheep to bring in

from the moor; water to carry to the hens in their distant huts; maybe cars and vans to dig out. Yet for all this, the country takes on a magic of white wonderland: trees of rarest lace pattern; sculptures of strange beauty; far-off glistening peaks; and all a stilly quietness of an uncanny nature.

It is nearly four o'clock in the morning, and if it had been spring the only sound left would be that from an early-morning lark high overhead, singing in a new day—a New Year?

In the big cities the gathering is not so intimate, so close, as in the Highlands, and the Highland families and crofts. There, the ordinary people come to tread under foot as bitter ashes their last hopes of the Old Year, its miseries they had survived, and to welcome the next year with hope and confidence that none could warrant, and none defeat. Bells ring loudly, little flat, black bottles come out of hip-pockets as if by magic, and nips are offered to friend and stranger alike; hands are then held in a circle (all this in the main street, mark you!)—unknown hands mostly—songs are sung and then a boisterous dance or reel trodden. 'Another dram'; 'Shure another wee dram will no' harrm ye, Andra'?' 'Och, aye'; and in the poor homes of these cities, 'Another dram and another thick slice of black bun, ma lassie'.

And that's the end of another year; and Scotland's motto carries on high 'NEMO ME IMPUNE LACESSIT'; or, translated in Glasgow-Scotch, 'Wha' daur meddle wi' me?'

*   *   *

At one of our village shops I picked up a pretty Gaelic Christmas card which I sent my English friends. I give the Gaelic first and the liberal translation later—

NOLLAIG CHRIDHEIL . . . AGUS BLIADHNA MHATH ÙR
GED THA 'BHLIADHNA SO A' DÙNADH
IS TÉ ÙR A' TIGHINN 'NA H-ÀITE,
'SE AR GUIDHE IS AR DÙRACHD
GUM BI 'N CÀIRDEAS MAR A BHÀ . . .

Hearty Christmas and a Good New Year
Though this year is ending
And a new one takes its place,
It is our wish and our desire
Our friendship will remain.

Another year. The sand-glass is running out; three hundred and sixty-five days gone by. How silently—yet how quickly again—has grain after grain, particle after particle, hour after hour, dropped in this glass. The beginning of a New Year is a time for serious thought as we commence on the journey of another one.

I have quoted a Gaelic greeting. It may be fitting, seeing I am English (and a Yorkshireman), to give the following as a New Year greeting:

> May the best you've ever seen
> Be the worst you'll ever see;
> May the mouse ne'er leave your meal sack
> With a tear drop in its eye.
> May your lum keep blithely reekin'
> Till you're old enough to die,
> May you aye be just as happy
> As I'd like you aye to be!

Critics may say there are one or two Scottish words in this Yorkshire greeting; but who cares. We are west of Garve! I know of a similar Irish one, viz.: 'May yer meal barrel niver run empty, an' may yer bread foriver be rough casted in butther'.

Sincere seasonal greetings are filled with something more than the old, old wish; although 'tis for ever new and welcome to our hearts. Maybe after 2000 years of affirmation of Christianity, the tide of the spoken word has turned, and we are now meant to prove that which previously has been merely assumed. *The world we view is the world made new.* Great events simply reveal and express a new set of values in this 20th century. Civilisation's progress is now rapidly unfolding. St. John's revelations on the Isle of Patmos were no séance, but of direct perception. Every individual belief and desire is a tributary of that great river called Progress; and every man, woman and child can play their part in creating a peaceful existence; a Christmas that extends all the year round. Man sows little brown seeds and bulbs in the soil, and his expectation is for something unspeakably richer and lovelier to burst forth from them. A tree needs to be pruned in order to bear fruit. This modern world is a slave to its discoveries and inventions; its politics, and nations' thirst for power. What we strive to get, we strive to keep. Vainly do we look ahead of Time for solutions to the world's difficulties; how eagerly most of us would love it to be Christmas all the time, so that the 'lion may lie down with the kid'. If all of us were so disposed, we need not experience Autumn and Winter, but perpetual Spring. 'Tis the living of life that matters, and once again, *the world we view is the world made new* . . .

As we turn back the pages, thoughts of many Christmases and New Years bury themselves in our minds as emblems of goodwill, and the spirit of giving.

Giving? . . . In some of the country districts of Germany even today, parents tell their children of a Christmas miracle which happened long ago in the old city of Strassburg. As snow and darkness fell, the Christmas Eve Service was beginning, and many well-dressed people were walking up the Cathedral steps. They were watched by poor, shivering, hungry little Hans as he sheltered close to the wall of the main doorway. He would have liked to have gone inside if only for the warmth; but he was a little beggar boy and was afraid. A lady in beautiful clothes and her small daughter came along. The little girl had a basket in her hand. Without any warning, the child ran up to him, and taking a large rosy apple from her basket, thrust it into his hand saying, 'This is for you'; and then quickly joined her mother and entered the church.

Hans looked in amazement at the apple, for he had rarely had such a present, and then in a sudden impulse crept inside the Cathedral as the singing of a Christmas hymn was commencing. He slipped into a back pew near the door. He didn't know what the service meant, but how glad he was to be warm, and the music and tall candle-lights delighted him—especially the very bright table up at the front, at the east end. He hung on to his apple and felt he was in heaven. Then he became afraid, for he saw some men walking down the aisles with plates taking up money as offerings to this feast; he wanted to run out into the cold snow-clad street, but the door had been shut. Inwardly he shivered with fear, for whilst he saw everyone putting in coins, he had nothing except his rosy apple. He couldn't part with that; besides he *dare* not, for what would everyone think or say if he put an apple and not a coin in the plate. What would the priest think; he would be angry; and God, too, might not He be angry? Oh! no! Then when the plate came in front of him, he unconsciously placed his apple 'mongst the money. Nobody uttered a word, and his apple was carried along the aisle, in front of the choir boys and up to the priest's table. Hans was spellbound, not knowing what might happen to him now; he might be beaten or he might be sent to the magistrates. But as the priest turned towards all those gathered in prayer, our little beggar friend Hans saw that his apple—the poorest gift of all—*had turned to gold*; and had taken on a shine of heavenly radiance. His gift must have pleased his Maker, and he felt no longer hungry, cold or miserable; instead he felt a great joy and warmth surging through his weak, thin body.

After the service, he saw the small child that had given him the apple leaving the Cathedral with her mother. He dared not go up to her to thank her, for he was only a beggar boy; so he just stood near the outside wall where she had first seen him. She turned and gave him a smile, and Hans took off his ragged cap and made a gracious bow. For he was no longer a beggar; he felt he was equal to those in fine raiment.

*   *   *

Whilst in Alexandria, Egypt, one Christmas-time, I came to witness another kindly action performed by the Greeks on New Year's Day—which day they think of, and keep, as a social feast, far more than Christmas Day itself, which is observed purely as a religious date in their calendar year. Some few days before 1st January, every Greek housewife bakes a cake rather like shortbread in taste, and a coin is mixed in with the flour. On New Year's Day, either at midday or evening meal, the cake is brought in and cut; and as each piece is sliced, the name of one of the persons present is called, and he or she takes her piece, hoping of course to find the coin in their share, which, it is imagined, would ensure good luck and good health throughout the ensuing year. It is all part of a solemn ritual; but the real point to be noted is that the very *first* slice cut is '*for the Christ*'; and this piece is put aside and later on given to a poor person. 'The Godly Act' it is termed.

Another instance of a foreign people's belief in 'the giving'; though their religion differs from our own.

Christmas! the spirit of giving; the spirit of tolerance and goodwill; and to my mind it doesn't matter two hoots whether 'tis 25th December or 25th June.

As I have said, this modern world is a slave, and we tend to forget our true nature and heritage; and our ignorance of what we are in bondage to is frightening at times. This modern world! By education, ventilation, sanitation, 'stratophiscation' and legislation we expect to bring about a new earth; trying nervously to draw back the curtains of the future is very apt to be a hindrance to our day-to-day living. Lots of new words and slogans are constantly being coined and repeated to excess. *Ecumenical* (a 'oneness'), mentioned before, can well be applied to Christmas Day, New Year's Day, Easter Day, All Saint's Day and any other special days in that this 'oneness' might come to be established day by day. But I suppose we must carry on as we were taught in our youth, 'sufficient for the day ...'. 'How long will I have to lie here, doctor?', a hospital patient once asked; and the physician's reply, 'Just one day at a time'. Adopting that outlook we conserve our strength in not frittering our energy away, worrying about a tomorrow that has yet to come.

Previously I made mention of the non-observance of Easter day up here; the Free and the Free Presbyterians looking upon *every* Sabbath as an 'Easter'. In the chapter *Eastern Interlude* I gave some details of the Greek Orthodox Church. In connection with Eastertide, the Greeks hold a very special procession which I once saw in Alexandria, and which is well worth recording. It reads, and appears, as though it was a New Year celebration. Sometimes out there, the East/West churches celebrate Easter Day perhaps within a week of each other, and on some occasions there is a gap of six weeks between them, *i.e.* between R.C.s., C. of E., and other Protestant bodies. The Orthodox Easter invariably takes place the first week of May.

Thursday in Holy Week is known to us as Maundy Thursday in the English calendar; to the Greeks it is known as 'Great Thursday'. Then it is that all the chapters from the four Gospels are read in detail, from the account of what happened in the Upper Room, to Gethsemane, the Trial and the Crucifixion. After this, the priest brings out the Cross—some five feet in height—placing it on the floor of the church. The figure of Christ is then screwed on to it, and the figure of His Mother is put on the right side, and that of Mary Magdalene on the left side. These figures are not in the nature of statues; they are of wood with the likenesses painted on—rather like 'cut-outs', being flat.

I have already mentioned the question of 'fasts' and 'fasting'.

On Good Friday ('Great Friday' to the Greeks) the Old Testament prophecies concerning our Lord are read, and at midday the church bells toll; thirty-three strokes, for the thirty-three years of our Lord's life. The priest then takes a cloth, and with great reverence removes the body of our Lord from the Cross, and then walks through the *ikonostassi* screen (*vide* Chapter 8), reappearing shortly, bearing a pall-like velvet cloth on which is a figured embroidery of the burial of the Lord. This is laid on a four-poster dias, whereupon all the congregation approach it, crossing themselves and kissing the cloth. The 'procession' is then ready to start late in the afternoon, when the church bell begins to toll, and a band leading the congregation plays various hymns. The procession would wander round the church garden and precincts, but where this does not exist, they parade up and down various streets. After hymns, the band commences to play Chopin's funeral march—to my mind, one of the greatest pieces of music. Amongst the procession are, of course, the robed choir boys carrying staffs upon which silver lamps are placed, all with a lighted candle. Then, other staffs on which wreaths are borne in the form of a Cross; other staffs still, with wreaths borne on six carved winged angels; and all these staffs are of silver. After all this, there comes the Cross with but a wreath upon it, for the Lord has been crucified and buried. Following this come all the church dignitaries, magistrates, consuls, and other V.I.P.s of the parish. Then four of the clergy in black robes, each holding a corner of the velvet pall. The Bishop is next, also in black, surrounded by further choir boys, some holding candles, others swinging 'censers' (for incense). That is the end of the procession proper; but then the general crowd of onlookers falls in behind, and all walk back into the church, so finishing the service.

That is Friday—Good Friday. The following morning is quiet, most people going to communion; but all foregather in the evening to celebrate the Resurrection, which service commences at 11 p.m.: Easter Eve. A few prayers are said, and then at 11.45 p.m. the congregation is led out of the church by the priest or bishop, both of whom are now wearing gorgeously rich vestments. Towards midnight, the priest knocks on the door of the church, which had been closed. The knock is repeated three times, and a deacon from within asks, 'Who knocks?' And the reply, 'The King of Glory'. The doors are thrown open. An ikon of the risen Christ stands against the *ikonostassi* (screen). It is wreathed with flowers, and the church is dimly lit. The priest, holding a lighted candle, then says, 'Come and draw a light from the Never Failing Light'. At this instance, the church becomes a blaze of light, and then each one of the congregation takes a candle, lighting it from the priest's candle, all singing 'Christ is risen from the dead'. These candles are put into lanterns and taken home. In Athens, which is built amongst hills, the effect of seeing all such people coming down from the various churches, bearing these lanterns, is truly fairy-like.

This is not all, though. For whilst the congregation is still in the church lighting the candles, pandemonium breaks loose outside. Squibs and Chinese crackers are let off and guns are fired—a regular Guy Fawkes affair! Once home, everyone eats a traditional meaty broth; then crack coloured eggs, so breaking their fast. The ikon of the Risen Christ remains in the church until Ascension Day. To most or all of us up in the Highlands, all I have described may appear to be theatrical to the highest degree; yet to millions of others it is the symbol and re-enactment of the Salvation of Mankind through the Cross. I have at least told you the story and explained the procedure to the best of my ability, in the hopes of it being of interest.

The Greek and Syrian Orthodox keep Christmas and New Year as we do in England, and according to the 'Gregorian' Calendar; they keep Easter, however, according to the 'Julian' Calendar. Although they inwardly admit the Julian Calendar is incorrect, yet they are loath to depart from their old traditions.

*   *   *

Whatever your religion, your faith, your beliefs . . . 'A Guid New Year to you—and on Earth peace *to men of goodwill*'.

I remember an old saying, 'There's nothing wrong with this old world—it's just the people in it!' However, whatever wrong there may be, there is nothing that cannot be righted— if we try. We may yet avoid Armageddon, the battlefield of the ages (the great plain of Esdraelon, or Megiddo) where the flags of all ancient nations were wet with the dews of Hermon, and where pageants of blood have swept through that war-devastated valley since the time of the Kings of Babylon to that of General Allenby. 'They gathered them together into the place which is called in Hebrew, Har-Mageddon.' *Har* means mountain; so we have the 'mount of Megiddo', the city of Megiddo being located on the slope of the mountains south of the plain. The Holy Land was chosen as the stage on which the two critical events of all history are set; and they were set on two mountains—Mount Calvary and Mount Megiddo. Two altars that dominate the world.

'A Guid New Year' can mean more than just four glib words, if we choose it to be so.

When the bugle's call sinks into silence
And the long marching columns stand still;
When the captain repeats his last orders
And they've captured the last fort and hill.
When the flag has been hauled from the mast-head
And the wounded afield checked in,
When the world that rejected its Saviour
Is asked for the reason—WHAT THEN ?

The years slip away and are lost to me, wrote Horace the Latin poet 2000 years ago in a Hogmanay mood. Each New Year means just that. The spirit of giving and of wishing one another greetings is verily a silken bond linking peoples together. The story is told of Sir Walter Raleigh who asked favour upon favour of Queen Elizabeth, to which she replied 'Raleigh when will you leave off begging ?' 'When your Majesty leaves off giving' he replied.

At Christmas and New Year most of us are drawn together— United we Stand; what a compelling force that can be. Divide the waters of Niagara into individual drops and they would be no more than falling rain; but in their united body of millions of tons of water cascading per hour they can quench the fire of Vesuvius—and still have plenty to spare to deal with other volcanoes.

CHAPTER 15

IN GENERAL

METAPHORICALLY speaking, it is better to travel than to arrive. Another familiar saying, used by a number of overseas visitors, is 'Getting there is half the fun'. To my mind a fair amount of enjoyment *is* obtained by the drawing-up of the itinerary as to where one is going, and where to put up *en route*. Some people make it up in the minutest detail, even reckoning out the distance to a half-mile; others take it as it comes. The miles in Scotland seem to be longer than elsewhere; and if you should happen to stop on the way to ask a local as to where so-and-so is, you'll probably be met with the answer, 'Oh! it's just round the corner'; but he wouldn't have said *which* corner he meant! Still, it's all fun, and as I have said on more than one occasion, *once you pass Garve, nobody hurries.* The operative word is 'dawdle'. So long as you know what day it is, who cares?

I think visitors coming up to the Wild West can be classified as follows: those who look to scenery as their main objective; those who are more interested in viewing historic places, castles and ruins dating back from the dawn of history; and those who look for any means of diversion from town habits and town life. At any rate those visiting the western seaboard and isles will find all three objectives in one. Alas! they may find all weathers in one; from brilliant hot days to brawling gales of Force 9 and 10, in which case they will wish they had lead-soled shoes or boots to ensure they had a good grip of Scotland, as they see the telegraph poles swaying and the wires sagging; the trees bending over trying to keep their natural vertical instead of their un-natural position of being parallel to the ground; sheep and lambs sheltering at the crofters' back doors; cows with their back-sides to the fury of the oncoming wind and rain; cats and dogs asleep before a peat fire; the crofter probably in the byre, sitting snug with his feet up on the cow's warm body, watching the rain pelt down. A visitor once said to a local, 'Doesn't it *ever* stop raining here?' to which the Highlander replied, 'It used to!'; the lochs whipped up into waves such as you see in the Minch on a winter's day, and the herring boats safely tied up to the pier, the crew in the hotel public bar spending their last week's pay, bonus included, and playing darts; the ferries moored and doubly anchored; the sea-birds flying backwards, and the dive-bombing skuas on holiday; the Loch Seaforth almost turning over on its journey to Stornoway; trout and salmon—being sensible creatures—lying snugly on the bed of the river, knowing full well there'll be no flies around today to gobble up—so the best thing to do (they reason) is to 'stay put'. It is true to say up here, the weather fashions the country and its life; and the country in turn influences the weather. Tourists will tell you that! But I am not being loyal in boosting these parts by penning or painting such a morbid picture; however, as a postcript I would say it is not so bad as all this, for the Gulf Stream doesn't let us down. Even so, think how bracing and invigorating all such weather as this can be. There is nothing better for one's complexion, without the aid of cosmetics, so on this score, I will have the fair sex on my side. Good!

Now the first thing in preparing for a holiday here is regarding the condition of your car, and most folk will contemplate giving it an extensive overhaul a few weeks beforehand, 'ere embarking on this 'perilous journey'. My advice is, don't. Years ago it was the custom, before going far afield, to put the car in the local garage and have it 'decoked', or decarbonised as it was later politely described, and valves ground in. That is now out of date with present-day fuel. I am all for a leave-well-alone policy; for if the local chap starts tinkering about with the timing, the distributor, and so on, the chances are you may find the car running worse than before. After all, you are not coming to an outlandish area, and any ordinary garage can put right anything simple. Of course if you run into another car in your careless driving, then you can't expect to find any expert body-builders around, north of Inverness. But that's *your* fault, not the car's. You should naturally see the battery is topped up, the oil-stick shows 'max', and you *must* not let your tank fall short of being quarter full—for garages up here are few and far

between. The tyres should be checked for the right pressure—
and inflated a spot more since you are carrying more luggage
and passengers (including Chummy, the dog) than in the towns;
and the spare tyre should be seen to as well; for this is very often
forgotten, and should you have need to change a tyre you will
—unless you had thought—find this tyre flat, or almost flat;
not only that, but well-worn, and may only take you a few miles
on your journey. So, take note, and beware. A car that has
been serviced regularly should not require any special preparation
or expense for your trip. It might be wise to carry a spare tube,
to safeguard against punctures or blow-outs and to save time,
on these 'awful roads!' (Some propagandist, am I not?) And
as you will encounter more than a few hills and steep gradients,
be sure to keep your eye on the hydraulic fluid reservoir, so that
your brake *does* function at the crucial moment. It is also wise
to have a spare fan-belt. You'll not need bulbs, for it is never
dark here in the summer. Even if it were, there are no police
traps around; and possibly your mahogany-coloured face
obtained in this splendiferous air, will prove sufficient light for
on-coming traffic! Should your road-fund licence, driving
licence, insurance certificate, even your car-radio licence be due
to expire before you return home—pay no attention! for this
is God's own country, and the odd P.C. you might (?) meet
in 500 miles wouldn't bother. He's too much of a 'chentleman'
to interfere or to ask questions. 'Chust that!'

    They are not out to fill up their pocket-book, or daily record
sheet, with such trivial items in order to advance their position
in the Police force. No, sir! They are human up here. Bless
them! And another 'hauf' won't do us any harm! As to
petrol, it should be remembered there are not too many pumps
in the Highlands; and if you are particular as to your own
special brand, you may have to travel miles for same; so when
a 'quarter-full', as I have said, you should think of refuelling.
Besides, many filling stations close early in the evening; and
most, if not all, are NOT open on the Sabbath. A gallon can of
petrol, carried in the boot, sometimes comes in handy.

    You're on the way, then; all set, and another piece of advice
if your next morning's journey is via twisting roads, is *don't*
have too big a breakfast; or else—; the dog included; for *he*
can be car-sick, too. Poor Chummy!

I have previously referred to the narrow roads met with up in the north; the many bends and blind corners, and that one needs to drive with extreme caution. In the interests of road-safety, it would do no harm to stress the following again:

1. In some places one should not only keep well to the left, but 'hug' the left; for you never know what mad driver may be rounding the bend well in the middle of the road-way. Someone remarked once, 'There are no bad roads ; only bad drivers'. There are plenty of both. Nearly every driver involved in an accident lays the blame on the *other* fool ; not thinking that such a saying implies that *he* too is a fool.

2. The passing-places are meant solely for passing, and not for parking. Should two or three cars be parked, there is no room for other cars coming in opposite directions to get by, and an awkward, needless congestion can arise. These passing-places are not meant as LAY-BYS such as one comes across in England.

3. Should you wish to stop to admire the view, only stop for a few minutes and then move on, so avoiding annoyance to others *en route*. Moreover, it may come as a surprise to many, that you infringe the Traffic regulations by doing so, and are liable to be charged by the police for obstruc-tion ; possibly finding yourself up at the Sheriff Court, Dingwall, one day.

4. By no means are these passing-places put there for over-night caravanning. This is most dangerous; and besides, who would want to sleep on the main highway? Yet some do!

5. If you are travelling at a modest speed and the fellow behind you keeps hooting in his anxiety to pass, well, let him pass; for you might be had up for obstruction! By all means let such a road-hog get ahead and get what may be coming his way. Wave him on with a smile, letting him see *you* have manners.

6. Remember this: more than any other physical act, accidents are caused by faulty RIGHT turns.

7. Whilst touring in the many light hours of summer, instead of sticking to motoring during usual hours of travel from 9 o'clock onwards, it is a good idea to start any *long* journey early; and by early, I mean around 3 a.m., when one would have got hundreds of miles 'away from it all' by the time the milkman was beginning his rounds in Inverness. You would have avoided the mass rush. Instead of sunsets on

the lochs, you would see brilliant sunrises on the lochs, and have had plenty of time to admire same without holding up traffic. The song 'up in the morning early is no' for me' would then be truly exploded.

I am not exaggerating these dangers. It is senseless to drive haphazardly, or with abandon, if you wish to safeguard your life and those of your passengers. You only need to have one accident—small though it may be—whereupon your whole holiday spirit is damped, to say nothing of the damage to your car. Of course should you have hired the car, you won't perhaps mind; but what of the other fellow's car? You must have a 100 per cent road sense and courteousness along these narrow tortuous highways. After all, you're not in a hurry, surely; you've no trains to catch, no appointments to keep. Unless this is clearly borne in mind and fully recognised, the only appointment you may have will be with Death. And one is a long time dead. Look well ahead, and be in perfect control of your automobile, be it car, estate car, caravette, motor cycle, scooter, or what not. Some drivers seem to think there can't possibly be any other people on these far-away Highland roads but themselves. They are in for a shock sooner or later; to say nothing of sheep and cows on the wayside. I have seen lots of glaring bad driving—'chance driving' I would call it; and 'chance' can play many tricks on the roads today. And of the 'crashing' of gears, there is no ending. I might well conclude this particular sermon by the well-known reconstruction road signs you see here and there, viz.: YOU HAVE BEEN WARNED.

*   *   *

Scenery, history, ruins and diversion, as I have said; and in the Western Highlands there is plenty to satisfy.

Even starting at Edinburgh, apart from the Castle itself, there is 'MONS MEG'—that great veteran cannon seen on the battlements, where you can think back into history to the time when men made war by throwing big cannon-balls at each other. This piece of medieval artillery is a national mascot. The idea that it was made at Mons in France—that village of memory of World War I—is an erroneous one, for this famous cannon was manufactured by a blacksmith in Galloway in 1455, and was presented to James II by the McLellan family (who had ordered its making) when the King arrived at Carlingwark, near Castle Douglas, with his forces to avenge the arrogance of the powerful Earl of Douglas (of Threave Castle) for his part in the hanging of Sir Patrick McLellan. The firing of the two granite balls from Mons Meg made the Earl capitulate. Legend has it that one of the balls broke off the hand of Margaret de Douglas ('The Fair Maid of Galloway') as she was seated at the table with the Earl. An act of Divine vengeance, it was called. The King created the town of Kirkcudbright a royal burgh, and gave lands to the blacksmith, whose wife's name was Meg. This great cannon was, thirty years later, taken from Edinburgh Castle and put into action at the siege of Dumbarton Castle by James IV in 1489. Nearly two hundred years after this (1682), Mons Meg burst whilst firing a salute to James II of England; the last of the Royal House of Stuart. After the 1745 Jacobite rebellion, the cannon was taken to the Tower of London and remained there for almost another one hundred years, when George IV gave permission for its return to Edinburgh Castle.

Whilst in Edinburgh there should also be seen the new Forth Road Bridge, the biggest engineering enterprise in Scotland this century, which cost over £20 millions; opened by H.M. The Queen on 4th September 1964.

Castles, abbeys, ruins and history. . . .

There is Stirling Castle with Bannockburn and the Wallace Monument near by. Bannockburn! in which fell in 1964, the 650th anniversary, and the 50th anniversary of the outbreak of World War I. There is a similarity between June 1314, which saw Scottish Nationalism triumph over its English 'overlord', and the valiant stand of Britain's 'Old Contemptibles' in August 1914. The Queen and Prince Philip were at Bannockburn when the statue of Robert the Bruce was unveiled. A remarkable statue indeed; the mounted figure on a charger, with raised battle-axe poised. A really marvellous piece of 27-foot bronze, valued nearly £30,000. The rotunda, detailing the battle, built around the old monument contains the Borestone where Bruce raised his standard on that memorable day. Thousands upon thousands of people are now visiting this historic site. The Scottish nation owes more to Bruce than to any other man. The geography of Scotland is such that the country has no large areas of flat country, but is divided up in all directions by ranges of hills and mountains, and by inlets of the sea, all of which made for an air of independence and love of freedom; and this has left its mark in the characters of even the lowest villager. This was to be found in the protest against the claims of Edward I in 1320, in the words of the Declaration of Independence (referred to earlier in this book) written on behalf of the Scottish people by the Prior of Arbroath. In it, the Parliament of Scotland maintained—regarding King Robert the Bruce . . . 'To him we are obliged and resolved to adhere in all things, both on account of his rights and of his merits as the man who has restored the people's safety and will defend their freedom. But if he should turn aside from the work he has begun, wishing that we or our Kingdom should be subjected to the King or people of England, we will immediately endeavour to expel him as our enemy and the subverter of his own rights and ours, and will make another King to defend us . . .'

This letter was also transmitted to Pope John XXII, and gained Papal recognition of Scottish independence from that quarter also.

Continuing, there is the Pass of Killiecrankie, near Pitlochry, where the army of William III was defeated by Jacobite forces in 1689. Culloden battlefield and Cawdor Castle (near Inverness), Glenfinnan monument (Loch Sheil), where Prince Charles raised his standard 19th August 1745. It was here that Bishop Macdonald blessed the royal standard and appointed a number of his priests to act as Chaplains to the Jacobite army. Urquhart Castle (Loch Ness); Inveraray Castle (Argyll); Dunvegan Castle (Skye); Arbroath Castle (Angus); Melrose Abbey (Roxburghshire); Fort Augustus Monastery; Dunrobin Castle (Sutherland); Eilean Donan Castle (near Dornie); Aros and Duart Castles (Mull); Dunollie and Dunstaffnage Castles (near Oban); and many, many others too innumerable to list—all well worth a visit.

As you travel up further along the royal route to Gairloch via Stirling, Callander, Strathyre, Balquhidder—long before reaching the famous Glen, Glencoe—you are in the heart of one of the most notorious clan-country, the MacGregors . . . Rob Roy MacGregor.

There are clans galore in Scotland; Ross-shire is really the land of the MacKenzies, though other clans in this county number the Morrisons, the MacLeods of Lewis (later Mac-Kenzies), the MacRaes, the Urquharts, the MacLennans, the Munroe's and the MacDonells of Glengarry. But the Clan MacGregor can claim much attention, for they were undoubtedly a very ancient and warlike clan. It is at Balquhidder (off by Strathyre) where Rob Roy the outlaw and his wife and sons are buried in the churchyard there (1734).

According to tradition, the clan is said to have descended from King Gregor, son to King Kenneth MacAlpine and grandson to King Alpine (*circa* A.D. 830). All MacGregors acknowledge the said King Gregor as their common ancestor, and signify that in their Gaelic slogan, ''S RIGHAL MO DHREAM' (Royal is my race). For centuries they owned large estates in Argyll and Perthshire; they had the dignity of lords, but destiny made them outlaws.

The deterioration of the clan began at the overthrowing of King Baliol by Robert the Bruce, as the MacGregors supported the former. When Robert the Bruce was crowned at Scone, Perthshire, on 2nd November 1306, among his first duties was to reward his supporters with lands expropriated from his defeated opponents; and so the MacGregors lost a large portion of their estates to the new government. The Campbells were guilty of several outrages against the MacGregors, for this infamous clan—of the bloody massacre of the Macdonalds at Glencoe fame—persuaded a subordinate clan to launch several assaults upon the MacGregors; although the wily Campbells were only using these hirelings to further their own ends. But the MacGregors were not slow in their retaliation, by slaughtering these aggressors as they fled away with their booty. Now, Campbell was an influential personage with the government, and falsely represented these affairs to the King in the manner that the MacGregors had unjustly set upon and butchered his neighbours, and demanded that punishment be inflicted in case such incidents were repeated with even more disastrous results. He received a commission to punish the MacGregors. The battles that followed cost the MacGregors a considerable part of their remaining estates; and of course Campbell saw to it that same became his own.

By 1500 the MacGregors had been dissolved into two groups; one at Loch Rannoch and one at Loch Lomondside.

A further incident which placed the MacGregors in bad relation-
ship with the high powers was the beheading of the King's
Under-Forester, Drummond Ernock, in 1584. He was a brother
of Stewart of Ardvorlich's wife. Coming across two of the
MacGregor band poaching the King's deer, he cut a piece off
their ears. The youths ran home and then returned with some
of their clan, catching the Under-Forester and quickly beheaded
him; and to add to this deed, his head was taken to his sister,
Mrs. Stewart of Ardvorlich, Loch Earn, who—being ignorant
of what had happened—greeted them and offered them a meal.
Whilst this was being set down, the bloody head was removed
from its sack and placed upon the table. Just that! The sight
drove Ernock's sister demented. Because of the alliance between
the MacGregors and the Macdonalds, the government issued a
'Denunciation of Fire and Sword' against the Clan MacGregor
for their part in this beheading. Lord Drummond himself
attacked Balquhidder and killed thirty-seven of the MacGregors.

On the 7th February 1603 the battle of Glen Fruin was fought
between the MacGregors and the Colquhouns of Luss (Loch
Lomond), in which the Laird of Luss's forces were annihilated.
It was unfortunate that Luss possessed a Royal Commission, and
so the MacGregors suffered greatly for this disregard of the
King's law.

Following this event, King James VI issued a proclamation
dated 3rd April 1603, stating 'the name of MacGregor shall be
abolished and those who bear that name shall renounce it under
pain of death'. The government thought that after two or three
generations with a new name, the descendants would have
forgotten all about their MacGregor ancestry. The government
was trying to exterminate this clan for ever; they were outlaws
who could be killed like vermin—and this applied to their
children also. Not until 1775 were the name and rights of this
broken clan restored. In the interval many of the clansmen had
adopted surnames from other clans, or formed them in various
ways to avoid using the forbidden name; so that a great number
of families of widely different names can today be connected with
Clan Gregor. The government even issued warrants for the
death of all the MacGregor participants of Glen Fruin; and a
reward was offered for every MacGregor head. The clan,
deprived of almost everything, turned outlaws and lived by

plunderings. Those who were unwilling to follow this hard and dangerous life dispersed throughout the land, becoming tenant farmers and generally taking the name of their new laird.

This, then, is the heritage from which Rob Roy came. He was born in 1671; and not only did he excel in his education—such as it was in those days—his robust and muscular frame together with exceedingly long arms made him most useful with the broadsword. His complexion was ruddy and his hair was red; hence he was called 'Roy', signifying in Gaelic these features. When Rob was only 19 years of age, his father was put in Edinburgh gaol for cattle-stealing. After two years he became ill, but the government would not allow his release, unless payment was made for the time he was incarcerated. Young Rob managed to secure the ransom money—we will not say how!—and his father was released in October 1691. When Rob Roy was only 21 he assumed the duties of Captain of the Glengyle Watch, being responsible for the suppression of violence and robbery in his district; particularly cattle-lifting! His reputation was enhanced in his encounter with a party of wild MacRaes from Wester Ross, who had lifted a number of cattle, and his dramatic killing of them and the stolen cattle being returned to the rightful owners. His name was now dreaded, and only a fool would dare cross swords with him.

In 1692, Rob whilst farming in Balquhidder commenced on his cattle-raising career, after marrying his cousin, Mary Mac-Gregor of Comar. Rob was a tenant of the Duke of Atholl, and not a very obedient tenant at that, and the Duke suspected Rob of being in league with Atholl's rival, Lord Breadalbane, a Campbell. In short, Atholl had Rob Roy captured in his house, but whilst he was being conveyed through Strathyre and along Loch Lubnaig, he made a bold escape. The Duke by this time was not interested in spending time and effort in pursuing the MacGregor, and in the end he persuaded Rob to take certain allegiance and oaths of faithfulness and obedience to His Lord-ship; and for these actions, Rob was granted a full pardon. For the next few years he led a peaceful life, keeping his hands off other people's cattle! He then started an insurance scheme. His clients would pay him a regular quarterly premium for assurance against theft; he guaranteed to either recover or to replace any of his clients' cattle that were stolen. Being Captain of the Watch, he could govern the movements of his men as he pleased and to his own advantage. He made a goodly business out of this idea.

In 1700 Rob Roy had become Chief of MacGregors, until his nephew, Gregor MacGregor, who had inherited Glengyle, became of age. Rob was prospering, but realised in a few years' time his nephew would claim the inheritance whereupon Rob would revert to a small and unimportant drover in Balquhidder. In the interim and to obtain more money to expand his business, he secured the interest of James Graham, Duke of Montrose, who agreed to give him funds on condition that the profits be shared equally. And so Rob assumed management of both cattle and money. A few years passed working in a very harmonious manner, Montrose and Rob, but then Montrose, who had been constantly advancing more money, became impatient for his profit. All might have been well if Rob had not entrusted a man named Macdonald with the droving and sale of the stock; for this scoundrel absconded with everything and was never heard of again. Montrose, rightly incensed, demanded that all the moneys he had made over be repaid, and with interest added.

And should Rob default, then Montrose would openly accuse him of fraud. MacGregor attempted to repay Montrose by mortgaging Craig Rostan, but this was only a temporary expedient. Montrose was now Secretary of State to Scotland (Lord Privy Seal) and his object was to annex Rob Roy's estates to his own, thereby considerably gaining in the matter of his outstanding cash debts. Rob could not openly oppose Montrose in court; it would be far too disrespectful; and his friends refused to associate themselves with his troubles.

At 41 years of age, Rob Roy being found to be a 'fraudulent bankrupt' was declared an outlaw, and his estates forfeited to the Duke. In November 1712, bailiffs and constables went up Loch Lomond to execute the order of seizure and landed at Inversnaid. Rob was away, but his wife and children were at home. The company, headed by John Graham of Killearn, stripped the house and property and ill-treated his wife shamefully.

Thereafter, a personal war existed between Rob Roy and Montrose.

In 1715, the Jacobites united for the cause of exiled King

James, but met with defeat at Sheriffmuir later in that year. Rob Roy had often carried on a guerrilla warfare on behalf of the Pretender (as well as for himself!), but for some unknown reason he did not attempt to engage in that battle of Sheriffmuir. After this, the clan were discouraged and returned to their glens and the rebellion came to an end. All the rebels received pardons. By now, Rob Roy was becoming too old to be following such a hard life as an outlaw and vagabond and he then found the Duke of Argyll ready to assist him, offering him his protection and a farm in Glen Shira. The Campbells and the Grahams were enemies, so Argyll was only too pleased to patronise Montrose's chief source of worry.

Rob Roy found himself longing for his own folk in Balquhidder. The Duke of Atholl, whose estates included Balquhidder, sent for him under the pretext of helping him back to a peaceful and law-abiding life. But treachery was afoot, and he was seized and imprisoned. However, Rob escaped, although he was wounded in the attempt. Rob Roy's relationships with Argyll now aroused new interests all round. Both Montrose and Atholl sought to discredit Argyll by proving him a Jacobite sympathiser and a traitor due to his friendship with MacGregor; but Rob would not betray his patron despite rewards or threats.

The MacGregor was now 50 years old, his life still full of uneasiness; under the Hanoverian rule he had been deprived of a peaceful normal life. A minor uprising of Jacobites occurred in Kintail in 1719, but their small force, amongst them our hero Rob Roy, was crushed at the battle of Glen Shiel, May 1719. Rob then obtained a sub-lease on a farm at Balquhidder; his Watch was reinstated, and he then petitioned to secure his freedom from all his outlawry charges. Montrose, the originator of the charges, was now anxious to end the feud, for it had been a costly affair all those ten years. MacGregor received his freedom wishes; and he spent the last years of his life in quiet retirement. He died in 1734 (aged 63 years) at Inverlochlarig farm, near Balquhidder.

Rob Roy MacGregor had not lived in vain, and he accomplished two outstanding things: one, he helped weld the Scottish people together against strong disintegrating forces; and two, he established himself as a national hero of the people for hundreds of years to follow. He can rightly be termed the

Famous Rob Roy MacGregor in the annals of Scottish history.

(I am indebted to my friend, Mr. Curtis A. Sisco, of Oakland, California, U.S.A. (descended from French nobility), for some of this subject-matter on the MacGregors, culled also from documentary evidence available at the National Library, Edinburgh). The MacGregor clan was the very last to stay beside Prince Charles at his defeat at Culloden, 16th April 1746.

Proceeding then from Rob Roy's locality at Balquhidder, we soon come to wild and barren Glencoe—the Glen o' Weeping —another historical landmark; the scene of the dastardly massacre, and one of the most awesome passes in Scotland in winter; a landscape without mercy, the Campbells butchering the Macdonalds (Papists and Jacobites) who were their hosts. Thirty-eight people, including two women and several children, were killed in cold blood in the early hours of that morning of 13th February 1692; and the rest, about 150 men, women and children, fled into the mountains to perish in a snow-storm. All under 70 years of age were to be put to the sword, was the order. Guests murdered hosts; it was, without doubt, Highland barbarism at its worst.

Even today, nearly three hundred years since, the name of Campbell is suspect; although I know of Campbells marrying into a Macdonald family, and at the Free Church in Gairloch, whose minister is a Macdonald, one of his elders is named Campbell. It is said King William III was primarily responsible for this massacre of the Catholic Macdonalds by the Protestant Campbell's. Aweel!

Continuing in historic vein, and not far from Ballachulish which is at the end of the Glencoe region, is the episode of 'James of the Glens', who stood trial for the Appin murder in 1752; and James's Gibbet near Ballachulish ferry. The Appin murder? Colin Campbell of Glenure ('the Red Fox') was shot in the woods of Lettermore that year. Although 'James Stewart of the Glens' was tried at Inveraray by a Campbell jury under a Campbell judge, the real mystery of who killed the Red Fox remains unsolved to this day; for whilst the name of the killer is known in Appin, the secret is kept as close as it was two hundred-odd years ago. In Appin they will tell you, 'Sorrow's stain still lies'. Caledonia stern and wild to be sure! In this locale one is not far from the Royal Castle of Dunstaffnage (four miles out of Oban), which has connections with the Stone of Destiny and with Flora Macdonald of Skye.

We are now drawing nearer to the north-west, and names like St. Columba (of Iona fame, where he landed on 12th May A.D. 563), Somerled of the Isles, from whose grandson Donald came the Macdonald clan, Robert the Bruce, Mary Queen of Scots, grand-daughter of James IV, Flora Macdonald and Bonnie Prince Charlie leap to our minds—and all wrapped up in legendary treasures, woven into many-coloured tapestries. On almost every hand we can come across some association with the Norsemen; practically every loch and creek has seen in its day, the arrival of the pillaging Vikings, and on every headland and shore the Highlanders in those days once stood to give them a welcome—of steel. The list is endless. The mingling of fact, truth, superstitions and fancy would surely fill page upon page. These were days long before the motor car and coach tours, and before electric pylons marched in regimental fashion over the hills; before the planes which make the journey to the many western isles in a matter of hours instead of days. Yet in the far-away places there is still the quiet and the peace of St. Columba's day when he—possessed with utmost faith and quite devoid of all attachments, wherewith he landed wiser, happier and more contented than his other fellow-voyagers, and careless of his own life and death—and his disciples landed at Iona and gave thanks to the Almighty for their safe arrival. Fourteen hundred years ago, St. Columba went up the little mound (the island is low-lying) overlooking the monastery and gave the following blessing:

> Unto this place, small and mean though it be, great homage shall be paid, not only by the Kings and peoples of the Scots, but by the rulers of barbarous and distant nations with their peoples. Thy saints also of other churches, shall regard it with no common reverence . . .

St. Columba was the great apostle of the Northern Picts, who were a race of people that formerly settled in the Highlands of Scotland, so named from tattooing themselves. The Celtic Cross combines a ring and a cross, the former intersecting the arms of the latter. It is quite distinct from any other form of cross. The Pictish stones have carvings thereon generally depicting a mirror and the cross; the mirror denoting self-awareness and meditation, the cross that of Christian self-sacrifice.

When one visits Iona, one may still hear St. Columba's last words uttered to his brethren around him in A.D. 597 '. . . that you preserve with each other sincere charity and peace . . .' and when one goes around the ruins and chapels, one feels hushed in the past, and one talks in whispers. One can even today witness the cathedral of Fingal's Cave at Staffa, where the sea rolls out a constant peal of carillons, as has been the pattern since the earth was formed; violent Staffa, peaceful Iona.

In all this you can, and will, thrill with the calm unspoilt beauty seen in all this land up here, especially as one sails through all the many sounds between the golden islands of the Hebrides and the deep indentations made by the countless sea-lochs on the western coast-line, even though spacecraft, travelling at 6000 miles per hour, and more than a quarter of a million miles, has thudded into the lighted side of the moon. In years to come it will no longer be 'Sunset on the Loch', but 'Moonfall *on* the Moon'. Then, we shall all be living in a 'new-look' world? We seem to be finding it more and more difficult to keep up with a world and life that appears to be changing so rapidly. As the old tom-cat said to his pal, 'Have you noticed that mice are faster these days?'

A 'New Look'—at the Highlands

We hear and read a great deal as to everyone who has the least bit of authority, trying to boost the Highlands; trying to flood the place with thousands more tourists; that the Highlands is lagging far behind in its so-called 'long term policy', and that strenuous efforts should be made to make 'attraction more attractive'. Personally, I think all this is a lot of ballyhoo. Commensurate with its resources (and its grandeur needs no words of mine to extol) the Highlands is holding its own in the national well-being. The superb settings to be found *everywhere* need no further gilding; its gold-leaf is there for the taking, and to tamper with nature will spell ruin. Recently some English visitors came and told me they had been to Ullapool and found it jammed full of cars and people, and ice-cream cones thrown on the pavements. They likened it to Blackpool (without

illuminations, of course), Bridlington and Brighton. But no
Mods or Rockers there! The very charm of the place was
blotted out. There is no need to fall over one another in stam-
peding to advertise Wester Ross or the Highlands and islands.
They all advertise themselves. Of course I know the Scottish
Tourist Board needs to prove its existence; but its upkeep can
surely be maintained in pursuing a quiet, ordinary course. They
are not, I feel, in business to produce stunning headlines. The
arc-lamps can be left to the film magnates. Otherwise, the goose
that lays the golden eggs will be killed. I know it creates a great
deal of egotism to be handling 'millions', but egotism in this
instance should not be countenanced.

In and around Aviemore—apart from the grandiose Cairn-
gorm snows—plans have been approved for a 3-million pound
holiday village or town, with all that that means; motels,
restaurants, bars, dance halls, and what-have-you; probably
fun fairs thrown in for good measure. Maybe girls from
Glasgow dancing the can-can; a Chinese restaurant with chop-
sticks and bamboo shoots and dishes such as chop-suey to add
flavour; and through the swing-doors of the bars set on lines
of the Western States' Las Vegas or Hangman's Creek joints,
we shall see men in 10-gallon hats like Mexican Pete, Dead Eye
Dick or Dangerous Dan Macgrew, all from the Rio Grande,
dashing through in search of fun at Black Mike's saloon, with their
fingers itching on their trigger guns, awaiting the entrance of
Eskimo Nell. It is only a phase, and like the Beatles, it will
pass in time. Merely a flash in the pan; for 'tis scenery up here
that is the tourist's magnet. What is needed is to preserve what
is best in the particular countryside. It needs taste and good
judgement and should not be left in the hands of 'foreign'
speculators. History shows that minorities are as often right as
majorities, if they have the truth on their side.

Up around Gairloch, the crofter and villager take in all the
visitors they can; every available house is full. To give a night's
lodging to a stranded visitor, I am sure the crofter and his wife
would sleep standing up like their cattle, so as to provide another
bed for the stranger. There's no need to put in a half-page advert
in the national press costing £500 and more to boost Gairloch;
it would be sheer waste of good money; and we don't want
two or three more hotels. The crofters and villagers are content;

the cow provides enough milk and butter; the eggs serve to pay the grocer's bill, their garden produce keeps the vegetable item low. A brisk season of letting, or bed and breakfast—and it *is* brisk and short—adds to the housewife's purse, and in the end helps her to buy a washing machine and other household goods, ready to make her spotless home even more spotless for the next year's visitors. And so it goes on, year after year. Maybe in the summer, visitors plus crofting is hard toil; but the good air, the contentment always uppermost, and the eagerness to welcome strangers, keep the good wife going. If it were taken to count, all the crofters and 'locals' accommodating visitors during the summer would be as great—perhaps greater —than the envisaged Aviemore project. Certainly the accent on personal contact and attention could not be questioned; for it is superb. And, what perhaps is more significant, the cash so spent would be far more widely spread. 'Laid-on' attractions may last for a year or so, but in the end 'tis grandeur and a quiet atmosphere that wins through. This is *not* journalistic fancy; merely pure unadulterated fact and common sense. What these crofters and villagers can't do by way of showering every attention upon a stranger, no one else can do.

A large number of people (23,000) visited the osprey habitat in 1964; but here again 'tis just a phase, and it may well never happen again. But mountains, lochs, straths and 'vastness' are like Father Thames—they carry on rolling along undisturbed, and sooner or later (most likely, sooner) folk will turn to the naturalness of this western seaboard. Its appeal is devastating.

And again, a London firm with millions to spend—these people always seem to have 'millions' on hand—is considering a plan to cash in on Islay, where they hope to build a luxury holiday village. Another South-sea bubble? or should I be more correct and say South-west bubble? The plan is to spend a million pounds on a hotel, motels, theatre, 750 summer cottages, and a shopping centre. I can visualise the top-less dress being exploited, and transistors (transistorised radio-receivers) carried about on every hand so as to bring 'life' to Islay in a big way. What a dreich affair? Imagine in such a small balmy island as Islay; and I use the word 'balmy' in all its senses. The syndicate so interested is hoping to crash into the tourist trade there with its massive development. Maybe 'crash' will be the operative word? The applicants stress the resort will cater for people wishing 'a quieter holiday'. I sometimes wonder how balmy reasoning can become.

Early in 1964—in February, to be exact—the government through the Secretary of State for Scotland, came out with a proposed TOURIST TAX on Scottish hoteliers, to help develop tourism in all its aspects. It was known as the fifty-bob (50/-) a year bed tax! Mr. Noble, the Secretary of State for Scotland, described this projected tax as merely a flea-bite. But a flea looks around for more than just one area to indulge in; he makes hops from place to place, and causes much discomfort! The fifty-bob-a-year tax met with much opposition; at least it is to the credit of seven Scottish Tory M.P.s who rebelled against it. The M.P.s were led by Sir Fitzroy MacLean of Bute and North Ayrshire, and were backed by M.P.s from West Aberdeen, Galloway, Ross and Cromarty, Inverness, Edinburgh South and East Renfrewshire. Only a year before, it was to be a sixpence-a-night tax upon guests by hotels and boarding houses. As both ideas were abandoned, some smart Alec from Whitehall will think up another suggestion 'ere long. Wait for it!

There always seems to be the tendency to treat taxpayers' money as though it really doesn't belong to anyone, and we therefore should give it away to someone! I am of belief that government should do for the people only the things the people cannot do for themselves.

Up here the Gairloch District Council held a conference in 1964, inviting most residents to attend, to discuss the various aspects of 'tourism' pertaining to this area; but not a single person ventured any pros or cons as to these taxes. No one seemed to realise the many implications involved. The boys in the Income Tax Department were forgotten!

I wrote a letter to the Northern press in the strongest of terms, and this appeared around the middle of February 1964. I give the text hereunder, and sent copies to the Prime Minister downwards. The government abandoned the idea two weeks after this letter was published—not without expressing their bitterness!

THE BEDROOM TOURIST TAX

We have heard a lot these past months of the Government's proposal to impose a tourist tax on Scotland; of a plan to raise

£200,000 a year by a 50 bob-a-bed levy on hotels, boarding and bed-and-breakfast houses, and which in many high quarters is welcomed by saying it would only amount to less than 1s. a week for each bedroom. Some of the smaller communities in the Highlands do not seem to be taking this proposed tax seriously enough, but unless an outcry is made now, it will be too late once the new Countryside and Tourism Amenities Bill becomes law.

I am strongly against any such tax, although I am in no way connected with the hotel or boarding-house business, being simply a retired Colonial living peacefully in my own house in the Highlands.

Let us first take this 50s. idea, dangled innocently before us as meaning so little.

In most parts of the Highlands, the real tourist season can be said to last for about 13 weeks in the year. So instead of a tax being 'less than 1s. per week', it would work out around 4s. per bed, per week—say £2 a week for a place having five double rooms. That's a lot of money for a small boarding-house to fork out. Then again it is not to be said that all beds would be occupied seven nights a week; moreover, many coming on a Saturday intending to move-on the next day (the Sabbath) would be refused accommodation. So we can whittle down the 7-nights-a-week, to a possible five nights full up; automatically increasing the aforementioned cost of £2 a week considerably. Such a tax would create anomalies and unfairness all round.

In the second place, what about those who live permanently in the Highlands, or for that matter in Scotland? If I wish to take a few days holiday from Gairloch to say Skye or Mull, why should I be taxed for going, in having to pay a little extra for my bed; for, make no mistake, this 'extra' will be added on to one's bill.

In the third place, there are interests other than hotels and boarding-houses, who benefit from the tourist trade, such as garages, shops, transport, travel agencies, pubs and places of entertainment. They are not being included in this tax. In short this is discriminating taxation of a most obnoxious nature. Then again, it is not every bed-and-breakfast house that will voluntarily give details of what they can provide, for then—sooner or later—they would be roped in by the Income Tax office! Such a tax as is outlined would require a lot of organising and would be expensive to collect as it would necessitate a horde of officials.

There is not the accommodation available for any tremendous influx of visitors up in the North, such as is envisaged by this advertising campaign. So where are we? It is quite common to find scores of cars along the sea coast at nights with families asleep.

Should a tax come about (and once again I strongly oppose it) then the only fair and reasonable way to my mind is to put a ½d.

in the £ on rates. The latest 1962/63 rateable value figures for Scotland amount to £100,106,000. A half-penny rate would give the £200,000 a year aimed at; no one would feel the impact of a ½d. rate. It could be easily collected by the local authorities with the rates, and they could charge the Tourist Board (or any special Council that the Secretary of State might appoint) in handling this money, say 2½ per cent, for such service.

Finally, we are by no means sure how and where the money would be spent. Believe me, there would be much misgivings as to same. The Cairngorms, Glencoe and other grandiose winter sports schemes would, in all probability, largely benefit so as to give the tax 'lime-light', but what of the small bed-and-breakfast people, and the poor crofters in the Highlands, who try to let a spare room or so in order to help them through their Winter months ?

Should they be called upon to pay a tax ? No, it is all wrong; and such a wrong needs righting—good and hearty. This bedroom tax is a piece of thoroughly bad legislation; unfair, ill-advised and fundamentally wrong.

In the Highlands, we don't look for money lavished on dual-carriageways or luxury hotels. The narrow roads enable the visitor time to move slowly and enjoy the scenery. Visitors just expect clean and comfortable quarters, and local food and dishes well served. They want it all 'our way' in this land of Fàilte and Slàinte Mhath. A year ago, the cry was for sixpence a night tax on visitors. Now some smart Alec has thought out another idea; and so we go on!

The Secretary of State for Scotland, Mr Michael Noble, can argue as he will, but the Highlands will remain as they are, taking in all the visitors possible, giving them more helpings of good, wholesome food than, I would say, anywhere else in Britain.

There are more ways of attracting new-comers to Scotland and the Highlands than a tax. As a writer I know that full well. In short, there are more ways of killing a cat than drowning it in milk.

As to tourism, I would again emphasize, visitors do *not* come expecting dual-carriageways and luxurious hotels; only do they come for clean, comfortable warm quarters, local food (porridge, not corn-flakes for breakfast!) well cooked and nicely served, *and* the joy of complete freedom 'midst grandeur. They want it 'our way' as has been the custom for generations ... and so it will remain; so it will long be remembered, make no mistake about this, those who may be in power at Westminster or Saint Andrew's House. I write from personal knowledge; personal contact with those who matter; those who inhabit this corner of

K

Britain. After all, the views of those directly acquainted with the facts of life appertaining to the Highlands, should be heeded !

I ask myself, why all this babbling anxiety over taxation to spend on more advertising of Scotland, when in 1963 well over 700,000 visitors *from overseas countries alone* paid us a visit, and spent nearly £22 million; and the British holiday-makers' contribution to Scotland's economy is at least four times that of the overseas visitors. Ten years ago only 250,000 overseas visitors came to Scotland, and the tourist trade was worth about £7 million.

Each year more and more people cross the border. It is thought nothing to send out 100,000 copies of the Tourist Board's small booklet 'Holidays in Scotland' free each year; so why all this brain-storm over searching to find some formula for a niggling, nagging, irritating tax of one's own land, when the country is already so popular? It is said some 25,000 people called in at the Board's Edinburgh information office last year making enquiries of a Scottish holiday, and the most popular region with these tourists (quoting from the Tourist Bulletin) is the Western Highlands. There is a large increase also in coaching parties. It seems to me, to embark on any further and intense advertising is just advertising for the sake of advertising.

Yes, every available house, nook and corner is full to capacity. Everyone is battling to cope with this welcome rush of visitors. I have even known people being accommodated at the Police Station, in the one cell there; and that *not* for drunkenness! And for yachtsmen, the beautiful safe anchorage in Badachro bay (south side) appears to be more and more attractive; millionaire's yachts included. It will soon be called the Cowes of Wester Ross.

We should not forget in all times of popularity and in most places made doubly popular by *artificial means*, that after the novelty has worn off, after shall we say, the 'Hosannas', there very often comes fast in its wake 'Crucify Him', biblically speaking; and that the crowds of today may well turn out to be but a handful tomorrow. So it may well be, after big business has exploited these quiet regions the cry will be for elsewhere; a 'more beyond' cry. At one time the coins of Spain were stamped with the two pillars of Hercules, representative, in Spain's early days, of the two promontories of the Rock of

Gibraltar, and the wording 'NE PLUS ULTRA' (no more beyond). But when Columbus sailed far beyond these pillars and discovered a new world, Spain changed her coins. The word 'NE' was struck off, leaving simply 'PLUS ULTRA' (more beyond). These are all plain facts, which should, I hope, safeguard the *real* Scottish north-west Highlands, and islands, from becoming urban in the slightest degree . . . or else. It was that great American Statesman and President, Abraham Lincoln, who said, just over a hundred years ago, 'Tell the people the facts and they will save the nation'. Travellers have a choice, not just a voice.

Soon people will be queuing up in Edinburgh to have breakfast in Gairloch the following week!

Our heritage in the Highlands is the tradition of humanism, which comes down to us from the ancient Greeks and the Judaic-Christian philosophy of man's unique nature. Socrates taught, as did our Lord, that it is not knowledge, or skill in a craft or science, that makes a man fully human; it is wisdom and virtue, and we need this wisdom in all this breathless propaganda of the Highlands. The most learned, the most erudite person in the world, may be wrong in some directions. And from the East came the voice of Confucius, the Chinese philosopher, who died in 479 B.C., ten years before Socrates was born. He also taught his followers that by learning, and above all by training in character, a man could become a princely person with a true sense of proportion.

*   *   *

The Red Deer

In the chapter 'Sport in the Highlands', passing reference was made to the red deer, since this lovely animal is indigenous to these northern parts. Its antiquity extends over many centuries. This cervine family is most fascinating, so much so that a little further study will not come amiss. The deer forests of Wester Ross form a corner of the largest, continuous tract of forest ground in Scotland, and cover over 50,000 acres of mountains and glens. The total forest area of Scotland is about $2\frac{1}{2}$ million acres—small really in comparison to game areas in the U.S.A. or Canada; but then, these are far bigger countries.

Whilst growing his new antlers, the stag looks for minerals, notably lime.

In stalking one needs to be not only familiar with the ground but with the 'carry' of the wind, for these animals have a most unusual sense of smell . . . more acute than any other beast. Light and shadow also play much importance, though their sight is poor. The social system of the deer is primarily of a family nature. The sexes separate into their own groups for most of the year; they keep more or less to their own boundaries. The breeding, or rutting, season lasts about six weeks. Each stag has his own harem of up to fifty hinds, and the rutting territory is invariably on the hinds' ground. They keep to the high ground —away from sheep, dogs and man. There is never any over-crowding; thirty acres or so per harem is thought a natural density.

Most hinds bear a calf each year, and a hind calves for the first time when four years old. Calving season is in June and July. It is a very rare occurrence for a hind to have two calves. It is estimated the average life of a deer is fifteen years. When the calves are born they become liable to be set upon by the fox, eagle or the wild cat, for the mother leaves its calf alone for a few days, whilst she wanders off a distance. A hard winter also brings about its toll, for should the hind be short of milk there is little chance of the calf surviving.

The roe deer is a small, shy, woodland beast; the red deer is not. The latter has an easy, long, trot whilst the former invariably 'bounds' along. As a group, deer are not quarrelsome animals; if hinds *do* pick a quarrel, then they kick each other. The 'velvet' is shed from the antlers during August. This velvet covers newly-formed antlers; it is a skin, and with the growth of the antlers comes excess calcification at the roots, thus cutting off the blood supply to the velvet so making the skin dead, and it commences to peel off. The animal helps in this peeling by rubbing its antlers against a tree or bush.

Whilst the hind makes a sound resembling a bark, the stag's 'roar' is confined to the rutting season only, which gradually tones down to a moan. The rest of the year its voice is silent. The 'roar' is indicative of sexual desire; the 'bark' symbolic of warning.

There are many works and treatises written on animals, their social life and behaviour. One of outstanding authority is Mr. F. Fraser Darling, Vice-President and Director of Research of the Conservation Foundation in New York, who was a lecturer at Edinburgh University in the 1950's. In a previous chapter I refer to Priest Island, one of the Summer Isles. I am told Mr. Fraser Darling made himself a hermit on this small isle, off Gruinard Bay, for a few years in order to make a close examination of seals, bird life and natural history relating to Wester Ross.

In the churchyard of Clachan, Loch Broom-side, there is the unusual tombstone of the keeper who was killed by a tame stag. The tombstone bears a Latin inscription:

TOT CERVORUM VICTOR NON SENECTUTI
SED CERVO CESSIT

'This man having killed many stags, succumbed to a stag himself—not to old age' . . .

Long ago in the Highlands, 'the chase' was accompanied by deerhounds (not unlike the Russian borzoi wolf-hounds), high-legged, lean, nimble and keen on foot as a greyhound, except they had heavier, curly, blue-grey coats; but with the advent of long-range rifles with precision sights, this method of coursing has become, comparatively speaking, a thing of the past. Years ago, a big pack of these trained deerhounds accompanying their masters, would be loosed, bringing the stags and hinds to bay, and then it became a simple matter. Peculiarly enough, these hounds had little scent, but relied mainly on their piercing eyesight.

*　　*　　*

Bird Life

Bird life is always a source of attraction. But up here we are not accustomed to being wakened by a 'dawn-chorus', for there are not the homely trees to attract the homely birds as in England; though I believe there are 97 different species of birds recorded to be found on the moors and hills here. To my mind, the song of birds has a beautiful, restful feeling; without this song our old planet would be dull. Not only that, without the colour of bird-life this earth would be more drab. For a bird is a creature of God—perhaps His most delicate and exquisite creation. Ceylon had an abundance of birds with wonderful colourings.

CHAPTER 16

EPILOGUE

SUNSET on the loch; on the Gair Loch, the Gairloch of Wester Ross. The Gairloch I knew when little more than a boy, when YOUTH was at the helm of the *Claymore*—the MacBrayne steamer I travelled on in 1914 and first discovered this ideal spot—and Hebe (according to legend) the goddess of Youth and Beauty, and cup-bearer to the gods, was the carved figure on the prow, holding high a torch unto all the oceans of the world ... oceans that were open to me at will.

Such was the enchantment of youth; but now twilight is stepping in to put *finis* to a crowded life. One can tell when one gets to advancing age without the aid of the calendar, by the fact when one's broad mind and narrow waist start changing places. Though I still possess a broad mind! One's life is comparatively short; one seems to be just beginning to find one's way about, when it is time to go. There is always one's girl friend at one's side—Annie Domini—with her constant Mona Lisa smile that seems to say 'I'll be back'; and so the years pass us with relentless and remorseless accuracy.

At the most, our longest day is short. Try as we will, we cannot bring Apollo's sky chariot to a halt, nor can we arrest the going down of the sun, which at times floods the horizon with all the spectrum of its vivid colours; not only its seven prismatic colours—its seven-spanned colours depicting Love, Meekness, Sympathy, Mercy, Kindness, Tolerance and Goodness—but all the other varied mingled colours such as one sees on a colour-chart when selecting a tin of paint at Kenny the ironmonger's. Nor can we fathom the hereafter, which we can only assume was—by one omnipotent Will, one omnipotent spirit—'thought' into existence. Once there was no heaven,

no earth; only a mist, which formed into twelve rivers of goodness. And out of the rivers, a fountain; and out of the fountain,
wisdom. In short, the earth was made by *A* power; the world
established by *A* wisdom; and the heavens stretched out by *His*
understanding.

We all have work to do in this world, and the time for its
execution has its fixed limits. We have no guarantee of any
allotted span, but even if we had, and even if it extended far
beyond the three score years and ten, there would still be no
time for idling. To the youth, life may seem long and leisurely,
but it looks very different in the retrospect. The young people
rejoice in the length of days to which they deem themselves
heir; the aged reflect on the brevity of life—there being no time
for trifling. Time's a hand's breadth, 'tis a tale; 'tis a short-lived
fading flower; 'tis a rainbow on a shower; 'tis a momentary
ray, smiling on a winter's day.

Our life is truly as a land journey; too even and too easy
over long distances across the plains; too hard and too painful
up the steep inclines. On the summit of the mountain we get a
magnificent, majestic, view over immense distances, and feel
exalted as a bird on the wing gliding on olive wings over a
vale of enchantment, catching glimpses of the shy deer darting
into the ravines and corries below the misty heights. But then continuing our journey and climbing *down*, we are too busy watching our footholds, so much so we then forget our summit joys.
How true all this is. Would that our human life might close
with music and pageantry, rather than our sliding into senility . . .

Life is full of cheerio's and hello's; of *au revoirs* and good-
byes; of slàinte mhaths; of tot siens ('not goodbye but cheerio'
in the Gambia, West Africkaana language)—and of that hack-
neyed phrase, 'I'll be seeing you'; together with 'Happy Days'.

There is another saying one sometimes comes across, 'Life
begins tomorrow'; in fact it was the title of a well-known
French film. But life *cannot* be postponed till tomorrow. We
live for today, for tomorrow, with its threats of nuclear warfare,
industrial unrest and so on, may never come. Life may be
likened to a dewdrop as it falls from the branches of a tree to the
ground; sometimes it never reaches the ground—it evanesces
in its downward journey. As I have said before, Adam was in
Paradise when he fell.

Gone are many of my old Gairloch friends; Morag (to whom I dedicated *And It Came To Pass*), Willie Fraser, Angus Fraser, also Annie Fraser, wife of 'Willie Lauder', a noble woman in her 86th year, whom I had been privileged to know for over forty years, Hecky, Murdo Fraser, Roddie MacLean (Badachro), My Lady Alice, Annie MacLean, Chrissie my neighbour, Roddie Bain, Katie MacLean, Katie Ann, Ina, and others—aye, even Thafne of Egypt days. Ah! me. I once saw an inscription on a sun-dial and I pen here its wisdom . . . 'To larger sight, the rim of shadow is the line of light'. Death is only a momentary rim of shadow so it would seem. Behind it—waiting—is the radiance of an altered and, one prays, a new life.

However, Fiona (derived from the Gallic FIONN, meaning white or fair) still remains my sheet anchor; steadfast, radiant, flawless as a blue sky, and like Esther, with light and gladness and joy in her heart, which throughout the years has been of such incalculable solace to me . . . a woman of genial sunny-hearted spirit indeed. Seldom does one come across a model marriage founded on sure love and cemented in mutual esteem; the man acting as a tender head, and the wife realising it all, sets forth what 'oneness' means, and ought to mean. In her eyes he is her all-in-all, finding the sweetest contentment in his company, his companionship and his fondness. For he is her 'big little world'. He in turn lavishes love on her. Their object in life is common, their wishes blend, their hearts become amalgamated and welded together, so begetting uniformity. Their affections are so united, it is hard to say where one begins or where one leaves off. And as age creeps on, the attachments and common ties and sympathy make light of any burdens that may arise, in further bonds of loving adoration. Astrologers tell us the stars impel, but do not compel. The same applies to love; you do not just say that you are in love and let it go at that, for LOVE—like a rare flower—needs tending and caring for each and every day; and all obstacles that stand in the way must be fought. It *must* be reciprocal; if not, it isn't love, but something far less.

To such a happily wedded existence, one might say . . .

> Endearing days, year by year,
> Even when fading light draws near.

At least it's 'myself' that says *that* to 'myself'.

As I look out at Gairloch's horse-shoe bay, I shall be setting
sail one day for its wide open mouth. It will be sunset; it will
be autumn—an incomparable season in Wester Ross—that comes
round once a year, and is determined, not by any man-made
calendar really, but by what happens in the sky. The 'fall' as
they term it in America.

Autumn, full of colour, full of peace, full of somnolence.
Setting sail, but whither? Not even the camel or the sphinx
can tell me. Would that we *might* know; on the other hand
'tis perhaps as well we don't know what is beyond us, as we pass
through the ivory gates of sleep into (this time) an uncharted sea,
where no more earthly sunsets will we be privileged to see; but
where CALA-NA-SITHE (haven of peace) will be one's future home
... we hope. And where, no doubt, we shall renew our sense
of mission and resume some forward march.

Interferences and sounds that started billions of years ago,
caused by dust and gas in the beginning, can—we are told—
when 'decoded', reveal the mysteries of the sun, the milky way,
and the universe at large. The sun is burning at the rate of
millions of tons of matter a second, and will burn for many
more million years; then explode, and the oceans will boil.
Truly we should feel honoured in living in such a wondrous
habitation, quite beyond human intellect and human understanding.

Nature in Gairloch, as remarked in earlier pages, always
presents a changing picture from my windows—a 'new look'
every day, even every hour sometimes—a new angle that can
bring a different purpose into living; comfort, hope and strength
if one looks for it in these unique surroundings. This 'new look'
is happening all over the world in our ordinary work-a-day life.
People and things that have made no impact on us, suddenly
say something, or act in some way or other as to give us a new
angle upon their worth and character—whether it be for better
or worse. We have a corollary in the New Testament in St.
Paul—Saul of Tarsus, the bigoted young Pharisee—who was
bitterly opposed to Christianity, and who considered THE MASTER
a fake messiah. But whilst journeying to Damascus he suddenly
came up against a blinding light, a blinding revelation, a heavenly
vision; a new look, a new angle of Him; and thenceforth he
became, as we know, in a flash an overwhelming and victorious

propagator of the Gospel. Strange, yet true ... 'Paul the Dauntless'.

In a previous book (*The End of the Rainbow*), I made mention of David Livingstone, that great missionary and African explorer; the discoverer of the Victoria Falls, where the spirit and his graven image brood for ever over the mists rising from the thunderous gorges, and where, on a moonlit night, you can gaze with wonder on the eerie magic of the lunar rainbow. There is a story told of him just before he set out from these shores on his last journey abroad. His friends begged and implored him not to go back again to the dark continent of Africa. He would die; wild beasts would maul him, and his flesh would be rent asunder by lions, and they would devour him. His very bones would be picked by vultures, and left to bleach under the parching, pitiless, scorching equatorial sun. But he said, 'I am going; for I have the word of a gentleman of the most sacred order, who said "lo! I am with you alway, even unto the end of the world"' ... And he went.

*   *   *

As I look out, I see the fishing-boats leaving harbour in the late afternoon, going slowly, but gracefully, to the open sea ... the Minch. The Minch said in English has an inoffensive sound, but hear the name pronounced by a Gaelic speaker, and you get every indication of the respect this crossing demands on a winter's night. One day, as I have said (when the sun shall have gone down whilst it was yet day), I shall be going with them, with—I hope—calm courage, and resolve, and with a company most honourable and blessèd—merchant-sailor friends (they that go down to the sea in ships, and do business in great waters), with a favourable wind and a star to guide; for the day dies with the night, and the glory of the world is tarnished with darkness—or so it seems. And yet again, it revives its own beauty, its own dowry as before; and the sun will once more tear open—nay, burst open—a new day. But I shall not be on board when they return to harbour. I shall be *en route* to Nirvana, for one cannot put a full-stop to advancing age. Even the human ear begins to die when we are but ten years old; and cancer, the hardening of the arteries, and such like, serve to remind us we are but feeble in the extreme. The wonder is, what with disease, decay and accident, we manage to grow up at all! Many medical men have devoted themselves to the scientific study of ageing, and have tried youth-giving potions, and graftings with interesting results. Yet there is no sign of the Elixir. Some try to live life at half-cock in hopes of living twice as long; but this cotton-wool existence seldom, if ever, works out. In primitive societies a man was faced in times of famine with the choice of eating his dog or his grandmother. Dogs caught seals; grandmothers did not. So he generally chose his grandmother.

* * *

This book is written with no attempt at drawing on the imagination; nor does it try to gloss over any defects in this land; for there are none to gloss over. It is written just as it appears to one living in its midst; one—a Yorkshireman and a Colonial—who left the world of the Far East after a quarter of a century there, and came to the West ... the north-west. (I was once told there was only one good man that came out of Yorkshire; Charles Peace, and they hanged him!)

Far from being a travel-guide, it is a vivid portrayal of a great country and a great people; so great in fact that the author was inspired to sit down and write eagerly about them *once again*; with an affection and a frankness that West Coast folk do not often—if ever—encounter. It should form a fitting companion to *And it Came to Pass*, for no other book has ventured to capture the real 'spirit' and the real 'feel' of these regions of the British Isles ... Wester Ross; where the people's livelihood, as I have said, may be aptly put as one foot in the sea, and one foot on the shore—fishing and cultivating the land; where, in a way, they let the world go by, except in so far as they dig the peats and catch the fish. Once again ...

> Will the peats dig themselves ?
> Will the fish jump ashore ?

When I go with the fishing fleet, and am being eventually ferried across the river *Styx*, I shall slip away—if it be ordained —with a love of this paradise of Wester Ross even better, perhaps, after death than before. Who knows ? For all you can hold in your dead cold hand, is what you have given away. Such

are the feelings I have of this great Gaelic-loving folk—
the young in heart. And I am sure I am not alone in this
regard.

> Had we never lov'd sae kindly,
> Had we never lov'd sae blindly;
> Never met—or never parted,
> We had ne'er been broken-hearted!

I shall also hold fond and tender memories of the East; and
of Ceylon and Egypt in particular.

Life is bottled sunshine; and death, the silent-footed butler,
sooner or later comes along and draws the cork. Would that
I could sack the butler! In this connection I am reminded of the
man who was to be hanged, and his remark, namely, 'the rope
was too short'.

I have often been asked whether I would wish to live my
life over again. On the whole it has been a pretty good one—
doubtless better than most people—but I see no point in repeating
it. After all, the point of a pattern is that it should be completed.
When nothing can be added without spoiling the design, the
artist leaves it. It would be as idle really as reading a detective
story over again, and you knew the ending. I have always lived
for the future, and I cannot rid myself of the habit of eternal
youth. Would that it could be so. One constantly walks
through life with death, hand in hand; and Death's hand is
warmer than one's own. Many intimate friends, as I have said,
have gone; both at home and abroad, and are seemingly forgotten. It is the way of the world. However, with some, I hope,
my memory will linger awhile. There is something within every
human being unconquered and unconquerable. That 'something' was not born, does not die at death, has never known
disease, has dwelt only in LOVE. It may lie undiscovered as a
jewel in clay. We are all so much greater within, than we have
dared to claim.

This I believe:

> The thoughts we think, the things we say
> Are the threads, strand by strand;
> That weave and turn, through the fabric of life
> The pattern is held in our hand.

This I believe:

> That the love we give is repaid in full
> And running over in measure;
> That the kindness we show and share each day
> Will fill our hearts with pleasure.

This I believe:

> That the world is run by rigid laws
> That are broken to our sorrow;
> That what we sow, that shall we reap
> On a not *too* distant tomorrow.

*   *   *

The stage has been set; the curtain is falling. Not on a play, but on fact ... Sunset on the loch; lighting up the Great Beyond.

On a crisp frosty evening, a full moon is seen coming up on the eastern horizon, *the same time* as the sun—a veritable ball of fire—is about to dip on the opposite horizon. Not often does one see this; yet it *can* be seen in Gairloch.

> Not for me, the crowded places
> Not for me, the cities' roar;
> Not for me, the worried faces
> You can see in every pore.

> But for me, the lochs and the mountains
> The air you can safely breathe;
> The cascading wayside fountains
> And friends you can truly believe.

> Give me this, and a clear northern sky
> With pearls in the morning's dew;
> All this, when saying goodbye
> Is given—to only a few.

Yes; only a few ...

I first saw Gairloch as a youth; sunrise. I am now seeing it at sunset. This part of our heritage, this story, should have a stirring appeal to those not only at home, but far beyond the seas, whose blood is Highland; and who may only in dreams behold their nativity. As I have said before, this is not a land of luxury. It is not the land of Ophir; but it *does* hold the tang of history and of belief. There are no nagging issues here, in this countryside, as in a town; no hard and fast barriers of wealth or station; the society is characterised by a well-mannered equality. And so it will remain—for 'tis the way of life here.

The patron saint of Scotland is St. Andrew. On St. Andrew's Day, 30th November, we should remember how much Britain owes to the restless and remarkable Scottish race. In this century alone, Scotland has given the nation no fewer than six Prime Ministers: Balfour, Campbell-Bannerman, Bonar Law, Ramsay MacDonald, Harold Macmillan, and Sir Alec Douglas-Home. In discovery, there were David Livingstone and Mungo Park (of Nigeria's fame). In science, the stars are many and indeed brilliant; to quote but two, Sir Alexander Fleming, discoverer of penicillin, and John Logie Baird, pioneer of TV. As for religion, the names of famous Scottish ministers are too many to enumerate.

All such have come from a nation, few in numbers—springing from an austere and difficult land, to be sure. And all this wealth of character and energy has poured out of Scotland to mankind's benefit and advantage.

'I am just going outside', said Oates, the sick explorer, fifty years ago, as he left the safety of Captain Scott's tent in the Antarctic one night, into a blinding blizzard, so as not to be a burden on his companions, or of jeopardising their chance of returning safely to the base camp. Fifty years ago—and it is not so long past—thus Oates let it be known where he was going; and many today, if they would but remember, are still inspired by that epic of courage—for courage it was.

When I set sail beyond the moorlands, the hills, the clouds and the many legendary treasures found wrapped-up in this land of Wester Ross; when I 'go outside'—with the sun descending beneath the western edge of the horizon, flooding the bay, its shores and the waters in a blue-golden light and which, within a short space of time, these golds and pinks in both sky and water are replaced by crimson, then purple, then grey and the sky begins to darken—yes, when I 'go outside', whilst the familiar horse-shoe bay of Gairloch momentarily holds the last light of day, I shall, I suppose, just find myself saying 'goodbye' (God be with you); and in the Gaelic DILEAS DO CHEILE ... be ye faithful to one another. Then steadfastly set course towards the New World—setting the helm for the *rising* sun.

Whenever I am asked, when all I have to do in this life would be finished, I answer 'never, as long as I am alive'—for one keeps on adding and adding; and when one puts one's hand to the plough, one should never take it away. He who kneads the dough has only the smallest share in the life of the ferment which he adds.

After a long and varied life, and the years slip by, one becomes calmer and more restful; despite the fact that some accident of metabolism appears to give me implacable vitality. How sorry I shall be to leave this land of crofters, their warm love, sympathy and compassion which are always uppermost; to say nothing of their collies that have to take burns and scree in their stride to seek and gather sheep from every corrie and corner; then coax them gently down like a flowing tide to their master with the stick below. And the crofters' sense of quiet humour also, which so often contains a depth of meaning. A Highlander called at the casualty hospital and asked to see Mr. Mackenzie. 'Which Mr. Mackenzie?' asked the old Scottish porter. 'The one who was knocked down by a steam roller' said the visitor. 'Oh, yes' said the porter, 'you'll find him in Wards 8, 9 and 10'.

And how loathe I shall be to leave the glittering red sunsets; so vivid that one small boy once said to his father, 'When the sun dips down, why doesn't it make a hiss in the sea ?'

This country here is not only vast, but seems boundless; the mountains are lofty enough for thoughts to rise in quiet dignity. They appear to make Time visible. Here is the Past still standing, thousands of years alive; and over all rests beauty and peace. The mountains and glens will be here when we have gone; even when men have forgotten where one's grave is.

From afar we can see where the rainbow comes down to earth, and we speak of the end of the rainbow as the place where all the gold must lie. But those who are in that spot cannot see the heavenly colours; they see no more than that the sun is shining through the rain.

This land in the Wild West is perpetually green, because it rains every fifteen minutes for a quarter of an hour!

When man has discovered the secret of blowing this world to pieces with a few bombs; when he is busy exploring the mysteries of outer space, does it matter *how* this world, or even how the Bible, came into our possession ? Does it matter ? What does it matter ? In my view it *does* matter.

Sunrise *after* Sunset . . . after sunset on the loch.

Sunset, the most impressive picture of all things superterranean, in which one becomes an eye-witness of the cosmos. When the amic ball of fire has dipped, all the festival and majesty of colours suddenly vanish and everything is blotted out. No earthly garden can compete with that of the firmament's; which has no noxious intruders, and no weeds; no annuals, no biennials—only eternals. No storms or gales, only the gentle breezes that help to produce the most varied colours (ephemeral though they may be) . . . colours that remain in our minds each and every day, as we tread through life, through the Corridors of TIME, and through the Years of Experience. Very wonderful; very inspiring.

'We're friendly people in Wester Ross' . . .

THE END